THE HEARTBEAT
OF IRAN

Erratum

On page 113, the last sentence on the page should read: "I'd ask Mrs. Clinton how she handled men in a world that's so dominated by them."

THE HEARTBEAT OF IRAN

Real Voices of a Country and Its People

Tara Kangarlou

PUBLISHING

New York, NY

Printed in the United States of America.
10 9 8 7 6 5 4 3 2 1

Ig Publishing
Box 2547
New York, NY 10163

www.igpub.com

ISBN: 978-1-63246-20-53

To my beloved Mom & Dad who gave me
the greatest treasure in life—humanity.

To people, whose existence can only continue through humanity.

تقدیم به انسانها , آنهایی که والاترین ارزششان انسان بودن است.

CONTENTS

Foreword

WHEN I WAS YOUNGER, I SPENT HOURS reading the incomparable poetry of Al Attar, Hafez, Khayyam, and Sa'adi. Their observations—some profound, others just playful—found its way into a lyricism that is still popular with readers throughout the world. And for Iranians everywhere, alongside the ingredients which blend to form their culture, it is the incomparable artistry of their poets which elicits their greatest pride—and justifiably so. Indeed, I have never met an Iranian who did not have a deep, almost visceral attachment to the loveliness of words when aligned so properly. And all of its content— whether literal or allegorical—is ultimately woven into storytelling.

Tara Kangarlou's book remains faithful to that tradition, and while she may be a modern globalist living in the West, she is still a daughter of Persia. Written in a style that is free-flowing and smooth, this compilation of highly readable stories stems not just from Tara's emotional connection to the country of her forebears, but also her recognition of the stubborn extent to which Iranians are still miscast in the popular perceptions of many living in the West, particularly in the United States.

Those bearded fanatics screaming "Death to Israel and the US" remain the default image for many living to the west of the Bosporus. So too is the belief that the current Iranian regime is utterly ruthless, executing publicly, for example, those convicted of offenses that took place when they were minors, or threatening the Middle East with disorder and extremism. While some of this may be true, and there are ordinary Iranians who are utterly unsavory—as you would find with people in every country—there are also many beautiful, complex individuals, many with a nobility of spirit, and almost all worthy of our complete admiration. Tara's book uncovers them wonderfully.

I have never been to Iran, but through her simple, intimate, and elegant storytelling, Tara took me to a saffron farm in the now dry farmlands of Khorasan; invited me to have chelow kabob in one of the oldest kabob houses in Tehran; to meet a blind Sunni environmental activist in the southern provinces of Sistan and Baluchestan; and to sit in a classroom in the rural village of Khansar, where the pain and promise of each child mirrors that of millions of other vulnerable children worldwide.

Put another way, Tara vividly conveys all of what she sees, hears, and feels—the vibrancy of the hues, the warmth of the personalities, their charm, the ambient noises, the scents. This is no monochromatic culture she is dealing with, but an extraordinary kaleidoscope of human experiences, all concentrated in a single geography that was once the home to some of humanity's greatest poets. I hope you enjoy this magnificent book as much as I did.

—Zeid Ra'ad Al Hussein
United Nations High Commissioner
for Human Rights, 2014–2018

Introduction

*T*HERE WAS AN HEIRESS SITTING TO MY left, the CEO of a Fortune 100 company to my right. The three of us were engaged in one of those awkward and politically correct conversations at a reception I had been obligated to attend. A casual question about my last name revealed my Iranian background, which led to a brief summary of my upbringing in Tehran. Suddenly, their gazes sharpened, and, as more wine was poured, the looks on the faces of my two dinner companions became increasingly perplexed. In the blink of an eye, I found myself floating in their preconceptions of my birthplace. To them, I was no longer an American, but rather an immigrant who proudly spoke of her Persian heritage and upbringing in Iran—a country that for much of the Western world is synonymous with rogue behavior, oppression, and turmoil.

In a room where half of the audience were paid to denounce diplomacy and the rest wrote checks, the heiress leaned in curiously and asked, "Did you guys escape during the Revolution? Is it dangerous to go back? I mean, it must be so hard to live there as a woman with those things they wear on their heads." Before I was able to answer her, the CEO chimed in with a patronizing question of his own: "But how can you speak English so well? You have no accent!" Sadly, this wasn't the first time I'd heard these kinds of questions.

As a dual national since birth, there is nothing I find more humiliating than having to prove my "real" identity—and there's nothing more terrifying than having that identity questioned by others. After all, what is a "real" identity, and who gets to define it? I consider myself a proud Iranian *and* a proud American; I embrace my upbringing in Tehran, my unique education in both countries, and the ability to call two of the world's most remarkable lands my home. By bridging these two cultures, languages, and mindsets, I have learned that there is so much more that connects us as human beings than what divides us on the global stage.

॰॰॰

As was the case at that dinner party, the duality of my "identity" has often been a subject of scrutiny, tainted with stereotypes and misconceptions—especially in the United States.

Growing up in my late teens in California, in order to fit into the mold, I frequently had to downplay my Iranian heritage—a familiar story for those who have undertaken the immigrant journey. No, I would tell people, my family did not escape a war, nor did they flee Iran after the 1979 revolution; I did not grow up in a desert, nor was I ever forced to walk around the streets wearing a long black veil. Between each one of these stereotypes lays infinite nuances that identify my upbringing and that of millions of other Iranians who live inside the country and beyond.

It's true, these days, as an American journalist I am not the most welcomed person by the hardliners and oppressive government forces in Iran; but that doesn't mean that my friends, family members or ordinary Iranians can't regularly travel back and forth to the country on holidays or for a visit. In other words, in order to understand Iran, one has to understand the ever-present dichotomies and become familiar with the many shades within the everyday fabric of life in the country— shades that are far from monotone, but rather a jarring mix of colors that will often leave you in awe.

One of these particular moments occurred in 2015, when I went back to Iran to cover the historic nuclear deal. Similar to any American or foreign news crew, we had a "government" designated "fixer" who was tasked to help "guide" us around. In reality though, he was our "minder," who delicately and oh so cordially shadowed us as we reported the news under the watchful eyes of the Iranian government. I'll never forget my last day in my birth city, when I wanted to take a few personal hours to visit my Dad's memorial site in Behesht -e- Zahra, Tehran's main cemetery. Little did I know that I would have to be chaperoned by a pseudo fixer in my home country just so I could visit my father's grave. Ironically, during the two hour drive to and from the cemetery, and the long walk through the crammed tombstones that were filled with my quiet tears, I somehow managed to see through the young man. We were roughly the same age. In those few hours he made me realize that underneath his guard was a smart, kind, and ambitious person who was only doing this job because of exactly what it was—a job.

A few years later, in the immediate aftermath of the tragic 2020 downing of the Ukrainian passenger jet that took 176 innocent lives, I realized that I was right—he wasn't one of them. I spoke to him again on the phone, where he emotionally opened up and told me that he had lost a close relative on that doomed flight—a life that was unfairly lost to the foolishness of the regime. During our conversation, it was hard to ignore his fuming rage and his resentment toward a system that he had once worked for and maneuvered through to make a career for himself.

When you live and breathe the nuances and are accustomed to the complexities of life in Iran, it is quite frustrating to see how often ordinary Iranians are portrayed through a narrow facade. Movies and television shows like *Argo*, *300*, *Not Without My Daughter*, and *Shahs of Sunset*, in addition to the ever-present political stories on mainstream media, are all that the world sees about a nation of more than 80 million. The nightmarish hostage crisis of the 1979 American embassy takeover, the unjust imprisonment of journalists, the unfair treatment of the Baha'is, the brutal crackdowns against political activists, and the host of fundamental human and civil rights abuses that exist in today's Iran must all be condemned. Without a doubt, such historic events, and current realities, hold a strong place in the country's fabric and should never be discounted by any means. However, it's only fair to see the whole picture. Like many other isolated and heavily marginalized nations, the Iranian people remain a mystery to much of the international community.

⊡

My own Iranian story begins with my parents, who came to the United States as green card holders in 1971, eventually becoming American citizens upon finishing their post-graduate studies. A few years after the revolution, they moved back to Tehran, and I was born as the Iran-Iraq War was coming to an end. My father was an oral surgeon who wanted to work in his home country and serve his own people despite his resentment toward the Iranian political establishment.

In 2003, while Dad remained in Iran, my mother and I moved back to the States so that I could finish high school in California and have an easier time preparing for college. For nearly eight years, until my father's death in 2011, we would travel back and forth to Iran during the summer holidays, and Dad would spend a few months with us in the United States. Thus, I was raised a citizen of both the US and Iran; and after so many years of living between these two estranged nations, today I feel like a child who's stuck between divorced parents. I love both places, but the two are always at odds; I respect both countries, but neither seems to see the humanity in the other; I can look deep into their hearts, but all they've ever focused on is hate.

⊡

I remember watching Roland Joffé's *The Killing Fields* with my father when I was eleven or twelve. I had always been passionate about writing and storytelling, but after seeing the film, I realized that I wanted to be a journalist—a profession that in my naive mind could make the world a "better place." From an early age, I started to believe in the power of storytelling— reporting on the issues that impact the core of humanity and people's livelihoods around the world.

Unfortunately, most Iranians—especially over the past forty years—have not been able to write their own stories; and if they are, they have often been obscured by oppressive forces in Iran, or those who control the narrative abroad. The Iranian story has often been told through political narratives, news channels, and those in the diaspora— which in and of itself is a cacophony of ideas, agendas, and political viewpoints.

These are precisely the reasons I decided to write this book and take you on this journey—a never before taken trip to Iran through intimate encounters with everyday Iranians. At a time when the world is divided by bigotry and political agendas, I believe in the urgency of building bridges, crossing divides, and uniting by way of understanding one another's stories—life stories that help us realize that we are all far more closer than any sanction, border, or wall.

The stories in this book are the realities of life in a country that the rest of the world does not get to see. For the first time ever, you will hear from ordinary Iranians in their own words—people whose passion, pain, and profound desire to speak mirrors that of millions of others worldwide.

Make no mistake, this is not a book about politics, nor is it meant to paint a rosy picture of a country whose people are suffering on a daily basis from repressive forces at home. Rather, it is an invitation for readers, particularly in the United States and elsewhere in the West, to take a glimpse into the hearts and minds of the Iranian people, and to view the intricacies of their lives in a unique environment unfamiliar to many living outside the country. While twenty or so portraits cannot ever capture the entirety of a nation of 80 million, the complexities of each story in this book can help bring readers closer to the textures, nuances and chasms of life in the Islamic Republic of Iran.

As I finish writing my introduction, I can't help but think of Margaret Atwood's words on how she hopes that people "will finally come to realize that there is only one 'race'—the human race—and that we are all members of it." As you read this book, more than anything, I hope you come to understand the values and humanity that you share with the average Iranian—an experience that will enable all of us to see beyond the surface, beyond the political headlines, and beyond the dark shadows of hostile governments. In doing so, you're already creating a path for discourse, dialogue, and engagement—all necessary ingredients for any form of progress, peace building, and change. Inherently, when people recognize their similarities, they become more tolerant and understanding of one another.

And when you finish this book, I hope you remember that it's the people of a nation who define their country, their values, and their history. By now, some of the people I've featured in the book may have left Iran, some may have changed careers, and some may have even died; but one thing will continue—and that is, or was, their passion for life.

Governments come and go, presidents change, regimes collapse, but what will forever remain is the pulse of the people who pump blood into the veins of their land—people who, in this case, are the heartbeat of Iran.

Hooriyeh Zeinali

T HE NINETY-THREE-YEAR-OLD WOMAN gets up slowly, holds on to her rolling walker, and strolls toward the window. No matter where she is or whose house she's visiting, she loves to sit by the window. It's as if she finds comfort in the open skies, in the spirited flocks of the birds, and the promise of a pedestrian who may or may not pass by.

Here, in her cozy two-bedroom apartment in Tehran's Niavaran neighborhood, she particularly likes to sit by the wide windows overlooking the Niavaran Palace—the one-time residence of Iran's late monarch, Mohammad Reza Shah Pahlavi. The view is partially obscured by hundreds of tall plane trees that create a green curtain across the vast grounds of the palace. Sometimes she looks down into the street, which occasionally gets cluttered with mild traffic unfit for this once-enchanting northern locale's narrow streets.

The woman's solitude is filled with many pictures of her children and their families that are neatly placed around the tidy living room. It's remarkable that she has lived long enough to see her grandchildren's grandchildren, none of whom currently live in Iran. There's a stunning antique chest in her bedroom. The hand-carved wooden masterpiece looks like a magical trunk through which you can go on a journey that not only tells the nearly century-long story of an Iranian woman, but also reveals the upheaval that her country has experienced during her lifetime.

"It was a big house, not too big, but comfortable enough for our family," she shares. "Initially, my father had a bakery business, but after the Russians first brought cars into Iran, he taught himself how to drive. He then sold his baking shops in order to buy trucks and cars and open a garage." Her vivid memory is astonishing—as if the 1920s were only yesterday.

She continues: "Father soon opened the first transportation business in Ardabil. The roads were nothing like today, so you can

just imagine how bumpy each journey must have been." She remembers how her father would ask his passengers to sign a waiver before getting on board— agreeing that in case the truck or car fell into a ditch, they would help the driver get the vehicle back on the road.

"My father was a very kind man. He wasn't academically educated and only knew how to read and write, but nonetheless he was a savvy businessman. He had a lot of land in Ardabil and later in Tehran, and while sharp at work, he was a gentle, humble, and extremely generous human being." She later tells me that her father's generosity ultimately led him to lose much of his wealth—a common fate back then (and even today) for many hardworking Iranians who trusted their associates, friends, and even family members.

⊡

Hooriyeh Zeinali was born on April 23,1926, just two days before the coronation of Reza Khan—a shrewd military commander who overthrew the seventh and final king of the Qajar dynasty, which had reigned over

Iran for over a century. In an attempt to restore an enfeebled nation that had been ravaged by the Russians and the British, Reza Khan established the Pahlavi dynasty. In less than a decade, the new "Shah" changed the country's name from Persia to Iran (*the Land of the Aryans*). Much of Reza Khan's nationalistic efforts were carried out against a militarized backdrop, until he was deposed by the British and their Russian allies at the dawn of the Second World War. His young son would then claim the throne—becoming the last monarch of Iran before the 1979 Islamic Revolution.

Hooriyeh's hometown of Ardabil, like the Persian Empire itself, has a rich millennia-old history. Over the centuries, Ardabil has endured the Arab invasion, the Mongol conquest, the Ottoman battles, and the forceful advances of the Russians. Located in the northwest, Ardabil is one of the thirty-one provinces of Iran, neighboring the Gilan Province to the East and Eastern Azerbaijan to the West. From the North, the province shares borders with the Republic of Azerbaijan—a territory that once belonged to Iran until, once again, Russia's gambit and Iranian ineptitude led to its annexation. After the "Russo-Persian" wars of the early 1800s, the two treaties of Gulestan and Turkmenchay were consecutively signed in 1813 and 1828 between the Tsar, Alexander I, and the second king of the Qajar dynasty. As a result, Iran's northwestern territories, which comprised modern-day Armenia, Georgia, Dagestan, and Azerbaijan, were annexed by imperial Russian forces.

In 1501, long before Reza Shah's mission to revitalize his weakened nation, in an effort to nationalize the then-divided Persia after centuries of foreign assault, a young man named Ismail founded the Safavid Empire. Born and raised in Ardabil, Ismail was a descendent of the great Sufi, Sheikh Safi al-Din Ardabili, whose tomb—a UNESCO World Heritage Site—remains the crown jewel of the city.

The Safavid Empire restored much of the country's social and political might, and throughout its two-century rule, reclaimed much of the Caucasus, parts of Turkey, Syrian, Iraq, Kuwait, Bahrain, all the way to Pakistan and Afghanistan as well as modern-day Uzbekistan and Turkmenistan. But perhaps the Empire's most significant mark was Shah Ismail's proclamation of Twelve-Imam Shia Islam as the country's official religion.

During the first fifty years of its reign, the Safavid throne was held a little over 100 miles outside of Ardabil in Tabriz—the current capital of the East Azerbaijan Province. Aside from its military and political strength, the Safavid Empire left Iran with some of its most glorious arts, architecture, and literary treasures. The two Ardabil Carpets, which were commissioned by the second Safavid king in honor of the late Sufi Sheikh, is one such masterpiece, underscoring the Iranian artistry of the time. Today, like many other Iranian national treasures, the pair of carpets reside outside its homeland, in the United Kingdom and the United States.

The province's eponymous capital is only hours away from the Caspian Sea and about sixty miles from Iran's third highest mountain, Sabalan. Atop the mountain's crater is one of the world's highest sweet water lakes, which is often frozen. The surrounding basin of the inactive volcano is known for its healing hot springs and silky honey that invite thousands of Iranian tourists into the region year-round.

Azeri Turkic is the native language of those living in Ardabil as well as the East and West Azerbaijan provinces; and while the country's official language is Farsi, millions of Iranians speak Azeri in the country's northwest region, helping to preserve their heritage, folklore, and culture. While geographically separated and politically polarized, the Azeri Iranians share the same language as those living in the Republic of Azerbaijan.

⁑

Hooriyeh speaks Farsi with the most precious Azeri accent; it's even more special when she speaks English—at least the few words she knows. After nine decades of life, the hospitable and warm woman puts forth an effort to respect, connect, and communicate with anyone who crosses her path—especially her grandchildren's American or European spouses.

Hooriyeh was the first child and only daughter of her parents and was treated like a little princess by her father. "I was really close to him, but not so much to my mom." She can't really think of a reason for this, but they were always distant. Hooriyeh's mother, Zeevar, passed away when she was a little over 100 years old. In her later years, she looked just like a little doll, with piercing blue eyes and snow-white hair. Her two perfectly braided pigtails rested gently against her thinly framed shoulders, making her petite physique look even more dainty and delicate. For nearly sixty years she lived in the same house that her late husband bought when they moved to Tehran. "She was young and never expressed her love and affection to me," Hooriyeh remembers. "My dad loved her so much, but she was always quiet. Unlike her, my father was my hero; he was everything."

When Zeevar gave birth to her second child, Hooriyeh found herself a playmate—a younger brother who'd become her closest friend and confidant. "I was around one or one and a half years old when my first brother was born. We pretty much grew up together and were inseparable. I loved him so very much. He was my best friend." The little boy's name was Karim—which translates to *generous and munificent*. Hooriyeh's mother gave birth to two other sons, but neither was able to take Karim's place in Hooriyeh's heart.

Hooriyeh was enthusiastically educated until Reza Shah proclaimed his infamous ban on the hijab—making it illegal for women to wear any sort of "Islamic veil" or cover-up in public. It was one of his many efforts to "modernize" Iran and import a European influence. "I absolutely loved going to school, but as soon as Reza Shah banned the hijab, many parents—including mine—no longer allowed their girls to go to school." Up until then, wearing the hijab, praying, going to the mosque, and being an active Muslim were not synonymous with following a political or religious agenda; instead, religion was subtly entwined within the society's culture and practices.

Reza Shah's 1936 decree was implemented with fury, with government forces pulling down women's hijabs on the street and banning the public wearing of the long veil, known as a "chador" in Farsi. "We couldn't go out of the house with our chadors. It was just an uncomfortable time. I was young but I remember the fear, the anger, and the confusion of those days." Hooriyeh's family wasn't particularly religious, but at the time, wearing a hijab was a regular part of everyday life, as well as being a long-embedded tradition that was hard to overturn quickly—let alone by intimidation and harassment.

Ten-year-old Hooriyeh was just finishing fourth grade when the ban took effect, and soon, like many of her classmates, she was left with no choice but to stop attending school. "I really wanted to go but my father and grandfather thought it was best if I stayed home. It wasn't that they didn't want me to study, they definitely did, but the environment had suddenly gone haywire and it just wasn't appropriate for girls to run around on the streets without a headscarf."

However, the young Hooriyeh didn't give up on her education. She began to read whatever books she could get her hands on in her father's library. "I started reading from a very young age and I soon became passionate about books. I didn't let anything stop me from continuing my education, even if it meant I had to do it on my own. I quickly grew fond of literature and history, not just Iranian history but world history like that of Russia, France, and England. I found it all quite fascinating. I read everything I could find."

⊡

Despite her young age, Hooriyeh was known as one of the most beautiful girls in Ardabil. (Her name translates to *a heavenly woman*.) She recalls how not a day went by that she didn't have multiple suitors knocking on her door. "I had suitors in every corner of the city. Every single night we'd have guests asking for my hand for their sons, but each time I said no. Every night guests would arrive after I had already gone to bed." Because of the hijab ban, women would leave their homes at night when they could discreetly wear their chadors without being harassed.

Hooriyeh remembers how her mother would often wake her up at night and ask her to join the unexpected guests. "One evening when my father was at work, he told one of his friends that he had to leave the office early on in order to get home on time and welcome a suitor's family. Apparently, his friend stopped my father right then and there and told him that, 'Hooriyeh is my own *Aroos*' (*bride* in Farsi)." The man was a respected businessman who worked in the same field as Hooriyeh's father. On her thirteenth birthday, she was engaged to Gholam Hossein—a seventeen-year-old who worked at his father's transportation company, helping with accounting and operations.

The Second World War had already begun when the young bride left her childhood home to live with her in-laws. "I was very lucky. My mother-in-law was a darling woman and so was her daughter. They were very kind and generous. I was respected from day one and they treated me like their own. There was no meal that we didn't have together. My husband was quiet, but he was incredibly respectful and cordial." Just like her father's house, her new home was quite spacious, and the young couple lived on the second floor of the villa. When Hooriyeh was fifteen, she and her mother-in-law—who was only in her thirties—simultaneously gave birth to daughters. Back then, women would often get married at a very young age, and thus the age difference between them and their children would be minimal.

⊡

On a hot summer day in August 1941, Iran found itself set ablaze by Soviet fire from the north and British attacks from the south. Reza Shah, who had declared neutrality in the war against Nazi Germany, soon realized that his country was stuck between the political might of two superpowers. The Allied Powers forced the once-great military man to abdicate his throne; he was replaced by his then-twenty-two-year-old heir Mohammad Reza, who, for the following four decades, ruled Iran in favor of British and American interests.

The turbulence quickly evolved into a more aggressive advancement by British and American forces, as well as the Soviets, who had their eye on the remainder of Iran's Azerbaijan region. The heat of the war and the pain of the battles left no one unaffected. In the final year of the war, Hooriyeh's blissful life fell into an abyss. "That year the Russians were as rampant as ever. One day, they stormed into my father's garage and confiscated his cars and trucks. They took everything he had ever built."

But what the Russians took from her family went far beyond material possessions; Hooriyeh lost her brother, Karim, to Stalin's soldiers, who at the time were occupying much of Iran's northern territories. "My world suddenly crumbled. He was around eighteen years old and was in the military when the Russians took him hostage." Though more than seventy years have passed, the memories of those woeful days still bring tears to the old woman's eyes. "My father's only wish was to see his son once more before he died—a wish that never came true." That same year, in hopes of finding solace and some financial relief, Hooriyeh's father left his hometown of Ardabil and resettled in Tehran. The hardworking man soon began to recoup his lost fortune by buying and selling land.

⚅

Karim's disappearance was followed by the birth of Hooriyeh's two oldest sons. While the joy of childbirth was heartwarming, the now twenty-year-old mother of three was soon to face another loss. "He had gone on a work trip to a nearby town and when he came back he was burning with a high fever. Overnight, a large black ulcer on his left cheek grew until it nearly covered half of his face. His fever kept getting higher and no doctor knew the cure."

After only five years of marriage, Hooriyeh lost her husband to a disease—essentially unknown at the time—called anthrax. "We didn't know what it was; the doctors couldn't figure it out. I'll never forget his face and the pain he endured. The day he died, it was as if I died as well. He took a big part of me with him when he left."

It's hard to imagine what the young widow must have gone through at the time. With three young children to care for, however, all she could think about was how to survive her grief. "I felt alone. And even though I wasn't really alone, there was an unbearable emptiness that weighed heavily on my chest."

Grappling with the loss of her two leading men, Hooriyeh wanted to leave Ardabil for Tehran and take refuge in the warm arms of a man whose love was an ever-present source of strength for her. "I wanted to take my children and go to my father's home, but my father-in-law said that I could either leave them behind or stay with them and marry my deceased ex-husband's younger brother. It was as if no one cared about my feelings. I had no choice but to stay—I suppose they thought that it was the best decision for the children."

In those days, no matter what kind of family you were born into, decisions were made by men. Children had to have a father and no "good" widow would live on her own. To Hooriyeh's dismay, her father supported the decision. "All they cared about was Gholam Hossein's children—making sure that they get what they needed at that young age. It was as if I suddenly had turned invisible."

In 1948, she married her deceased husband's younger brother, who shared the name of her lost brother—Karim. "He was seven years younger than me and hadn't even reached puberty. It was as if I was marrying a child. I remember the times I would help him get dressed for school and now I was forced to call him my husband." It took the newlyweds over a year to consummate their marriage, and while Hooriyeh never loved Karim the way she loved his brother, she slowly grew fond of his calm demeanor and charm. "Love? I don't know. I never knew what to call my feelings for him. I don't know if it was love, respect, companionship. I don't know."

Unlike his older brother, Karim was a painter, poet, and writer who'd spend much of his time among the literati of the 1940s and was a close friend of Sadegh Hedayat—one of the greatest writers of modern Iran, who committed suicide in 1951.

□:
:□

That same year, Hooriyeh's in-laws decided to relocate to Tehran and rebuild their lives away from the painful memory of Gholam Hossein's sudden death. That same year, Prime Minister Mohammad Mosaddegh, one of Iran's most beloved figures, nationalized the country's oil industry. As a result, the nation was instantly hit by foreign intrusion, which was the direct result of the immense influence of the Americans and the British within the Pahlavi regime. It didn't take long before Mosaddegh's democratically elected government was toppled by a CIA- and MI6-orchestrated coup d'état that led to the man's imprisonment and eventual house arrest, where he would remain until his unceremonious death in a village outside of Tehran in 1967.

In 1958, Hooriyeh delivered her sixth and final child. "Karim was an extremely loving father and cared for everyone equally. For him, there was no difference between his brother's children and his own—everyone was treated the same, but he was especially affectionate toward his daughters."

Hooriyeh was still getting used to her new life with Karim when tragedy struck once again. "For the longest time, he suffered a sharp pain in his lower stomach area that he pretty much ignored, until he could no longer bear it," she recalls. Karim underwent hemorrhoid surgery—a procedure that led, after a series of complications and internal bleeding, to his death at the age of twenty-five.

At the age of only thirty-two, Hooriyeh was once again forced to weather the pain of losing a husband. Her youngest daughter was only eight months old, and Karim's two other children were only six and seven. Fortunately, both Hooriyeh's father and father-in-law were incredibly supportive of the widow and her children, and they continued to live in utmost comfort and care. But there was a part of her heart that forever remained broken. I asked her about the time when she felt the happiest. There was a powerful silence in her response—a long pause that in itself was a loud answer. "I don't know; maybe when I was a young girl—young enough to have no worries in life."

It almost seemed as if Hooriyeh's life was cursed. Then a miracle arrived at her door. "One day we received a letter from Ardabil. It was a letter that was originally addressed to my parents' old house before they moved to Tehran. It was Karim. He was alive!"

Hooriyeh's brother was once again back in her life, except he was now a grown man who had survived the brutal atrocities of Stalin's gulags in Siberia. After being captured, the young Iranian soldier had been taken back to Russia and sent off to the infamous labor camps that imprisoned and killed hundreds of thousands of opposition members, intellectuals, writers, and ordinary citizens. After Stalin's death in 1953, Karim's camp was dissembled, and the surviving detainees set free. Karim soon found himself in Moscow, where he was given the opportunity to attend the university and, after years of internment,

start to rebuild a new life. "For the first few years his letters were not being delivered to Iran," Hooriyeh remembers. "There was no way for him to inform us that he was alive. Russian and Iranian relations were sour, and he didn't have any means to contact us." Hooriyeh soon found out that her brother had become a veterinarian and married a Russian woman.

It wasn't until after the Islamic Revolution that Hooriyeh was able to reunite with her beloved brother. Her father wasn't as fortunate. "My father never had a chance to see Karim nor his three daughters. He died in 1979, when I was visiting my second daughter and newly born granddaughter in the United States. My mother and I finally managed to get our visas in 1982 and visit Karim in Moscow. I'll never forget the day I saw him for the first time since his departure to join the military. It was just the most memorable moment." You can sense the exuberant joy each time Hooriyeh speaks of Karim—a tall, handsome man with blue eyes, who nearly lost his life to the Soviet dictatorship. "He finally came back to Iran after forty years, and he also brought along his first daughter." She told me that one of the most joyous days of her life was when Karim stood by her side at her youngest daughter's wedding in Tehran in the late 1980s.

⠿

Hooriyeh never remarried after the death of her second husband, instead devoting the rest of her life to the upbringing of her six children, who were also cousins. This peculiar truth did not come out until the children were able to fully comprehend the reality—children who learnt from their mother's strength, resilience, and selflessness.

In the late 1950s, her father purchased a stunning villa in Damavand—one of Tehran's most scenic regions—which would be cherished by Hooriyeh for many years to come. Tucked away in Iran's lush province of Mazandaran, Mount Damavand is the nation's tallest mountain peak. The volcanic mountain is located in the middle of the

Alborz Mountain range, which stretches from the Azerbaijan Province all the way to the eastern province of Khorasan. Damavand's snowy peak is often visible from Tehran, and its mesmerizing meadows and hillsides are a most inviting sight throughout spring and summer. While the mountain itself is in Mazandaran, the village is located about fifty minutes away in the province of Tehran.

This countryside soon became a magical getaway for Hooriyeh, her children, grandchildren, and her two brothers and their families; and while a few of her children would later buy their own villas in Damavand, the old country house will forever be treasured by Hooriyeh. She tells me that nothing can ever compare with those lazy summer days when the kids would play in the vast cherry orchards, picking walnuts from hundred-year-old trees, and swimming in the sparkling stream that ended in a whimsical thicket called the "Heaven's Gate" or *Dalan e Behesht* in Farsi. Hooriyeh would spend tireless hours in the cucumber fields along with their many gardeners; she would find herself making the most delicious fruit rolls, known as *lavashak*, only to see them instantly devoured by the kids.

As time passed, Hooriyeh's oldest daughter married a lawyer, her middle daughter a dentist, and the younger one an architect. Her sons and middle daughter finished their higher education abroad. Today, all her children and grandchildren except for her oldest daughter and her husband have left Iran and are settled in Europe, Canada, and the United States. Like so many Iranians since the Islamic Revolution, they have decided to build a brighter future for their families outside of their homeland. Most of them are dual citizens or have green cards. Her oldest son, who has lived nearly half of his life in Canada, managed to get Hooriyeh her Canadian citizenship, which helps her travel frequently and allows her to spend time with those she loves the most.

Every few months, one or two of her children return to Tehran to look after their mother. For the most part, a nurse takes care of Hooriyeh, though her oldest daughter visits on a regular basis. Hooriyeh misses the days when everyone lived in the same house or nearby. "It was so wonderful when it was busy around me—when everyone lived in the same city and close to one another. It's just terrible now; simply terrible—everyone is living in a different corner of the world."

You can close your eyes and picture a large kitchen in either of her daughter's homes, where the beloved grandmother of eleven would be cooking for her family. Cooking is one of the greatest prizes of Persian culture. It's a tradition woven with love, compassion, and hospitality, reflective of Iran's rich history and culture. Azeri women in particular are known for their unrivaled culinary abilities—a talent mastered by Hooriyeh and her daughters. One of the most precious memories she's left for her grandchildren is when she'd gather them all to make *Ghottab*, a traditional Azeri dish in which minced herbed meat is placed on a small round bed of homemade dough that is folded in half and then fried to perfection.

Over the course of her nine-plus decades on earth, Hooriyeh has braved some of the most devastating heartaches a woman can endure; her resilience in the face of tragedy perfectly captures the ethos of Iran over the past century: two kings, a world war, a coup, a revolution that completely pulled the nation apart, followed by an eight-year war.

Today, Hooriyeh's memory is as sharp as ever, and her skin is clearer than that of a thirty-year-old, which makes you wonder about the secret to her youthful glow. Could it be because she never wore makeup? Or that, despite all her pain, she has always been loved by all those who have come into her life?

Her long, thick black locks that her middle daughter loves to trim whenever she visits from the US have turned grayish-white. Hooriyeh has promised to visit her daughter in California, but there's always a competition between her children, who all want to have "Maman" stay with them.

Her phone rings constantly; it's one of her brothers, or the grandchildren, or some other family member calling to say hello. Sometimes you'll even find her on Facetime chatting away with one of her children abroad. At any moment, one of them is ready to get her a ticket to leave Iran, but all Hooriyeh wants is to live in peace, sitting by her window, in the house she bought when her youngest son got married in the mid-1990s, and for the first time in her entire life, she had to live alone.

One wonders where her final resting place will be. Ardebil? Damavand? What about next to her children in Canada or the US? Perhaps it doesn't make any difference, for she'll always remain the paragon of life for her children, their children, and the generations to come, no matter where she's laid to rest. The likes of Hooriyeh will forever live on as the exemplar of the true loving Persian mother—the jewels of a bygone era.

All that she wants these days, however, is for her children to be happy. "That's all I want. I want them all to be happy, healthy, and at peace; that's my only wish."

Ali Nassirian

*B*OB HOOP, BOB HOOP!" HE QUIETLY LAUGHS as he repeats the famed American comedian's name in a sweet Persian accent. "I remember Bob Hope and Charlie Chaplin so well, but I loved Bob Hope the most when I was a young boy. I would laugh so much watching him," recalls the Iranian film legend whose career can be compared to the likes of Hollywood stars such as Marlon Brando, Al Pacino, and Robert De Niro.

In more than a half century of professional acting, he has performed an incredible range of roles, including an orthodox Jew, a Wahhabi Mufti, and a pious married Muslim in modern-day Iran who falls in love with a younger woman against his proclamations. He has brought kings, fools, and nationalists to life. In many cases, his performance was the sole reason the film was successful.

Yet despite his unparalleled celebrity, he remains one of the humblest actors in Iranian cinema. In a 2018 interview, Oprah Winfrey told *Vogue*, "Fame doesn't change you if you already know who you are." This sentiment vividly resonates with him. "Respect," he says. "You need to respect your work and yourself."

He is a megastar whose strong presence puts you in awe; but in all his glory, those who know him or have worked with him swear by his humility, professionalism, and exuberant respect for others. Among his colleagues and friends, he is known as a mentor for the younger generation of artists, writers, and actors. "The new generation of artists should remember one thing: perseverance," he says. "Our youth need to believe in their craft—they need to full-heartedly pursue their dreams with tenacity and never underestimate the powerful value of self-education."

The grand actor worked before the 1979 Islamic Revolution and has continued to work after it, shining in each era—proof that superb acting can transcend political turmoil. "Excellence in work and life only

comes with genuine resolve and hard work," he insists.

One of the beautiful subtleties in Farsi is how a person's manner of speaking can immediately give away their age, education, upbringing, even their religious and political beliefs. The old actor's tone, choice of words, and eloquent recollection of the past reveals his unassuming sophistication and cultured persona. His elegant speech is embedded in his love for Persian poetry, literature, and Iranian folklore—which he believes must be passed on to the next generation of Iranians who "need to know that our poets and writers have left us the greatest of assets and investment. Our culture, literature, and poetry are our birth certificate—our only identity."

⊡

Ali Nassirian was born in Tehran on a cold February day in 1935—a year before Reza Shah banned women from wearing the veil in support of his ambitions of modernizing an Iran that the rest of the world still knew as Persia. Back in a time when most families had no less than four or five children, Ali was an only child. "I was a lonely child. I didn't have anyone to play with, so I would entertain myself in my lonesome using everything that came my way."

In the 1930s, Tehran was far from the congested city it is today. Uncontrollable traffic, ominous pollution, and office buildings that creep through residential areas were all in the distant future. Back then, much of the city was comprised of dusty roads and farmland. The more developed parts were made up of beautiful villas and homes separated by narrow alleys and wide roads where people walked while carriages, bicycles, and cars crossed their paths with ease.

In those old streets, young Ali would watch performances of the classic forms of Persian theater, from the peasant fool who blackens his face in *Siah Bazi*— literally, "Black Play"—to reveal the treachery and dishonesty of his master through his own self-degradation and clown-like idiocy; to the passionate plays mourning the innocent deaths of religious martyrs and fictional heroes in *Tazieh* ("Mourning Performance"); to the allegories and mythical tales told by a single Naqqali "oral performer." This dramatic street life excited the young Ali. "I would rush home, take my mother's rouge and find a coal from the basement, fix my makeup, and start reenacting the stories I would see in the *Siah Bazi* or *Tazieh*," he recalls vividly. Among the three forms, *Tazieh* survived the revolution and is still commonly performed today in villages and more conservative states—mainly due to the fact that its religious nature is not seen as a threat. Figurative heroes, the desire for innocence, or "mazloom," the fight for legitimacy, and the strange feeling of fulfillment in mourning all live and breathe in Iran's private, public, and political spaces. These are all elements that have lived on through *Tazieh*.

Ali also remembers the popular *Tasneefs* of the time, which were ballad-like Persian classical poems turned into songs accompanied by traditional Persian music. "I would go buy the lyrics sheets to these *Tasneefs* for one qiran on Lalezar Street and come home and perform for myself." (One qiran is equivalent to less than 1/10000 of a US dollar today.) Ali also loved the atmosphere of weddings. "Gosh, they were so grand and carnivalesque. It wasn't like today where these, what are they called . . . DJs . . . would play. We had dancers and musicians with great costumes. Of course, the production varied depending on the party's budget, but it was always so fascinating for me to watch these performances, dancers, singers; it was the most magnificent sight for my childish eyes."

Unlike many Iranian parents then—and now—Ali's mother and father didn't fuss over their son's studies, and ultimately, his profession. "My parents were easy with me and let me explore," he says. Growing up as an only child, his solitude enabled him to learn how to perform, entertain, and connect with others. "Everyone loved my singing; whenever the uncles, aunts, and the family would gather, I was the first act—they would all say, 'Ali, Ali, come sing.'" His gentle laughter is a testament to a childhood where he was allowed to freely navigate his interests, which soon led him to acting.

⊡

It wasn't until the eighth grade that Ali Nassirian stepped foot on stage. He auditioned for Bahman Forsi—his then-schoolmate—who later became a respected playwright, director, and author, and who left Iran for London during the revolution. "I'd heard that there was going to be an audition, and that this tenth-grader was doing a casting call for his show. I did not hesitate for a minute and went for the audition." He recalls all of this as if it happened yesterday. "I was a thin boy and somehow they gave me the role of a street thug who had to act super macho and sing—it was so ridiculous," he shares with a laugh. That performance convinced Ali to continue acting in high school.

At Pirnia High School in Tehran, Ali was a classmate of some of Iran's most notable acting talents, including Esmail Davarfar, Jamshid Layegh and Fereydoun Farrokhzad—the brother of famed poet Forough Farrokhzad, who died in a car accident in 1967. While Forough was a pioneer in feminist confessional poetry, her brother Fereydoun became a flamboyant standup comedian, singer, and vibrant actor who was also an ardent critic of the Islamic regime. In the late 1990s, he was murdered in Bonn, Germany, in a case that is often associated with Iranian intelligence. "We made a group and started acting and putting on shows—Fereydoun would usually play a female role," Ali says with a big laugh.

After finishing high school, Ali attended the theatrical academy Jameye Barbod. There, he learned the basics and theories of acting and theater while performing minor roles. However, it wasn't long before the young actor would find himself on a famous street that many consider to be the birthplace of modern Iranian theater.

⊡

Long before Ali pursued his theatrical career, King Naser Al-Din Shah of the Qajar dynasty, who ruled Iran for a half century in the mid-nineteenth century, spent much time and money to modernize the country. The art-savvy, music-loving, and photography-obsessed ruler was the first modern Persian monarch to travel to Europe or "Farangestan" (an older term used by Persians to refer to Europe) in search of the latest innovations and trends.

In the late-1870s, inspired by a visit to Paris, the dandy king ordered that a replica of the Champs-Élysées be built in Tehran. The result was Lalezar Street, a wide boulevard filled with boutiques, cinemas, theaters, restaurants, and cabarets that for the next century would be a grand hub for luxury, fine outings, and of course, the arts. It was on this very street that one of the fathers of modern Iranian theater, Abdul-Hossein Noushin, set up shop in the 1940s. Inspired by Russian, French, and British playwrights and philosophers, Noushin was a force who modernized Iran's theatrical space. His teachings and techniques also greatly influenced a generation of professional stage actors and writers—including Ali Nassirian.

In addition to the arts, Noushin was also a devout Marxist. He and many other leftist writers, poets, and intellectuals were part of a movement that opposed the Pahlavi monarchy, as well as foreign influence in Iran—particularly that of the United States and Great Britain. In 1949, after a failed assassination attempt against Mohammad Reza Shah Pahlavi, Noushin was arrested. While in prison, he wrote the *Art of Theater*. and with the support of his wife, the Armenian-Iranian actress, Loreta, continued to influence his followers from behind bars. "I remember reading Noushin's *Art of Theater* while he was still in prison and immediately signed up to join his theatrical group in the Saadi Theater," Ali says. "There we practiced and learned about writers like Gorky, Maeterlinck, and Oscar Wilde." But the eighteen-year-old Ali's time at the Saadi did not last long. In 1953, the US and Great Britain's coup d'état toppled the democratically elected Prime Minister Mohammad Mosaddegh. The Saadi was among the many theaters, newspapers, and publications shut down by government forces in the wake of the coup.

Following the closing of the Saadi Theater, Ali worked with Armenian-Iranian dramatist, writer, and scholar, Shahin Sarkisian, who even more than Noushin, was influenced by European, French and American playwrights. Under Sarkisian's coaching, Ali learned the Stanislavski method and reenacted plays by Anton Chekhov, Henrik Ibsen, August Strindberg, Luigi Pirandello, and Arthur Miller. "We did so much and spent hours and hours at Sarkisian's home, and also the theater."

During the early 1950s, American movies were regularly popping up on the screens of Lalezar Street's glittering cinemas. One of Ali's great joys was to save up money and treat himself to an American film. "I always loved watching western movies when I was younger," he recalls. "I loved the headdresses and makeup of the Native Americans— somehow they reminded me of our own *Tazieh*." One American actor in particular caught Ali's attention. "Marlon Brando. I still remember him in Tennessee William's *A Streetcar Named Desire*. I still think it's one of the best performances of all time."

During the same period, the twenty-two-year-old actor wrote his first play. Inspired by Iranian writer Sadegh Hedayat—a pioneer of literary modernism—Ali wrote *The Golden Serpent,* a love-story rooted in Iranian folklore. In 1959, he wrote his second play, *Bolbole Sargashte* or *The Wandering Nightingale*—a tragedy where a wicked woman, in love with her stepson, kills the boy and feeds his body to his father; justice

prevails at the end when the boy's sister resurrects her brother's soul in the form of a nightingale. The story is a textured tale that maneuvers through the ever-present themes of mazloom—the innocent, the mourning of the dead, and the resurrection of truth.

Ali's play became a smash success. It went on to tour the country, and eventually ended up at the International Theatre Institute ITI (Théâtre des Nations) in Paris—the world's largest performing arts organization, founded in 1948 by UNESCO in collaboration with some elite performers of the time. *The Wandering Nightingale* was Iran's first theatrical performance in the west.

During the 1960s, Ali helped produce and starred in dozens of theatrical productions for Iran's then-privatized television network. "It was really then that the public got to know us," he says. "Television truly changed the way we performed." Ali Nassirian would go on to play many leading roles alongside some of Iran's greatest actors, writers, and directors. One of his most well-regarded masterpieces was in Dariush Mehrjui's 1969 film, *Cow*. Released during a turbulent period of heightened censorship, the film explores many deeply rooted social issues within the rural population, including delusion and misgivings toward the "enemy," and the lack of boundaries in people's public and private lives.

At the height of the 1979 Islamic Revolution, many of Ali's colleagues left Iran. Ali himself left for a brief period to perform some of his plays in the US and Canada, but soon returned home to Iran. "I spent time in Los Angeles, New York, and some large cities in Canada. Many people there regarded theater as a weekend activity, a way to pass time, not as an art," he says, recalling how tickets for his plays were sold at the Persian Markets—still a common practice for many Iranian performances in the West. "It wasn't serious. It's like moving a plant from its soil and forcing it to grow in another soil—a foreign soil—a soil that's so incompatible with its natural habitat and natural place of growth. For that plant to grow, thrive, and reproduce, you need to have it where it belongs, where it's rooted. I couldn't leave my roots. I belonged to this culture, to this society."

The first few years after the Islamic Revolution, the television and film industry was going through an ambiguous phase. Those prerevolution artists who stayed were not sure of the new government mandates or what was going to be censored by the new regime. "Who would have thought that some of the greatest talents of Iran's cinema would appear in those years." Ali recalls. "There are hidden talents in our country today and they all have exceptional potential to shine," says the timeless actor, who praises prerevolution filmmakers and writers like Kiarostami and Mehrjui, but also embraces postrevolution geniuses like two-time Academy Award-winning writer and director Asghar Farhadi. "Today, there are eighty million new outlooks and perspectives in Iran. The young minds are forward-thinking and with that, will only grow new ideas."

Unlike many other industries, cinema—in its restricted nature—has somewhat thrived in postrevolution Iran, giving birth to powerful works that speak to the nation's social issues. Actors, actresses, directors, and writers have all found creative ways to share some of the most deeply disturbing realities of life through their storytelling, writing, and performances. It is ironic that under censorship and constant control, Iran's postrevolution cinema has produced some of its most outstanding pictures. One of Ali's most regarded postrevolution roles was as Judge Shareh in the 1982 television series, *Sarbedaran*, which told the story of the historic revolt of the Persian "Sarbedaran" army of Khurasan against the Mongol invasion of Persia.

Looking back at Ali's work, it becomes obvious that he has always been immune to external pressures—a clear testament to an unconditional commitment to his craft, his country, and family. Despite his long and distinguished career, today, his wife and three sons are his most treasured possessions. "Aside from my integrity, my family is all I have in life," he says. He met his wife when they were both young, as they were family friends. She is a typical caring Iranian housewife who loves to nourish and support her husband and children. When you call their home to talk with Master Nassirian, she speaks to you as if you were her own child. (Ali's beloved wife passed away in 2019.)

Though Ali has remained in Iran, his three sons left their homeland for the United States. When you ask about his children, you can sense a stifled grief in his voice. For a man who so fundamentally loves his family, you can imagine how hard it must be to have his children live abroad. He was a lonely child growing up, and these days the solitude he feels in the absence of his sons is inescapable. Luckily, one of them has come back. "One of them has returned recently. He actually lives nearby," the old man says with pure joy.

The humility that so many associate with this legend is evident in his only remaining wish. "My only wish at this stage of life is to preserve my dignity, respect, and name." Then, in his typical calming tone, with his usual elegance, Ali recites a poem from the great thirteenth century Persian poet, Saadi:

" نام نیکو گر بماند ز آدمی، به کزو ماند سرای زرنگار"

"It's much better if instead of gold, a person leaves a respected reputation behind."

Mohammad-Ali Abtahi

*W*hen I was young boy, I would cry a lot during prayers, asking God for a bicycle and a Super 8 camcorder. I remember one time, *Agha Jaan* (an old-fashioned term for father) came to me and asked, 'my dear son, what is it you want from God so desperately that makes you cry like this?'"

He laughs with a boyish energy as he remembers the day. "There was a young guy who worked at our house and we became friends when I was a little boy," he begins. "The two of us decided to go to the Imam Reza shrine to buy a camera. There was a guy nearby who sold Russian Lubitels and I remember paying him ten toman to buy the camera. It was the most exciting thing. I took my friend and we went inside the shrine. It was midweek and the place was empty. We soon found an open door that led to a staircase and decided to climb all the way up."

Little did the boy know that the long fractal staircase would take him and his friend into a forbidden place where they would capture some of the most remarkable images of what's often referred to as the "Holy City of Mashhad," home to the largest mosque in the world and the resting place of Imam Reza, the Eighth Imam of the Shia Muslims. "Apparently we had ended up atop the minaret."

While the city of Qom—the resting place of Imam Reza's sister, Masoumeh—remains the main hub for Shia jurisprudence in Iran, Mashhad's unparalleled significance is predominantly spiritual and cultural. As a result, the shrine is equally revered by religious and nonreligious people alike. "It was just spectacular. I have no words to describe the view, my feeling, and just everything we felt at that moment. We quickly started to take pictures of each other. I'd take some of him and he'd do the same for me; and then we'd switch again." Their innocent fun abruptly came to a halt when the guards of the holy shrine suddenly noticed the boys up above the minaret. "They rushed through the door and started yelling at us and kicking us out. I mean we were technically intruders and were absolutely not allowed to go through that door, let alone be up the minaret taking pictures. But I mean we didn't really know where that door was going to take us." He laughs again.

Ayatollah Mohammad-Ali Abtahi is a Shia Muslim cleric whose name is synonymous with reform for many Iranians. He was twenty years old when the Islamic Revolution overthrew the Pahlavi monarchy and forever changed Iranian history. He does things that regular Ayatollahs don't. He puts on his turban and cloak when he is going to an official

meeting, ceremony, or making a television appearance; when off duty, he wears regular khakis and an Oxford shirt like an ordinary man. More than anything, he has humanized the clergy. He seems sincere, modest, and in some ways, even cool. He's an avid fan of theater, a movie buff, and a music enthusiast. "I think Woody Allen makes incredibly powerful films. Have you seen *Midnight in Paris*?" he asks me in a questioning tone, as if he's keen to hear my opinion of the film. "I've also recently watched *Snowden*, which I think was fascinating; same with *The Social Network*. But what I love are the movies that somehow merge human spirit and values with other more contemporary motifs. For example, I really enjoyed *Me Before You*."

All these movies are "technically" banned by the Iranian government, and would only air on public television after going through several layers of censorship; but in reality, the ever-flowing stream of foreign entertainment is covertly consumed by everyday Iranians as if there's nothing to stop them from watching, listening, and downloading the same content that is consumed in North America or Europe. There was a time, in the earlier years of the Islamic Revolution, when entertainment was severely controlled; but nowadays, high-speed internet and technology have made it much harder for the regime to stifle every inch of life in Iran.

It's hard to believe that this arts-and-culture aficionado was once part of a repressive regime that continues to censor artists, filmmakers, writers, and musicians in Iran. "I think one of my biggest accomplishments in life has been my ability to distinguish and differentiate between the various aspects of my life," he proclaims proudly. "In other words, I have always tried to be the best cleric while being the best father, at the same time understanding literature and following cultural movements. At this very moment that we're speaking, I can comfortably say that there are no famous novels or books (both domestically and internationally) that I have not read. Even during some of the most hectic and turbulent times of my life, there was not a week that would go by without me watching at least one title from IMBD's top movie list."

He was also a pioneer in Iran in the use of technology and social media. "I was the first *akhoond* (cleric) to have a web log and use the internet to connect with people," Abtahi tells me with obvious pride. He was also the first government official to use a mobile phone to take pictures and share them with his followers. "I'll never forget when I heard that there were mobile phones coming that had cameras on them and could take pictures. I asked one of my friends in Dubai to get me one; and as soon as I got my hands on the phone I couldn't stop taking pictures from government meetings, of administration officials, and just everything and anything I wanted, and then post it on my blog."

The "Blogger Ayatollah" soon became a somewhat popular figure among Iranian youth—who to this day are still deprived of unfiltered online freedom. "I feel my blog was the single source of communication between the administration and the people," he states. "Other channels were often closed, censored, and just nonexistent, so in a way the blog turned into a reformist outlet for millions of Iranians. I never missed a single day of blogging and posting new content on the blog. The only day I missed posting was the night I was arrested back in 2009."

While social media was growing into a worldwide phenomenon over the past few decades, it was being turned into a feared commodity by the Iranian government, particularly under the Ahmadinejad administration. Twitter, Facebook, and many other websites as well as phone messenger apps were all filtered (and still are to an extent.) On a larger scale, the regime will even disconnect the country's entire internet apparatus if it feels the need to—as seen in the aftermath of the November 2019 protests that opposed the government's sudden hike in fuel prices. Despite these restrictions, savvy youth use VPNs (Virtual Private Networks) to circumvent the constant filtering and maintain an active social media presence. As a result, Iran has the highest number of internet users in the Middle East—a powerful reminder that the Iranian people have a strong voice and a fervent desire to belong to the international community.

"Entering the virtual space was an incredibly important thing for me," Abtahi says. "I have fifty, sixty thousand followers who are teenagers. I try to understand what they say, what they want, what they read, do, listen to—what young boys and girls do. There's nothing more important than to be part of the society and learn about the youth. They (the government) don't understand that virtual space cannot be banned; they don't understand that they need to define society based on their needs. You know, like it or not, want it or not, social media is a reality and the youth are active there—we too need to be out there; we too need to connect with this population."

Abtahi's father, Agha Jaan (an old-fashioned term used in Farsi for father), was an old-school and well-respected cleric in Mashhad. "He was highly respected by many," Abtahi shares. "Agha Jaan had some land and I guess was what you call a landlord in his own right; he had many friends who were reputable merchants and traders at the time."

Abtahi is the oldest sibling of a family that includes his two younger brothers and sisters as well as a half-brother from his father's second wife, with whom he grew close after his mother's death in 2008. The family grew up in a religious household—a large estate where his father hosted fellow clerics and other religious authorities. "I don't remember that we ever sat together for a meal." Abtahi recalls. "There was always something happening in our house. Agha Jaan would always have guests over and my beloved mother's kitchen was always on. She was the kindest and most generous woman."

Growing up, Abtahi was exposed to many of the pioneers of the Islamic Revolution, including the man who would later become Supreme Leader. "When I was a teenager, I would attend Ayatollah Khomeini's lectures in Mashhad. I also really liked Dr. Shariati and would read his writings and listen to his lectures. I was also heavily influenced by my uncle, my mother's brother—a more vigorous religious revolutionary—who was martyred in the beginning of the revolution by the MEK."

Ali Shariati was born into a family of clerics outside of Mashhad. In 1964, after finishing his PhD at the Sorbonne, the charismatic revolutionary returned to Iran and began a series of radical lectures in Mashhad and then later in Tehran. He is still regarded as one of Iran's most notable sociologists and philosophers. He was imprisoned and placed under house arrest on multiple occasions by the Pahlavi regime. Two years prior to the revolution, Shariati fled Iran for the United Kingdom, where he soon died from an "apparent heart attack" at the age of forty-three.

Shariati is credited as one of the most prominent figures espousing anti-Shah narratives, which helped ignite the flames of the revolution in 1979. In his lectures and writings, he was heavily critical of the monarchy and the shallow "Westernization" of Iran, while supporting the revival of traditional religious values—in this case Shiism—in the nation's fight for social justice. While Shariati's work was entwined with Shia values, many conservative clerics and mullahs of the time were critical of his "enlightened" views of Islam—a prejudice that drove him out of Mashhad and forced the young visionary to settle in Tehran.

Abtahi began his religious studies after finishing fourth grade. He was partly home schooled, and also attended religious institutions. "These days *rohaniat* (clericalism) has become political, but back then, the clerical sects and political actors were separate entities. You know, politics is earthly (*zamini*), politics is not ethereal (*asemani*)." While some shared Abtahi's moderate vision at the time of the revolution, the burning desire for change following the Shah's overthrow, along with the sanguine promises of the opposition—and ultimately in many cases, the ignorance of the masses—led millions of Iranians to follow Ayatollah Ruhollah Khomeini. "I used to pass out leaflets myself when I was only sixteen, seventeen years old," Abtahi says. "The air was filled with a revolutionary energy—it was busy times." However, this revolutionary activity began to create some distance between Abtahi and his father. "I was excited to be a part of this change, but I found myself drifting away from my father, who wasn't taking part in the revolution."

While Abtahi's father, as well as his brothers, did not take part in the revolutionary activity sweeping Iran, his uncle, Abdolkarim Hasheminejad, was an ardent follower of the ayatollah, and ultimately became Khomeini's man in Mashhad. However, just three short years after the revolution, Abtahi's uncle was assassinated by a suicide bomber outside his office in Mashhad. It was later confirmed that the assassin was part of the infamous "Mujahedin-e-Khalq" (MEK), commonly known as the National Council of Resistance of Iran (NCRI) in the West. In their steadfast opposition to the Shah, the group was initially an ally of the ayatollah and his followers, but after the revolution, its allegiance turned into an armed animosity over ideology and direction. This fallout led to a bloodbath that saw executions and murders carried out against the Mujahedin by the newly formed Islamic Republic. Simultaneously, the MEK turned rogue and carried out suicide bombings and murders— including the assassination of Americans—and later sided with Saddam Hussein during the Iran-Iraq War.

The MEK is resented by almost all Iranians inside the country and abroad, and for the longest time was designated a terrorist organization by the United States and Europe. However, in 2012, after decades of lobbying and funding by "certain" governments, the group was removed from the terrorist list and soon found itself a new office five minutes away from the White House. Since then, Washington hawks, warmongers, and politicians like Rudy Giuliani, John Bolton, Tom Cotton, Mike Pompeo, Robert Torricelli, Joseph Lieberman, and Mitch McConnell's wife, Elaine Chao, have supported and received payments from the MEK to lobby , attend or speak at their events. To many people's disdain, the much-respected American war hero and one-time presidential candidate, Senator John McCain, was also a supporter of the group.

⊡

"I always loved reading, but in those days, we didn't have much access to translated books," Abtahi reminisces. "But I knew this guy who was the son of one of Mashhad's clerics who gave me my first translated copy of a foreign book." It was *Sartre on Cuba* by Jean-Paul Sartre—a revolutionary book that takes the reader into the anti-colonial Cuba of Fidel Castro and Che Guevara. "The book had a strong impact on me, and I found it brilliant. I didn't have much general knowledge of the world, so this was an incredibly eye-opening read." Abtahi became a voracious reader. "Slowly, more and more books became available and I began to vehemently read whatever I could find. I recall being enthralled by Bangladesh's independence from Pakistan. I found it to be the most fascinating international phenomenon of the time. I also started reading Arabic books and grew fond of Sayyid Qutb and former Egyptian President Gamal Abdel Nasser. As you know, Qutb was convicted and executed by Nasser's government for an attempt to assassinate the president. It's funny because to this day I find myself faced with a paradox. How can it be that on one hand I support Nasser and on the other hand find Qutb important?"

In addition to being an avid reader, Abtahi is also a lover of tea, and he asked me several times during our interview if he could be excused to pour himself another cup. His casual level of comfort is a reflection of his confidence and especially his pecululiar authenticity, which is a rare quality to find in government officials or religious figures, regardless of their nationality. "Let me think. It could be anyone?" he says in response to my question about which famous person he'd choose to have tea with if he could. "Ah . . . If I could sit and have tea with anyone in the world—dead or alive—I'd choose Ahmad Mahmoud. I wish we could just sit in one of those houses from his novel *Hamsayeha* (*Neighbors*) and just talk—talk about everything and anything. Of course, if Bolour Khanoom allows." He chuckles as he alludes to the young vixen who seduces the naive protagonist of the novel.

Ahmad E'ta, known commonly by his pen name Ahmad Mahmoud, was a well-respected Iranian novelist and a pioneering force in social realism. His critical outlook toward the Pahlavi monarchy, imperialism, and devotion to the daily struggles of the poor and the working class made him an enemy of the state. He was one of the many young and fervid followers of Mosaddegh who drew inspiration from the pro-democracy movement of the early 1950s. Many of his novels, including *Neighbors,* were banned under the Shah for political reasons and later censored by the ayatollah for containing sexual improprieties.

In the immediate aftermath of the 1979 revolution, the newly established theocracy drafted a new constitution and began to purge academic textbooks of any westernized or pro-Shah narratives, inserting their own language that conformed with the Islamic government's ideology and agenda. The so-called "Cultural Revolution" disrupted universities and the entirety of the academic system in the early to mid-1980s. In a 1989 referendum, the government made some amendments to the 1979 constitution, with the Supreme Leader claiming the authority to appoint the head of the newly named Islamic Republic of Iran Broadcasting (IRIB).

It was during this time that young Abtahi was assigned to his first broadcasting post in Mashhad. "I was probably the only cleric who knew something about tv, radio, films, and things as such," he shares. "I was also respected for my religious background, so immediately after the revolution the higher ups recommended me to be in charge of Mashhad's radio programming. I was the only cleric who the radio folks would be okay with, I guess." Soon, Abtahi was transferred to head the radio stations in Bushehr and Shiraz—two critical capitals in the Bushehr and Fars Provinces—during the early years of the Iran-Iraq War. Eventually, he was sent by the IRIB to Tehran, and appointed to run Iranian radio. "My first daughter was only a few months old and my wife was still in Mashhad," Abtahi recalls. "It was early on in the war and she didn't want to move to Tehran. But we had no choice and had to go. I moved my small family to Tehran, and have stayed here since."

Back then, the only way that information could get in and out of Iran was through the country's physical borders. Radio and television were fully controlled by the government, and books, magazines, cassettes, and any other type of media was checked before being allowed to leave the country. Even women's sewing patterns were impounded by the Islamic Revolutionary Guard Corps (IRGC). Nothing could get by the vigilant eyes of the *Pasdars* (another common word for the IRGC forces), or through the country's tightened security apparatus. "It was as if I was the only ally of the entertainment folks in those days," Abtahi recalls. "I was never conservative and never wanted to impose any tough regulation or restrictions. The people—especially the clergy—who would enter the radio and television were not popular at all among the employees and professionals, but I always tried to become friends with the rest of the team even though I was under an enormous amount of pressure from the outside and above." Even though there were still some moderate voices during the early stages of the Khomeini regime, they had minimal power and a limited reach—especially pertaining to national security and intelligence matters. There was only so much they could do given the hardliner's large influence, which was supported by the country's highest authority, the Supreme Leader.

When it comes to media censorship, Iran remains one of the most highly controlled countries in the world—especially for journalists, writers and filmmakers. Despite this, there has been an exponential loosening of those early postrevolution limits. For example, ordinary people would rarely talk politics with strangers, impermissible music playing in a car would have meant detention or a fine for the driver, and women's hijabs in public were heavily restricted. Nowadays, women's headscarves are loosely worn, people publicly curse the regime, and you can hear Cardi B, Beyoncé, or deep house music blasting from cars stuck in the jam-packed traffic of cities nationwide. Similarly, while there were very few Iranian women on television postrevolution (and they were always forced to wear the chador), today you can find more color and ease on many television shows and Iranian-produced movies. After the revolution, the only entertainment from the West allowed were depressing foreign dramas and cartoons that had been heavily censored and altered; today, nobody watches IRIB, and most households—including those of government officials—have satellite channels that give them unprecedented access to the global stage. "A lot has happened over the years," Abtahi says, "and I think the patience of our filmmakers, and cultural figures should be heavily admired and respected. They have been very patient."

Abtahi was only twenty-seven when he joined Mohammad Khatami at the Ministry of Culture and Islamic Guidance—an organization that restricts cultural, literary, or artistic activities that are deemed as threatening to the ideology and security of the Islamic regime. Khatami, who would serve as Iran's president from 1997 to 2005, was a well-known reformist. "I really wanted to work with Khatami and when he asked me to join him at the ministry, I immediately left the radio and went on to become his cultural attaché," Abtahi says. "The job gave me the opportunity to travel all the time; there were few countries that I have not traveled to and I think these journeys enabled me to have an even wider outlook and a much more open perspective." This extensive travel allowed Abtahi to build cultural relationships throughout the world, which would prove key to his reform-based ideas. "I was so fortunate because I was constantly meeting counterparts who were heads of this theater or that cinema, this art gallery or that publication, and in general got the opportunity to be exposed to an international cultural and arts sphere. In Iran, we were also part of the reformist camp, so this was the first steps toward my efforts to building a better relationship with people."

In 1992, under the presidency of Hashemi Rafsanjani—a once conservative pillar of the Islamic Revolution who in the later years of his life put on the mask of a reformist—Khatami was forced to resign from the Ministry of Culture. His resignation came only four years after the end of the Iran-Iraq War, and was one of the first public examples of domestic turmoil between the reformists and the hardliners who, while small in number, continue to have a strong grip on the country.

A faithful follower of Khatami, Abtahi too left the ministry and soon found himself back in radio—this time heading the country's bureau in Beirut. "I just didn't get along with the management. They were from the other side and so they sent me to Beirut just so they could keep face, but still keep me away and out of sight."

Five years later, in 1997, millions of women, students, and intellectuals—longing for change after nearly two decades of repressive rule—came out to support Mohammad Khatami for president. With almost 70 percent of the vote, Khatami won the election and became the first "reformist" president of the Islamic Republic of Iran. "I got myself back to Tehran and was soon appointed as the president's chief of staff," Abtahi proudly tells me.

Khatami's presidency was the first example of a stark difference between the government and the regime. As primitive as it may sound, the main reason Khatami was so beloved by ordinary people was that for the first time since the revolution, Iran was represented by a man who knew how to speak English and who seemed to value globalization, engagement, and social justice. On the international stage, Khatami is perhaps best known for presenting the "Dialogue Among Civilizations" to the United Nations, which resulted in the UN naming the year 2001 after his initiative.

Unsurprisingly, Khatami's presidency was dominated by a polarized political rift between the reformist agenda of the one-time revolutionaries—who after nearly two decades were dissatisfied with the course of their revolution—and the hardline conservatives who were backed by the security, religious, and intelligence apparatus. In opposition to Khatami's presumed support for press freedom, many reformist newspapers and dailies were shut down by these forces. This led in July 1999 to the largest student led protests since the revolution. Students were beaten, arrested, and tortured—with some even reportedly killed in prison. In the end, nearly no one was held accountable. This divide left many ordinary Iranians disillusioned with the idea of major reform.

"We did what we could. I for one did all I could," Abtahi states mournfully. In some ways, he feels that some of the harshest criticism of the Khatami administration came directly in opposition to his moderate views. "Honestly, I feel some of the biggest hits to the administration came because of my push for reformist policies. They thought I was an effective force in this effort." During Khatami's second term, Abtahi resigned from his post as the Vice President for Legal and Parliamentary Affairs.

"One of the biggest problems of this regime is that it has made it quite easy to be its enemy," Abtahi declares. "Meaning, when they say women who don't conform to full hijab are 'enemies of the government' then whoever wants to show their rage toward the system will mess with their hijab. Why should a strong government be so easily poked at?" He believes the only way the country "can grow and succeed is to have people of different beliefs coexist amicably and be respectful of one another," whether they be conservative or moderate. "I believe that neither forgoing all religious values nor constraining people in the name of Islam will lead to the society's success. We can have everything in balance and moderation, and that's what we need."

In one of his talks that aired on Iran's version of YouTube, Abtahi said that the emphasis on the religious viewpoint by the country's ruling class has damaged Iranian society. "I'm worried about the demise of any real religious values," he states plainly. "When one has introduced personal expectations as religious demands and in ways have taken every single right or freedom away in this guise, people would naturally say that they want to live their one life instead of abiding by the mandates. When they see this 'religious' interference with every aspect of their life, they choose living over religion. This is what concerns me. In reality, faith and life should be entwined and complement one another, but now our people are forced to choose one or the other." Abtahi believes that these issues stem from the ignorance of the religious conservatives: "I feel part of it is that there are those who want to completely deny the reality, while there are others who truly don't know any better. They feel information is provided by the newspapers, but in reality, no one reads the paper these days except for themselves. It's as if they're communicating with one another without being in touch with reality of life and the people."

In 2009, Abtahi was arrested during the so-called "green movement" that apposed the re-election of President Mahmoud Ahmadinejad. He was directly involved with the campaign of one of the two reformist candidates, both of whom were placed under house arrest. What followed was an unprecedented uprising by millions of students, political activists, and ordinary men and women in support of the "reformist" leadership. Unfortunately, the movement was suppressed by hardline forces, with thousands beaten and arrested, and many killed. Along with other reformist figures, intellectuals, journalists, and political activists, Abtahi was detained and sent to the notorious Evin prison. There, Saeed Mortazavi, Tehran's then-Prosecutor General and one of the most ferocious figures to ever hold a government post, personally took on the task of abusing the cleric, telling Abtahi "to write his will." In the aftermath of the failed revolt, Abtahi's former boss, Khatami, was also placed under severe scrutiny and banned from making any press and public appearances.

"Those days were not good and I really don't want to talk about it," Abtahi says with obvious anguish. "It hurts. There are so many anxieties that still remain. What worries me today is what's going to happen to Iran? What's going to come out of these fractions and polarizations. Every day I think about what could happen on these streets," he says with a heavy sigh. "I still see my therapist every other week. It's funny because people in Iran don't publicly talk about therapy, but it was one of the most important things that helped me get through this."

Aside from therapy, Abtahi's wife and three daughters were the main force that got him back on his feet. "My wife was always there for me. I don't know what I would have done without the support of my family. Oftentimes, I worry about whether or not I was strong enough for my family. I wonder if these events ever made them think that I'm not there for them. That thought troubles me a lot. I worry about them; I worry that I don't disappoint or embarrass my wife or my children. Over the years, they were my rock; I hope they know how much I'm grateful for them."

Abtahi was only eighteen when he married his then-fifteen-year-old wife. "Those days, they just wanted to make sure guys got married, so they didn't get into trouble or commit any sinful acts. So my mom was very keen in finding me a wife," he says. His wife ended up being his cousin—a teenager whom he didn't meet until the day of their wedding. "It was super traditional back then; in the family gatherings, women only spent time with women and the men were always separated, so I never really had a chance to see her face-to-face." Despite their young ages when they married, the two of them have managed to build a happy life. "We were both kids," he says in a kind voice. "We pretty much grew up together. Our marriage grew into a friendship that I think was beautiful—something that has made our marriage strong." With three daughters, the cleric is surrounded by women, which he believes to be a blessing: "I have three girls and I think that's why our life is filled with kindness and a gentle softness."

Unlike their own marriage, he and his wife have not interfered in their daughter's futures. "Both my girls who are married chose their own husbands and met them on their own; my youngest is still at home working on finishing her degree in the arts."

Today, the retired government official spends his time reading, writing, going to the theater and movies, and listening to his favorite music. "Music is a little tickle that comes and warms one's heart, and this heart does not always want the same thing," he says with the music of his voice. "Sometimes it wants happy music, sometimes it wants pop, sometimes it needs foreign music, and sometimes it needs traditional Persian songs. I've always said that the best music is the one you can connect with at that given moment." He also has his particular Iranian favorites. "I have to say of all these Iranian singers, Ghomayshi was always special for me. There's a warm melancholy in his voice—one that invites you to move with him. So many people have the same melancholy, but his makes you want to walk along with his music." Siavash Ghomayshi is one of the many singers who fled Iran after the Islamic Revolution; his music continues to be banned by the regime.

Abtahi also has a love for *ghelyoun*—also known as hookah or shisha in the Western world. "I love to go out with my wife, just go shopping, walking, and sometimes go to my favorite café. There's a great spot I love that has the best ghelyoun and tea. I just love going there with her to relax for a few hours." It is easy to picture him with his wife, driving down to his favorite café on Kheradmand Street in central Tehran, listening to a Ghomayshi oldie in the background. "I just want people to be happy, I want them to enjoy life. I want to enjoy life myself, and you know none of that is in contrast with my beliefs and values."

Abtahi believes that Iranians are inherently nonviolent, but have sadly been labeled the opposite by much of the world. "Iranians are some of the greatest and smartest people in the world, and I think labeling them negatively has hurt them a lot over the years. We are often framed as the bad guys. You see, we passed a revolution, an eight-year-long war, and sanctions, so—based on the Western belief—80 percent of our population should have ended up as terrorists. No? But in none of these terrorist attacks do you see one single Iranian. Why? Because we—as Iranians—inherently don't want violence."

His favorite Islamic word is *Allah*. "I think it's the most important word; it reminds us that there is a single God—one that we all believe in despite our religion and origin. And you know, this single power, this single God almighty has not created us to kill each other. He created us with love; he is *rahman e raheem* (the beneficent and the merciful). As a Muslim man, I know my God as that—as rahman e rahim."

Back when he worked for the government, as part of his travels, Abtahi went to the United States on a few occasions, visiting New York, Washington, Missouri, and Los Angeles. "Everything seemed so big, the cars, buildings, the people." He also noticed something that made him understand why people voted for someone like Donald Trump. "One of the things that fascinated me the most was how simple-minded they were. They are good people and very kind, but were quite simple. Based on my observation, they have been fed this idea that they are the greatest and most powerful nation in the world, but really don't know what to do with it or what it even means. I also think it's quite remarkable how religious many of them are and how much it affects their politics. In a way, when you look at their politicians you see that they are part of the same fabric. I think I now understand where Mr. Trump got votes from and who were the people who voted for him."

These days, Abtahi spends much of his time working on his novels— stories that have not been granted permission for publication by the same Ministry of Culture and Islamic Guidance he once worked for. "I love storytelling and writing novels. My first novel is about this family and all the complications they endure during the 2009 uprisings. It has really shaped up to be a beautiful story, but unfortunately, it has not been approved for publication." While his novels are yet to be released, he received permission to publish an anthology called *We Lost* in 2017. The book is a collection of his blog posts from 2004 to 2005, during the final year of the Khatami presidency.

If you scroll through his Instagram account, you will see that he's passionate about books—foreign titles that are translated into Farsi and published in Iran. His captions are well thought out and he's always inviting others to share their views. Among his recommendations are *Everyday Is Extra* by former US Secretary Of State John Kerry, *Becoming* by Michelle Obama, and Nobel Prize Laureate Svetlana Alexievich's *The Unwomanly Face Of War*. Of his many posts, one seems particularly special. In it, he writes about the day he visited his youngest daughter's photo gallery exhibition at Tehran University, a display of her thesis project entitled "Tehran: Fear, Solitude." "Wherever you are born and raised is called your city," reads his daughter's words from the project. "The place is commonly known as your homeland; a homeland that shapes the experiences of your existence—birth, life, laughter, tears, family, love, separation, pain, depression, happiness, and worst of all, solitude and fear. My city is called Tehran. It's a large city filled with dichotomies, contrasts, and cohesions; filled with different classes and sympathy; filled with murder and mercy; filled with intertwined highways and anxious traffic; filled with communities and neighborhoods with unique cultures and unfamiliar migrant faces; and most importantly a place of creating and making decisions. While beautiful and exciting, it can also be terrifying. The minute this fear curls around your solitude is when the most enduring of feelings fills your heart and soul. Whether big or small, in this project, I searched for the terrifying experiences that those close to me have experienced in this tumultuous city—a city that's homeland, a homeland that's the flesh and body."

When I asked Abtahi what he would like Iran to be like in fifty years, when his daughters are old women, he told me he wants the country to be a powerful regional force whose people are also prosperous and successful. "It would be incredible if both can be achieved at the same time. I'm the happiest when I see young people who are happy—young people who are hopeful for a better future."

Faezeh

"THERE IS NOTHING MORE TRAITOROUS than living life as an outsider, like an outcast. There is nothing more painful than feeling as if you're living life in limbo." Her beautiful thick brown hair accentuates her fair skin, and her unruffled smile leads you to stare into her brown eyes—piercing through with an undeniable vigor. It's hard to imagine that until recently, this petite girl—with her bright red lips and red nail polish—shielded herself beneath a dark black veil, filled with judgment and prejudice against the West, the United States, and all things secular and free. "Before, it was the public who would put on a mask in front of me," she says sadly, but defiantly, "but now, I'm the one masking my true identity from my family and those who belong to my colony."

This duality of life is nothing out of the ordinary in today's Iran; but what's striking is how a twenty-something-year-old managed to resurrect herself by breaking away from one of the darkest and most confining strands of current Iranian society—the conservative "true believers." They are the powerful minority who believe fervently in the regime's narrative, "Velayate Faghih," or the "Guardianship of the Islamist Jurist," and in the country's Supreme Leader. They are the vassals who make up the intelligence apparatus, the Islamic Revolutionary Guard Corps (IRGC), and the Basij forces. They're the custodians of the revolution; the ones who fight Russia's war in Syria; the ones who beat people during protests; and the ones who impose the hardline rules of the regime across Iran. In reality, the majority of government officials

and regime insiders engage in many of the activities they deem "haram" or "un-permissible" in public. From drinking alcohol, watching and listening to the music and programs they ban, to womanizing, selling drugs, and money laundering, they do it all.

One of the lasting ironies of the Islamic Revolution is that the hardliners failed to successfully embed their version of Islam into the private lives of most ordinary Iranians. Instead, by force-feeding them their inflexible ideology, they created an inherent resentment against religion and its practice among much of citizenry. As a result, most Iranians have learned how to hide their private lives in order to blend into the confines of the regime—maneuvering through the didactic rules of the government while practicing their freedom behind closed doors. The more the regime shoved its narratives down people's throats, the more resentful the people became. So much so that today, religious ceremonies are only attended by supporters of the regime and those employed by the government.

While most people in modern-day Iran grew up learning how to live this public/private duality, the young girl never learned that trick, which caused many of her friends and family to turn against her. "Ever since I was a little girl, I remember my dad would always praise me for my beliefs, my love of Islam, my devotion," she says. "But now they see me as a pariah, as a rebel. There were so many times that my friends would judge me, point fingers at me, and tell me that I'm starting to dress like a prostitute or speak like an idiot—all because I was finally realizing my free will."

⊡⋮

The term "one-eye Chadori" is a colloquial way to refer to an ultra conservative woman who is fully covered, with only one eye showing from beneath her long black veil.

Faezeh was once one of them.

She was born and raised in an ultra-conservative family in a rural section of Tehran. Her father is a retired IRGC official who continues to be a rigid supporter of the regime. Her mother is a traditional religious woman who believes her sole purpose in life is to support her husband and raise her children. "We grew up in what I call a cultural colony—a colony that the *Sepah* (IRGC) creates for its employees," Faezeh tells me. "We were around the same types of people, with similar beliefs, political views, and employment. It was only natural for us to grow up believing in an incredibly narrow perspective that was dictated to us all our lives."

There was no music allowed in her home, no films, and no foreign media. The only entertainment permissible was state television. And it wasn't just her family. "Everyone around me was like us," Faezeh shares. "Our neighbors, family, friends, they all lived like this, so it was only natural for me to be resentful toward the others who didn't live like us, those who thought differently, those who looked differently—the rest of the society and the rest of the world. We didn't know any better. I didn't know any better."

As a youngster, Faezeh was more of a tomboy than a girly-girl. Her biggest wish was to play with the neighborhood boys in the street and ride a bicycle. "Gosh, I still remember how much I wanted to ride a bicycle. They told me boys do that, or it's not safe and permissible to ride the bicycle on the streets. Sometimes I feel I didn't get the chance to experience the simplest moments of my childhood."

When she was fourteen, her father decided to relocate the family to a more conservative community. Faezeh explained that her father was concerned that their already conservative neighborhood was at risk of becoming home "to other less conservative people and families"— deeming this a threat to his family. "He freaked out and moved us to Parand—a newly built community near Imam Khomeini International Airport. It was a new community and only IRGC and hardcore government employees were living there."

Together with her older sister, Faezeh attended Koran classes and the mosque. Even though Faezeh had a passion and talent for drawing and art, she was only permitted to draw landscapes—portraits and figures were not allowed. As she became a teenager, she started to worry about her chastity, how well-kept her hijab was, and how she could be a more devout Muslim. "I remember I was fifteen years old and wanted to wear colorful clothes—nothing too fashionable, but just a colorful scarf or something. But my dad told me if you decide to do that, you need to wear the black chador (the long black veil)." It was then that she learned how to hide her true desires. "It was as if I had to cover my interest with a black veil in order to be good, to remain devout, and to stay true to the teachings of our community, and so I did."

Because of her father's work, politics played a large part in Faezeh's youth. "We were all told to support one candidate, to respect one leader, to think in a specific way—we didn't see the other side and grew up only knowing one singular narrative—only one way to see what's right and what's wrong." Anything other than "Islam, the regime's beliefs, and the government's narratives" were and still are big taboos in her house. More than anything, she explains that the "Velayate Faghigh" was and remains a redline for her family.

Faezeh took all this to heart. As a result, she became more religiously conservative than her mother and older sister. Faezeh recalls how, during her teenage years, she was constantly analyzing her devotion to Islam. "I was always scrutinizing myself when I was young. I was incredibly closed-minded and remember how my biggest worry in life was whether or not I was covered enough. I was constantly questioning whether I was religious enough. Or politically devoted enough."

One of her main interests was reading. However, she only had access to her father's narrowly curated library, which was filled with conservative books on Islam and the revolution. "It was as if I was reading the same book over and over again, except authored by a different person. Everything was the repeat of the same conservative ideology and I was being injected with those beliefs book after book. My dad's books became my entire life—my entire source of knowledge and wisdom; you can only imagine the level of fanaticism." She admits she was not in a healthy state of mind. "The right and wrong of my entire life had to go through a religious filter—a very narrow interpretation of religion defined my entire being as well as my political views."

After finishing high school, Faezeh was ready to choose her university major. "I was at a crossroads. I was so close to moving to Qom to attend a seminary and become a theologian. My obsession with Islam and my paranoia about being a good-enough Muslim, entwined with political pressures, made me want to study it for the rest of my life."

Yet somehow, the eighteen-year-old realized that if she attended the seminary, she would forever miss out on the "college experience." "I remember thinking, 'What if I miss out on the exciting experience of college?'" Even though she wasn't connected with the outside world, Faezeh had seen on state television what college could potentially look like. "I loved this Iranian TV series—I forgot its name—where a bunch of college girls lived together and they shared their problems, views, life, everything . . . it was so much fun—I was afraid I might never experience that."

Based on a fantasy on a state-produced television show, Faezeh made a life-changing decision. "I wanted to study philosophy, but my dad didn't accept it. I suppose he was afraid that I'd be exposed to a whole new world of thinking." It was a moment that transformed Faezeh into the brilliant young woman that she is today.

⊡⡀
⡀⊡

Other than majoring in philosophy instead of going to the seminary, things did not immediately change for Faezeh once she started college. "In the beginning, I was still the same conservative girl," she recalls. "I would go to university with my chador on, participate in the student Basij forces, and only hang out with people like myself." It was 2009, the height of the unrest against one of Iranian most hardline presidents, Mahmoud Ahmadinejad, an unprecedented moment in the post-revolution era where, for the first time, millions of people took to the streets to voice their anger, anti-regime sentiments, and to call for reform. Faezeh didn't take part in any of it. "When your political views get entwined with religious beliefs, you stop questioning," she reflects. "Then you stop contemplating between right and wrong." For Faezeh and her like, there was no other choice better than Ahmadinejad. It was as if he was manually programmed into their brains.

It was during this time that Faezeh was torn between the conservative ethos of her upbringing and the new ideas she was being exposed to. "I was a mess," she remembers. "I was reading Sartre, Kant, Hegel, and all these great thinkers, and all I could think of was how little I knew and how different the world really was from what I was told." It was around this time that she wrote an article on the "Iranian Identity" for the university's Basij publication. The piece was immediately rejected, and she was asked to edit her entire analysis. "In my article, I was insinuating that there was no one single Iranian identity," Faezeh recounts. "We have religious identities, ethnic identities, geographic identities, and nationalistic beliefs, which ultimately led to my assertion that in Iran there is no singular identity. But as soon as I took it to the Basij, they changed it all and told me, 'No, this is all wrong. We have an identity and that's the Islamic Republic's identity.'" Perhaps Faezeh was ready to leave her past behind, but this conflict with the Basij publication was the spark that led to her finally giving up the entire foundation she had been raised to believe in.

"If I could use one word to describe myself or to feel closest to, it'll be freedom." But for Faezeh that freedom did not come easy. While the great philosophers and thinkers were catalysts in bringing about Faezeh's transformation, one man in particular enabled her to experience something that made her feel truly alive for the first time in her life. She was twenty years old, and going on her first date. "I don't think anyone can ever understand my true feelings. It was the first time in my entire life that I experienced freedom."

While in university, Faezeh's curiosity, brightness, and commitment to her lessons had attracted a fellow classmate. Unlike Faezeh, this young man came from a totally different background. "He was completely from the other side of the spectrum," she says. "He was very smart, middle class, and hardworking. He was anti-government and anti-religious and was the exact opposite of my family and my background." Yet somehow, her sense of intrigue and his curiosity brought the two of them together. "When I was getting ready to go on our first date, I felt as if for the longest time—in fact all my life until then—I had only been a spectator of other people's lives and the whole experience of living. This time, it was as if I was experiencing what it's like to live. I always watched others fly from a distance; this time it was my turn—I was experiencing life up close."

The two met for dinner at one of Tehran's most beautiful architectural sights, *Pol-e-Tabiat*, or the "Nature Bridge." Over the bustling streets and jammed highways of the city, the bridge soars forty meters high across the Modarres highway, connecting two parks. In a country often viewed as hostile to women, this masterpiece was designed by a female architect—making its lush and green ambiance an even more exciting ground for Iranians.

The 300-meter-long bridge is divided into two main floors that house multiple coffee shops and restaurants. There, on the second floor, in a cozy restaurant, over some pizza and coke, Faezeh experienced the ultimate high. "I can't explain my feeling. We both came from different worlds, but he believed in me, he seemed to understand that I wanted to change, and he was there to support me. After dinner we went for a stroll next to the highway—it was just such an incredible feeling."

Of course, all this was done in secret, as Faezeh's family didn't know of her ideological metamorphosis and had no idea that their daughter was on her first date. "I had told my parents that I was with one of my girlfriends whom they trusted," she recalls with a bashful laugh. "My friend didn't even know I was on a date, but I knew she wouldn't tell either way."

⊡⋮

These radical changes in her intellectual and personal life helped Faezeh understand that it was okay for her to think outside of the confines of her strict upbringing. "I slowly began to accept the new woman that I was turning into," she shares. "I was beginning to realize some of the very basic desires that for the longest time I had deemed wrong—like wearing nail polish, wearing colorful clothes, or listening to the music of my choice. I was slowly beginning to accept that it's okay to not be scared."

It was difficult, however, for Faezeh to share her self-transformation with her family. "Everyone criticized me so much, everyone would tell me how unstable I was, how low I had become, and how 'immoral' I was as a woman, as a person. So many people left me. Even my own sister became resentful toward me; she still is—we don't have the same relationship that we had when we were young."

For the first year of her change, Faezeh went through a painful isolation from her family and old friends, but one that she now deems worth it. "I grew up in a world that stole your free will, your agency, and your ability to think for yourself," she says. Faezeh explains how during her transition, she reached a point where all she wanted was to make her own decisions. "I got to a point where I didn't want anything else but to be in charge of my own life, my own thoughts, my own choices. I wanted to have the right to choose for myself, and even though it made life difficult for me, I still wanted to be the decision-maker for my own life, I wanted to be responsible for my own choices."

After graduating from college, Faezeh's desire to expand her horizons went in yet another direction. "I wanted to study fine art, but my dad didn't agree—he didn't even like me to read art history. Every other picture in the textbooks had some sort of nude and of course he didn't deem it appropriate," Faezeh recalls. "After being rejected by my community, I needed something that was uniting, something that was peaceful in its nature, something that was inherently unifying—and that to me was art." It took her a year to get accepted to graduate school, but when she was, it was as if she had entered a whole new world.

Today, she teaches art to a group of youngsters and also works part-time as a kindergarten teacher. "I always looked at art as a tool to bring about social change. Look at all the amazing female artists throughout history—they all had something profound to say and they said it through their art. I believe in that. I believe in the profound power of the performing arts."

⊡

Faezeh was once the epitome of what the Islamic regime deems the ideal "Muslim woman," but now, the atheistic young lady sees religion and Islam as an "impediment" to one's free will. "You need to understand that I'm someone who has experienced Islam in the deepest and most profound way possible and today—with confidence—I can tell you that

it's the most restricting thing, that will to seek one's entirety at all costs."
When asked to define Islam, she compared it to a "dictator father," who,
unless obeyed, can be the most terrifying and harshest of people, but
once obeyed, will provide you with kindness and calmness—as defined
by himself. "But all of that calmness and kindness comes in exchange
for your freedom and free will," Faezeh states. "In Islam, you need to
sacrifice your own agency in order to become a good Muslim." Her belief
in "agreeing to disagree" and the "peaceful coexistence of opposites" is
what keeps her up at night. These are disciplines that she fundamentally
believes in and prays one day can govern her society.

Faezeh believes that Iranian women need to get in touch with their
own free will, no matter their religious beliefs. "Whether it's conservative
women or ordinary women," she says with conviction, "Iranian women
need to get in touch with their own ability to think freely, and with their
innate power to be the decision-maker in their own lives—starting from
their homes, all the way to outside society. This is the only way women
can bring about change in today's Iranian society." Faezeh believes that
breaking these societal chains—in the same way that she broke her own
individual chain—is the first and necessary step toward true progress.
"What makes me sad is that these days, despite all the 'reforms and
freedoms,' there's a major cultural deficit among Iranian women. You
can blatantly see that in the social media spheres, just out and about in
the society and in different communities." Much of this, according to
Faezeh, is due to the regime's effort to "dumb down" women via basic
reforms that offer them trivial freedoms that have no long-term or
profound impact. She believes that women must put aside their fears
and instead use their free will. "Creating fear, creating a taboo, creating
a desperate need to fit in the society as defined by the government are
all elements that keep our women behind—women need to put those
fears aside and use their own free will to rescue themselves from their
enslavement," she says. "So long as women are afraid to be true to
themselves, they will continue to be suppressed."

One of the sad things about Faezeh's transformation is that it has made her a virtual foreigner among the people that were once closest to her. "I'm an alien to my parents, to my family, to my friends that I grew up with," she laments. "I'm a foreigner simply because they can't accept me or the likes of me; they don't know how."

Though quite cynical toward the conservative world she was raised in, she still believes it necessary to share her views and experiences with young women who are of the same socio-religious background as her: "They have such great potential to change, and all of it depends on whether or not they get the opportunity and courage to leave their fears aside." Faezeh is in touch with many teenagers who remind her of her younger self, when she was trapped behind the walls of religion and oppression. "I speak to quite a few of these girls regularly and can see the sparkle in their eyes," she says. "If I can help one of them change her life, I feel I've done something." She knows a few girls who have chosen a path like hers, though most girls with similar backgrounds still enter into very early marriages or get involved in an "empty superficial life that's combined with useless and baseless religious beliefs." Faezeh believes that even though the group of young regime converts may not be a large one, they can nevertheless be a powerful force in Iranian society if they fight through and break the chains that have indentured them in the name of Islam.

Despite this hopefulness, Faezeh, like many other young Iranians, is disillusioned by much of what she sees around her, and wonders if change is ever really possible. "*Change*. What a heavy word," she says with a rueful smile. "I think if there is to be change it has to come from within the government. The problem in Iran, though, is people are not united; reformist intellectuals and moderate voices are very divided." Faezeh argues that the reformist voices that can potentially bring about the desired changes are busy arguing over "petty stuff that leaves no room for agreement and progress toward the bigger problems and the more important goals."

Ultimately, her biggest dream in is to live somewhere where she can think freely and act as her free will guides her to. Sometimes, she thinks about leaving Iran for the United States to work on her PhD in Art History: "I want to study and research at a top-grade university, and I think that's only available in the US. I want to learn and be part of feminist voices, female thinkers and intellectuals—I want to belong to that group—to be able to learn how to speak my mind through art."

These days, the once "one-eyed Chadori" reads Immanuel Kant and Irvin Yalom, and if she's not swooning to the beauty of Ella Fitzgerald and Louis Armstrong, she is busy listening to Bob Marley and Pink Floyd. "When I'm happy I listen to jazz, and when I'm sad I listen to rock—I'm obsessed with Pink Floyd's 'Hey You'—'Hey you, don't help them to bury the light. Don't give in without a fight.'"

She laughs in a girlish tone when I ask, if she could have tea with anyone in the world, who would it be? She chooses Simone de Beauvoir and Jean-Paul Sartre. "They are my favorite couple, favorite intellectual duo—I would want to spend time with both of them." She goes on to quote Sartre. "'We have no choice but to make choices. We are forced to take actions to become our free selves—to become who we are—to become a human being.'" The way she quotes him is as if he was a savior that opened her eyes to a whole new world.

From her new life with Sartre and de Beauvoir and Pink Floyd and dating and colorful clothes, she flashes back to being a child again. "I remember when I was a little girl, there was a book I would read about a little white bird who was in a cage and we as the reader had to finish it on our own." Faezeh recalls how each time she'd open the book and read about the little bird, she'd end the story by setting the bird free. "I would always set her free; that was my ending for the little bird. Today, I feel I have set my own self free—I feel my life ended up being like that bird's—outside of a cage and fully liberated.

Rabbi Harav Yehuda Gerami

THE WORN DOWN BUILDING IS less than a five minute drive from what used to be the Israeli embassy, up until the 1979 Islamic Revolution. But today, it continues to stand strong, about a kilometer away from what turned into the PLO embassy, on a boulevard that was renamed after Palestine. The two-story synagogue was built back in the 1960s in the Yousef Abad neighborhood—home to the thousands of Jewish Iranians in Tehran.

Palestine (also known as felestin) street is a long swarming boulevard in central Tehran that stretches from Fatemi Square to one of the Shah's former residences, known as the Marble Palace. The street used to be called Palace, but its name was changed after the revolution, as were the designations of many other streets in Iran. Royal titles gave way to the martyrs of the Iran-Iraq War; American and British politicians and monarchs—like Kennedy and Elizabeth—blurred into a fog of revolutionary figures; Islamic clerics and those opposing the Pahlavi monarchy took over the names of squares, intersections, and alleys across the country—and Fatemi was one them.

Dr. Hossein Fatemi is one of the rare historic figures who is respected by many factions in Iran—nationalists, the clergy, and even some royalists. He was a journalist, scholar, and a politician. From 1951 to 1952, he served as Iran's Foreign Minister under the country's revered Prime Minister Mohammad Mosaddegh, who credited Fatemi with the idea of nationalizing the country's oil. Soon after the CIA-led coup in 1953, Fatemi was assassinated by the Pahlavi regime.

Adjacent to North Palestine Street, about 600 meters from the

Iraqi Embassy and a few blocks from Iran's Justice Department, is the Abrishami Synagogue. The exterior of the building is modest; inside, its simple architecture and humble ark and bimah look more like a quaint temple in the United States than the kind of ornate religious structure you would ordinarily see in Iran. For the synagogue's young rabbi, this simplicity is what inspires him in his quest to keep alive a centuries-old religious tradition that allows Iranian Jews to practice their faith to its fullest within the borders of their homeland. "We love Iran and we want to stay here. You see, religion should bring people closer to one another—not just in Iran, but around the world," says the rabbi. "The most important teachings of religion are morality and the principles of life, and that's what matters the most."

The rabbi, who began teaching the Torah and Talmud when he was only fourteen years old, takes immense pride in the fact that he is the only academically trained rabbi in Iran. Yet it is his humility that makes his mission so appealing, which is to educate the next generation of Jews and Jewish faith leaders in the Islamic Republic of Iran.

Rabbi Harav Yehuda Gerami was born into an educated family;

his father was a physician who wanted his only son to follow in his footsteps. However, from an early age, Yehuda knew that he wanted to be a man of God. "When you're given a gift by God, you need to use it in his service and the service of others," he says. "Since I was a child, I was a good speaker and had a way for communication, so thought I should use the gifts he gave me in his honor."

If you close your eyes and listen to him speak, you can easily think he is twenty years older than his actual age of thirty-something. There is a strong sense of command, language, and conviction in his voice that is surprising coming from someone so young. "Not that many people have reached my level at this age," he shares. "I feel that there's a boat and I happen to be its captain. I feel responsible to lead the boat to safety." He goes on to explain that in today's Iran, Jewish leaders are mostly *hakhams* (Torah scholars) who are accustomed to the ancient and traditional teachings of Judaism. Yehuda's beliefs and aims are more contemporary. "My main goal is to be a modern rabbi with a strong and comprehensive academic background," he tells me. "In Iran we've only had hakhams with hundred-year-old traditional customs, but I'm the only rabbi with academic training and accreditation."

As a child, Yehuda went to a regular public school in Tehran, and studied alongside Muslim students. In Iran, there are Jewish schools for Jewish students, Christian schools for Christians, and public/private schools for the majority Muslim population. While there is no law that bans religious minorities from attending public school, many prefer to attend their own schools given that they're usually located within their neighborhoods, and their families want their children to assimilate within their communities from an early age. The one religious minority that remains ostracized to this day is the Baha'i community, who are discriminated against on various fronts including access to any form of higher education. Yehuda, however, never felt uncomfortable being part of the minority in public school. "I never felt any prejudice against my Jewish community as a child or while I was studying in the public school system," he says. "Of course, you always have naughty children and kids just being kids—but the teachers were always respectful toward my faith." It wasn't until he went to the United States that he learned about the fear and ignorance of the Western world toward his home country: "It was then that I realized the negative image that foreigners have of Iran and Iranians." The young rabbi believes that anti-Iran sentiments exist solely to "benefit certain groups who want to create fear against Iran."

In his late teen years, Yehuda left Iran and spent a year studying at one of the world's most prestigious Yeshivas in Israel. "As a teenager, I would spend hours and hours reading; I continued to do that in the university." He then went to the United States, where he attended the Ner Israel Rabbinical College in Baltimore, Maryland. There's a common belief that Iranians aren't allowed to travel to Israel, and while this may be the case for majority of the population, members of the Jewish community are free to take the religious pilgrimage to Jerusalem. The situation is similar for Iranian Muslims who want to visit Saudi Arabia for the annual Hajj pilgrimage. The Islamic Republic of Iran and the Kingdom of Saudi Arabia are regional archrivals who have not seen eye-to-eye since the 1979 revolution; however, the Iranian government allows its citizens to participate in the pilgrimage to Mecca and Medina. "The issue that Iranians have with the Israeli regime is a political problem," explains the rabbi. He goes on to say how "the same level of intolerance and resentment toward the Israeli regime exists within many Jewish communities in Europe and the US, where Jewish people are not supportive of the Israeli government—that's the same in Iran."

The history of the Jewish people in Iran actually dates back to biblical times, when Persian kings such as Cyrus, Darius the Great, and Artaxerxes regarded religion as a way of belonging, purpose, and identity for their people. "So few people know that some of our prophets like Daniel Hanavi, Mordechai, and others are buried in Iran," Yehuda tells me. Today, the largest number of Jews outside of Israel in the Middle East live in Israel's enemy state of Iran. While the current number of 25,000 is a far cry from the approximately 80,000 Jews who lived in prerevolution Iran, it is a sign that Jewish people can live freely in the country. There's even a Jewish member of Parliament who often accompanies the Iranian government delegation to the UN General Assembly meetings—a little known fact for many westerners who are constantly fed Iran's anti-Jewish narrative. And while much of that is PR tactics by the regime, the reality is that the violence and turbulence of the early years of the revolution have substantially calmed down over the last few decades.

During the 1979 revolution, many Iranian Jews left the country for Israel, Europe, and the United States. However, the reason for this complex mass migration is often misunderstood. In the United States and the West, the common narrative suggests that they left because the Mullahs and Islamic clerics just "hated" the Jews and wanted them "killed." The reality, however, tells a different story. While the new-to-power ayatollahs executed many members of the various political and religious factions they deemed "anti-revolutionary"—especially the vulnerable Baha'i religious minority—their main fear regarding the Jewish population was the relationship of many affluent Jewish-Iranians to Israel—their arch-enemy. They did not care so much about their religion, but were afraid of the strong ties that prominent members of the Iranian Jewish community had to the Israeli regime—a fear that still exists today.

In the immediate aftermath of the revolution, a culture of "ambiguity" governed Iran. No one knew what was going to happen next, who was going to be killed, or who was going to be condemned by the newly installed revolutionary forces. The residue of this culture is visible to this day; but over the years, much of the Iranian regime's redlines have become obvious—if you're smart, you won't cross them, but if you do, then it's game over. However, the real danger remains in the gray zone; and while many of these "red lines" are quite obvious, there are still those ambiguous and unjustifiable arrests, disappearances, and at points, executions that one can never anticipate or explain.

A 1979 *New York Times* article encapsulates this opacity as it applied to the Jewish community:

"What can I tell you?" said a rabbi who is a prominent leader of Tehran's Jewish community. "We have no problems. There is no trouble." Asked a few minutes later for the correct spelling of his name, he shrank back in horror. "You're not going to use my name?" he cried. "That would only cause trouble." The incident sums up the situation. While there are worries, no one is willing to speak publicly for fear of making things worse. Nor are there specific incidents that can be confirmed.

. . .

Serge Klarsfeld, a French lawyer who specializes in hunting down Nazi war criminals, came here during the weekend to investigate the situation. He met with Dr. Yazdi, who told him that Mr. Elghanian had been executed only for crimes against the state and his closeness to the Shah. Dr. Yazdi asserted that "Jews have nothing to fear" as long as they do not violate Islamic law or endanger the nation . . ."

Habib Elghanian was a prominent Iranian-Jewish businessman during the reign of the Shah. His empire included a variety of industries—among them textiles, plastics, machinery, and real estate. After the fall of the Shah, the fear of the unknown prompted many Iranians, especially those who had been close to the former regime, as well as religious minorities, to sell their belongings and leave the country. While Elghanian's family quickly resettled in the United States, the businessman returned to Iran in hopes of selling his assets—only to be detained by the Islamic revolutionaries, who condemned him as a spy for the "Zionist" regime of Israel. His execution was a dark chapter that amplified people's worst fears about the new Islamic Republic.

In 2012, the then twenty-five-year-old Yehuda returned to Iran as a rabbi. "I saw a void in Iran and made it my mission and priority to fill it and be of service to my community," he says emotionally, thinking of his father, who passed away only six months after his return. But his father's death did have one silver lining, leaving the young rabbi with an inheritance that enabled him to expand his teachings to the Jewish community in Iran.

In addition to his faith, Yehuda also has a strong sense of devotion to his homeland. While many of his relatives left Iran in pursuit of better financial and educational opportunities, he chose to stay—as his father had. "When you go to Istanbul, Turkey, you can't freely walk into a synagogue—they have guards who will question you ten times over. But in Iran we have none of that. The Muslim community respects the Jewish community and vice-versa," says the rabbi in describing the little-known reality of religious coexistence in Iran. "We freely pray, work, go to our religious events, and even have a say in politics," he said as he explained the challenges of being Jewish in Iran. "In Iran, there are general challenges that affect all people, not just religious minorities. From economic and financial hardships, to high divorce rates, and soaring expectation among the youth, you have categorical challenges that affect all communities—some more and some less."

A day in the life of Rabbi Gerami means waking up before the sun rises and going to bed long after the sun has set. His work can include officiating at Jewish weddings (he is also the only rabbi in Iran who can annul marriages), teaching the Talmud, Torah, and other religious classes, as well as offering private tutoring and holding religious ceremonies and various public and private events. "In my nightly classes you can see students as young as nine to men as old as eighty," he says with a smile. "I try to teach in such a way that everyone can take something from my lessons."

From morning prayers to as many as four classes per day, Yehuda's daily life is filled with everything he can offer to his community—mostly for free, as he makes no salary as a rabbi, nor from performing his religious duties. His only source of income is the rent he receives from a few apartments his father left him. "Religion is wisdom," he states. "But unfortunately, these days it is used and manipulated for all the wrong reasons. But it has to be there to ground us, to humble us, to bring us down from our egos." It's so easy to hear the compassion in Yehuda's voice, which manifests itself as a sense of duty toward his community and his students. "Sometimes I think if I can't think or comprehend, one day I'll die—it's then that I'll have nothing else in life," he says.

His sweetest memory of his life as a teacher was when he was still a teenager, teaching at a synagogue where his now-wife was a young student of his. "I remember her being my student, but I never thought she'd be my wife one day," he recalls with a kind laugh. "It wasn't until I returned from the States that my dad made the introductions, but yes, she was my student when I was still a teenager."

At the end of our conversation, his little son comes over and sits in his lap. I ask Yehuda what his biggest wish is for his children. "To be in the service of God," he replies. Then he leaves me with this thought from the Torah: "*En Od Milevado*"—there is no other power other than that of God in this universe.

Author's Note:

This is a story about one person and his family with utmost respect to those who lost their loved ones and faced difficulties during the Islamic Revolution and thereafter. No two stories are alike, and not everyone shares the same fate. There is no doubt that stifling and persecuting individuals based on their faith is an evil act and should always be condemned—wherever it may be in this world. .

Ashkan Khosropoor

*A*U FOND, VOUS SAVEZ, MON SEUL RIVAL *international, c'est Tintin! Nous sommes les petits qui ne se laissent pas avoir par les grands. On ne s'en aperçoit pas à cause de ma taille!"* ("Really, you know, my only international rival is Tintin! We're both little fellows who won't be got at by the big fellows. Nobody notices, because of my height!")

These are the words that General Charles de Gaulle once said in praise of the petite blond teenage reporter whose adventures, curiosity, and compassion continues to entertain and inspire young minds all over the world.

Miles away from France, Tintin and his white fox terrier Milou were the Iranian boy's inspirational play friends in early 1990s post-Iran-Iraq War Tehran. The child's timid yet curious demeanor mirrored that of the fictional boy reporter. "I remember when I still didn't know how to read, and I would ask my mom to read me Tintin's adventures," the now grown man recalls with a nostalgic smile. "I would ask her to read it over and over again. She would finish one story and as soon as she was done, I would ask her to read it again." Like millions of other children worldwide, the imaginary world of the young reporter wheeled the young boy to faraway lands and kindled his love of "discovery" and "writing."

During the early years of his childhood, the boy, his parents (and later his younger sister) all slept in the same room in their small apartment in the Shahr-e ziba neighborhood of Tehran. "When we were going to sleep, my mom would read me stories; but in reality, she was the one who would get tired, and I would only want to hear more."

One of the boy's fondest memories was spending time at the Tehran International Book Fair, a yearly festival that brings in books and authors from all over the world. "I was either in the second or third grade and I remember picking out a lot of books at the fair," he says. "My mom was quite shocked when she saw me in the queue. The total

came to about 5,000 toman. This was during the time when her monthly salary was about 60,000 toman."

Books and reading weren't the only joys in the young boy's life. "I also loved to draw," he tells me. When he was five or six years old, he found a notebook and some colored pencils in a neighbor's home. There, he would sit quietly and spend hours drawing the fair-skinned teenager with his golden spiky hair and the rest of Hergé's characters who accompanied Tintin on his many journeys. "Back then, all the neighbors were friends and whether it be in the backyard or on the streets, everyone would hang out with each other," he remembers. He was also a lonely child who spent a lot of time in his own imaginary world. "I was the only child in my family (before his sister was born), so no cousins and grandkids were around for a while. I spent a lot of time in our neighbor's home—spending hours and hours drawing on the corner edges of a notebook I had found." In the years following the Iran-Iraq War, some of the most basic items were hard to find—even in Tehran. There were no lined notebooks, and color-pencils were rare; products like milk, rice and cooking oil were still rationed; and there were nearly no foreign goods available to the public.

As a child, the boy also read *Gol-Agha*—a weekly satirical magazine that was launched in 1991 by Kioumars Saberi Foumani, a writer and satirist. Beneath the censoring eyes of the government, *Gol-Agha* created an invaluable space to critique and rail against the political and social turmoil of a pre-social media era. Flipping through the pages of *Gol-Agha* and *Gol-Agha Youth*, the boy realized that humor could be a powerful tool in conveying serious matters. He also found himself mesmerized by the colorful cartoons and caricatures that were and still are a rarity in the Iranian public media sphere. Twelve years after publishing its first issue, *Gol-Agha* ceased publication. Two years later, its founder died of cancer. "I learned the word *jarayed* from *Gol-Agha* and I kept wondering what it meant," he shares. "I recall drawing Tintin and whatever adventure he was on and I would write *jarayed* underneath my work. I didn't know what it meant, but I thought it would make my work look more important." *Jarayed* literally translates to "the press"—which is still censored, stifled, and monitored by government forces in Iran.

When the now teenager entered tenth grade, Pouya Lotfian, a reporter from the newspaper *Shargh*, visited his high school, encouraging the students to sign up for a journalism workshop in order for them to launch their first school magazine. "At first, about thirty-five students signed up for Pouya Lotfian's workshop, but soon there were only a few of us who remained," he remembers. From reporting to interviewing and editing, Lotfian taught the aspiring young journalists the ins-and-outs of the craft. "He taught us everything, and truly went above and beyond," he recalls fondly. "I knew then that this is what I wanted to do. I worked so hard to do my best in the school's magazine."

For the magazine, the teenager wrote mainly satirical pieces and conducted interviews. "We tried to challenge and be critical of the school administration around issues that bothered the students and were important to us—and that wasn't quite welcomed by the principal." He explains how the student's dealings with the school administration were similar to the struggles Lotfian warned them against in the real world. "I remember we had the most dismal library with a horrible book selection and some random cassette tapes," he says. "I can't tell you how many times we wrote about this and published pieces to express our concerns. I'm proud of what I did; with our writing, we finally managed to bring attention to the issue and successfully have the school administration renovate the library and turn it into what I can recall being a fantastic library."

A few months later, Lotfian helped the teen and his fellow students enter the country's then respectful "Medade Kamrang" (light pencil) youth journalism competition. "I'll never forget the field trips we took for that competition—it was right around the time when the Bam earthquake happened, so there was quite a lot of news going on," he recalls. "The events and places they took us to and the stories we were able to cover were all surreal." It became even more surreal when on the final day of the program, the aspiring young journalist was announced as the winner of the national competition for his reporting. "I couldn't believe it. I was just a student and there were so many other students from all over the country. Not only did I realize 'wow there are other student journalists and publishers out there,' but I also was hit with the reality that I wanted to do this professionally."

Ashkan Khosropoor grew up in a humble family. His father, a shopkeeper and merchant, wanted his son to become an engineer while his mother, perturbed by the volatile nature of journalism in Iran, was wary of her only son's decision. In an attempt to please his parents, Ashkan studied industrial engineering at the university for a while, but soon found himself disinterested in a subject that he felt had "nothing to offer and [he] did not understand." During the same time, the young writer started to freelance and eventually managed to have his work published in some of the country's major newspapers like *Shargh* and *Hamshahri*.

In the late 1830s, a court intellectual named Mirza Saleh Shirazi published Iran's first newspaper. Shirazi had studied in England, and upon his return to Iran, brought the first printing machine to the royal court of the third King of the Qajar dynasty. By the early 1900s, as Iran's Constitutional Revolution was in full swing, there were quite a few newspapers in circulation, where many politicians, philosophers, religious figures and writers published their work in order to try and sway public opinion.

The press has always been used as a vehicle for change in Iran—so much that in the early 1950s, in an attempt to strengthen his grip on power, Mohammad Reza Pahlavi, the last monarch of Iran, ordered the closure of many liberal papers and the arrest of leftist journalists and intellectuals. In the days following the 1979 revolution, many journalists, editors, and reporters who had worked in the prerevolution press were either detained or forced to flee Iran; for those who stayed, working under the new and in many cases blurry confines of the Islamic regime was and remains a difficult mandate to follow.

In 2018, *Time* magazine named four journalists and one newspaper as its Person of the Year. A slain Saudi journalist, a Filipino news editor, two *Reuters* reporters in detention in Myanmar, and the staff of the *Capital Gazette* newspapers in Maryland were collectively recognized as the "guardians" of the truth. Worldwide, more than ever before, the flag-bearers of the truth face an ever-increasing hostility that makes their work more frightening and vital. Countries like Turkey, China, Egypt, and Eritrea have long banned freedom of expression and the press, while Gulf nations such as Saudi Arabia, Qatar, Bahrain, and the United Arab Emirates all have strict regulations and codes of conduct for journalists, public expression, and the press. Even in the United

States—the so-called freedom-of-press capital of the world—there are still redlines that can tarnish one's journalism career; the same goes for the UK and Europe. Then you have journalists in Latin America and Asia who suffer from repression while standing up to hardline regimes.

Like many of these countries, Iran remains a police state when it comes to press freedom. In the years since the Islamic Revolution, many reformist and moderate publications have been shut down, and untold numbers of journalists, editors, publishers, and web bloggers whose only crime was practicing free expression have been arrested, tortured, and in some cases, put to death. On the colorful newsstands of Tehran, you won't find a single daily newspaper that doesn't belong to a political fraction whose aim is to promote and advance a specific interest or agenda. For example, the *Keyhan* newspaper belongs to Hossein Shariatmadari, a close friend and ally of the Supreme Leader; *Hamshahri* is owned by the conservative former Mayor of Tehran, Mohammad Bagher Ghalibaf; *Shargh* and *Etemad* are run by a group of reformist politicians, writers, and activists; and one of the country's oldest newspapers *Ettela'at,* is currently managed by a conservative cleric and his compadres.

In a country where at any moment the government can deem your work a threat to "national security," journalism is a dangerous business. "Why do you do it? Why do people go to war zones and report from chaos?" Ashkan asks. "Because they feel the rush; because they feel it matters. I don't think I would be happy doing anything else. Yet, there are other things we have to do in Iran to make money." Ashkan explained how many young journalists and reporters like himself need to get freelance gigs in public relations, marketing, and other types of non-news industries to make ends meet. "We have to do it all, because journalism doesn't have the same respect and stature here that it does in many counties overseas."

These days, Ashkan works as a reporter and translator at one of the most popular biweekly magazines in Tehran, *Danestaniha*, which covers science, technology, and culture. (The name translates to "Things to Know.") He writes book reviews, reports on scientific discoveries, and covers cultural events. He's particularly interested in innovation, education, technology, and sharing stimulating stories that can inspire his readers and the millions of Iranian youth who spend most of their time roaming different social media platforms and not gravitating toward newspapers and the daily press. He explains how "telling unique stories" is what satisfies him the most as a journalist: "I get quite excited when I uncover stories about unique people, cultures, and events." Ashkan attributes much of his zeal for journalism to the lessons he learned from his mother: "Be truthful and don't ever lie. This is what she would always tell me and later my sister when we were growing up. It had nothing to do with being religious or anything—it was something she believed in so much and passed on to us."

Nonetheless, Ashkan is also aware of the downsides to working as a journalist. "Working in the press, especially as a journalist, is like driving in Iran," he says with a sneer. "Overseas, you know that there are clear rules and regulations for driving; you stop when the light is red, you don't turn without signaling, and you don't cross or enter when you're not supposed to. Here though, there are no rules, so you as a pedestrian need to be careful to not get hit by cars. The cars drive as they wish, and you're just supposed to have your eyes all around to make sure nothing is coming your way."

There is also the aforementioned lack of financial security. "Not only is journalism a risky craft, but it also doesn't make any money," he says with frustration. "All this for a monthly salary of 1.5 to maximum 2 million toman that equals to 100 to 200 dollars with a 1- to 10-dollar conversion rate." He has always admired journalists in America, not only for their greater freedom to report on issues, but because their profession can be financially viable. "I was always jealous of you guys, of American journalists—not just for the freedoms you have, but for the fact that your work is financially valuable," he says. "I've heard that journalists can make an average of $1000 per month. Here, if someone gets paid 2 million toman, they are on cloud nine."

⠿

Ashkan's love for writing initially flourished when he was twelve years old. "I remember one day I got a standing ovation from my classmates for an essay I wrote and read in the class," he shares. "The teacher had asked us to write about one of Ferdowsi's work and his famous verse, ("I built a tall palace from words that'll be immune to the wind and rain.")

"پی افکندم از نظم کاخی بلند   که از باد و باران نیابد گزند"

Ferdowsi—perhaps the greatest figure in Persian literature—composed the longest epic poem ever written by a single poet. In his book, *Shahnameh*, he masterfully depicts Iran before the invasion of the Arab Muslims in the mid-600s BC, recounting the literal and metaphorical history of his ancient homeland. To this day, *Shahnameh*—a collection of 50,000 couplets—remains the crown jewel of Persian literature and an undeniable symbol of Iranian nationalism.

"My essay was quite emotional," Ashkan recalls. "In my last sentence I wrote how as Iranians we should help continue Ferdowsi's mission, and since he has left us with this treasure, we have to make sure that we preserve it forever. Even my teacher applauded—he was quite a serious man and would never give anyone the highest grade, but that day I got a twenty (equivalent to an A+). It was unreal."

One of Ferdowsi's greatest gifts in *Shahnameh* was his effort to preserve the Zoroastrian identity—the first official religion practiced by the Persian kings such as Cyrus the Great and Dariush, as well as millions of other Iranians, until the defeat of the Sassanian Empire by the Arabs. While many believe that the world will end in blazing fires and roaring flames, Zoroastrians believe fire is what gives birth to life—regarding it as the most sacred symbol of life and divinity. The principles of the religion are embedded in a person's divine nature and the constant battle between the pure energy of goodness and the dark forces of evil. Zoroastrians believe that in the journey of life, one can prevail over the dark forces through constructive thoughts, wisdom, free will, and goodness. For them, fire is light, light is guidance, and guidance is what will help a person reach ultimate wisdom.

"I remember covering a piece on the Zoroastrian holiday of Farvardingan for CHN (the Cultural Heritage News Agency, a news site

that was launched in 2002 to cover stories pertaining to Iran's cultural heritage)," Ashkan recalls. "It's the celebration of the deceased in the religion and takes place in Farvardin (the first month of spring and the first season of the year on the Persian calendar)." This led to Ashkan gaining recognition among the Zoroastrian community, which in turn led to him being asked to write for the Zoroastrian's biweekly magazine, *A-Mordad*. It was the first time he had received a paycheck for his writing. "It was such an incredible feeling, the idea that I will get paid for my work was very special," he recalls with pride.

"Saying good, doing good, and thinking good," has been the motto of Zoroastrians since the days of Zoroaster—the religion's prophet. While there are no documents to certify Zoroaster's date of birth or the year of his death, his teachings were quite prevalent during the Achaemenid dynasty, which was established by Cyrus the Great and grew to its zenith under King Darius I, who reigned from 549 to the mid-480s BC. A devote Zoroastrian, Darius, the "King of the Kings," promoted ethnic inclusion, religious freedom, and fairness across ancient Persia. *Nowruz*—"new day"—is perhaps the most glorious of these ancient traditions that has survived to the present day. It's what Iranians regard as the new year, a turn of the season that leaves behind the cold and darkness of winter in favor of the warmth and beauty of spring. Nowruz is celebrated by Iranians all over the world as well as by many people across Western Asia and the Caucasus. It marks the last day of winter and takes place on the exact start of the vernal equinox.

"My family was never really religious," Ashkan explains. "It was when I got older that I learned more and more about Zoroastrianism. I then realized that the values were always present in my life and in my parents' teachings." Today, Ashkan is one of the estimated 20,000 Zoroastrians who remain in Iran. While the population who practice this ancient religion of peace and virtue is small, they are nevertheless highly respected by the predominantly Muslim society. "Growing up, I didn't feel discriminated against at all," Ashkan tells me. "I mean sure, there are always naughty kids who cause problems, but it wasn't a big thing. I recall during my teenage years there was a boy who would say, 'oh you guys pray to fire' and make fun of me, but that was just kids being stupid."

Unlike the Bahá'í faith, which is strictly persecuted under the current Islamic regime, Zoroastrianism is celebrated freely across the country. The representatives of the religion have seats in parliament, are employed by the government, and are not politically and socially scrutinized. Zoroastrian students have the choice of either attending Zoroastrian schools, which teach the same basic curriculum as public schools—in addition to Zoroastrian religious classes—or going to regular public schools. Similar to other religious minorities in Iran, if Zoroastrian students decide to attend public school, they do not have to study the Koran or Islamic religion; instead they are able to take a religion class specific to their faith. Up until high school Ashkan attended Zoroastrian schools, before enrolling in a regular high school. "These days, sometimes it helps being a Zoroastrian in the newsroom," he says with an innocent laugh. "I don't get involved in the daily politics and office drama. Somehow there's a deep sense of respect toward our community."

Right around the time when the Arabs began their conquest, thousands of Persian Zoroastrians fled their homeland for the west coast of India, settling in Gujarat. Today, India is host to the largest community of Zoroastrians in the world. "I think the most beautiful story that will explain the true Zoroastrian spirit is when the Iranian immigrants were rejected by the Indian governor in Gujarat," Ashkan says. "The Indian governor sent the Zoroastrian immigrants a full bowl of milk that was filled to the edges. His aim was to politely refuse their settlement in a society that he deemed fully populated. In return, the leader of the Zoroastrian immigrants added sugar to the milk and send it back to the Indian king." Ashkan tells the story with colorful detail and a sense of pride. "You see, the Zoroastrian leader wanted to demonstrate that they, the Iranian immigrants, would not take up much room and would not hurt the already crowded Indian society; rather, he wanted to show that they would live with the Indians in harmony and peace, with the only aspiration of adding 'sweetness' to their society."

It's perhaps hard to believe that thousands of years ago, a bowl of sugary milk managed to build peace, and that an ancient religion can keep its fire alive for several millennia. The secret is their humane principles, which are clearly embodied by Ashkan. "Calmness, to live in peace and in calm; that's honestly my biggest dream—my biggest wish," he says earnestly.

At the end of our talk, he tells me "*Roozkarniak.*" It is a phrase in the Zoroastrian Dari language, an ancient form of Dari that's nearly extinct but still spoken in parts of Yazd and Kerman. In Farsi, it literally translates to *Roozegarat Neek*, which means "May your days be good." "This is my favorite phrase in Dari," Ashkan says with a smile. "You say it in the morning to greet someone. I remember learning it in my Zoroastrian kindergarten, and it has always stayed with me. It always will."

Khalil Koiki

*H*E WAS BORN AND RAISED IN THE ancient city of Qasr-e
Shirin ("Shirin's Palace" in English). During the Sassanian
Empire, Shirin was the lover, then wife, of King Khosrow II. She was
a Christain, and he practiced Zoroastrianism—the common religion
of many Persians before the rise of Islam. Khosrow and Shirin's love
story remains the crown jewel of Persian literature, punctuated by the
beautiful writings of the eleventh-century poet Nizami Ganjavi.

Qasr-e Shirin is tucked away in Iran's Kermanshah Province,
beneath the grand mountains of Zagros, which extend over 900 miles,
beginning in the northwest and ending at the Strait of Hormuz in the
Persian Gulf. Kermanshah is one of three provinces that are home to
the country's third largest ethnic group, the Kurds, who have long
lived in the northwestern region of Iran that borders Iraq and Turkey.
In ancient times, this mountainous city was adorned with palaces and
gardens that had been built for Queen Shirin by her husband. It was a
city of passion, power, and religious plurality—where Jews, Christians,
Muslims, Zoroastrians, and pagans all lived together in peace.

At its height in the seventh century, the Sassanian Empire
encompassed the entire Levant, the Arabian Peninsula, Turkey,
Afghanistan, and Pakistan, reaching all the way to Uzbekistan from the
east and Egypt from the west. However, in 651 AD, under the reign of
Yazdgerd III, Khosrow II's grandson, the Sassanian dynasty collapsed as
the Arabs invaded and forever veiled the land with Islam.

Centuries later, Qasr-e Shirin was once again invaded by Arab soliders. This time it was the Iraqi Ba'ath army who stormed the city during the early months of the Iran-Iraq War. In September 1980, Saddam Hussein's army—backed by the United States and other allies—attacked Iran. Hundreds of thousands of people died on both sides during the eight long years of warfare, which included thousands of Iranians who were killed by Saddam's lethal chemical attacks.

"Speaking of war is not pleasant," he says, despair still present in his voice even after all these years. "Three decades have passed since Iraqi fire blazed through the city, but it still hurts. It still breaks my heart thinking of those days." He was only fifteen when the Iraqis attacked his hometown of Qasr-e Shirin. "We felt it in our lives—every day. There was no light, no water, no gas, nothing. Every day we waited to see if this was the day it was going to hit our home—every night it was either two homes to the left or four home to the right. Dinner was served under rockets; life was lived under RPG noises; it was hell."

As the Iraqi forces ravaged through Qasr-e Shirin, his childhood

was uprooted piece by piece. His playground, boyhood friends and the fields of reed he escaped to as a child were all destroyed. "The city that was once so peaceful, beautiful, and pure was burning in the flames of violence," he recalls. "The war took many things, especially the innocence of those who witnessed the bloodbath and survived to experience its memories for years to come."

Khalil Koiki was one of those survivors. Today, he is a well-regarded calligrapher and painter who is revered for his unique talent in combining the two mediums. His art is a marriage of aesthetics and technique, entwined with the depth of Persian poetry—all of which was inspired by his upbringing in Qasr-e Shirin. "My art background is from where I lived as a child—not in my learning and practice of the art itself," Khalil shares. "Through your art, you reflect yourself, your true self, your childhood and roots. You see me through my art."

At the age of sixteen, along with his parents, two brothers, and two sisters, Khalil left Qasr-e Shirin for Arak—the capital city of the Markazi Province, 300 miles to the east. A year later, the family settled permanently in Tehran. For Khalil, the sharp memories of his life—the first half spent breathing in the pain and loss of war, the second half remembering Qasr-e Shirin and the many friends he lost there, still bring tears to the middle-aged man's eyes. "As a child my biggest fear was to lose my friends. You won't believe it, but I had thirty to forty best friends growing up in Qasr-e Shirin. It was unreal. For me, each of them was a lifeline."

When war broke out, Khalil was too young to join the army, so he contributed to the cause by painting calligraphy handouts for soldiers' families and writing public announcements. "I did my part through my art—they asked me to write something and I would do the job," he says. Eventually, Khalil found himself with the somber task of recording the names of the dead. One day, he was asked to write the name of one of his dearest friends. "It was in the afternoon when they came asking me to do a calligraphy of a young martyr's name on a white piece of fabric," he recalls with a slight quiver in his voice. "It was a common thing for families to do. They'd wanted to hang their son's name on their door and in the neighborhood to commemorate his martyrdom. At first, I couldn't believe what I heard. It was the name of one of my best friends—he was gone, and I was alive to write his name. Why? I still don't have an answer."

Today, thirty years into his professional career, Khalil shares his childhood pain and memories through his art. "My essence is rooted in the place I'm from, not where I live now," he says, recalling the hours he'd spend as a child in the massive fields of reed on the outskirts of Qasr-e Shirin. "Rows and rows of reed dancing beneath the breeze and looking straight into the setting sun—to this day it's the most magnificent sight I've ever seen," he says with a nostalgic smile. "Each day, an hour before and after school, I would escape to the fields, lay down among the reeds, and gaze into the blue sky. I'd always cut a reed to play music with it; and each day it was the reed I'd carry home that would reveal my hideout to my parents." Khalil laughs as he remembers his visits to the fields as the "most exciting yet stressful moments" of his boyhood. "Each day, the anxiety of confronting my parents as they'd worry about my whereabouts, mixed with the excitement of getting lost within the reed fields, were the two most stressful and sensational feelings of my childhood," he says.

In Farsi, reed is called *ney*, and refers to the plant as well as the ancient musical instrument. The tall, thin, wooden cylinder exudes a deep and despondent sound—as though the reed itself is crying. Historically, it was popular among Sufis in search of the self, mystics in praise of the divine, and lovers lamenting their loss. It also became popular in Persian miniature paintings of the Safavid dynasty of the sixteenth century.

The use of the reed was also a common metaphor in Persian literature and poetry:

> *Listen to the reed, how it complains*
> *and tells a tale of separation pains.*

These are the first two lines of Rumi's *Masnavi*—a collection of six books of poetry that the Persian Sufi wrote over the span of fifteen years, until his death in 1273. The search for the divine, the divinity of man himself, and the mystical bond that connect the creator with creation are all inextricably written down in the poem's more than 25,000 verses. Rumi sums up the entire message of his work in the opening eighteen verses of the first folio, entitled "Ney-Naame" or "Reed Letters."

A few years ago, Khalil suddenly noticed a strange phenomenon—

the reoccurrence of straight lines in many of his paintings. These repetitive vertical brush strokes had a resemblance to the exalting reeds that had captivated his imagination during his childhood. "After almost three decades, I'm just now realizing that perhaps the lines are delicate manifestations of the reeds," he says.

His paintings are filled with layers of colors dancing through prose, poetry, imagery, and figurines that are all woven together in the most eloquent, yet mysterious of ways. The intricacies of his art mirror the depth of the poetry of Hafez, Saadi, and Rumi. When you read those ancient Persian poets, you lose yourself in the complexity of their thoughts and ideas, yet so effortlessly find yourself gliding through each stanza. It is the same with Khalil's art.

From the United Arab Emirates to France and Southeast Asia, Khalil has held solo gallery shows and art exhibitions in countries across the world. He is also respected among his students in Iran, and currently teaches at an all-girls arts college. But despite his cultured and global outlook, he has never thought of leaving Iran. "The promise of life outside of my own country was never enough of a reason for me to leave," he says. "What I want in life is not there; it's here, in my own land, on my own soil, with my own people. I live with these people, I believe in these people, I live with their love." Khalil's only wish is for some of the basic societal and economic opportunities that exist in Europe and North America to become available in Iran.

While social challenges may weigh heavily on Khalil's mind, at home he is at peace. He got married late in life, but found a woman whom he calls "the essence of love, pure love." She is not an artist, but the head nurse of the oncology department at one of Tehran's prestigious private hospitals. "She is very sensitive and emotional with an incredibly challenging job," he says with pride. "I believe for the families she counsels, she is the angel that gives them love in some of the most devastating moments of their lives."

Together, they have two daughters. Part of Khalil's calmness stems from living in an all-female household that is filled with "sensibility, honesty, and love." "Being honest is the most important thing in life," he says. "Something that was a bold trait among Iranians—especially those in Qasr-e Shirin." Despite his deep artistic connection to his home city, Khalil never moved back, as he doesn't believe there is a place there for him, or his art. "What can I do there?" he asks. "The level of poverty is so extreme that when people are still desperate for basic necessities like education, housing, healthcare, they don't need art—how could I have been of service to those people with my line of work? My lack of contribution would only hurt me more." One of Khalil's brothers did move back to Qasr-e Shirin after becoming a medical doctor, an altruistic act that few migrants from small villages in Iran do—especially after they experience the comforts of life in Tehran.

What pains Khalil most these days is the demise of honesty, honor, and integrity in Iranian society. He believes that he can only replicate those values and traits through his art. "The only place that I can be the most honest is in my work," he says. "I spend the majority of my time in my studio because I can be honest with my paintings and they'll be honest with me." For Khalil, art is an honest place, where his audience can go to ask questions about larger societal concerns, as well as feeling safe from the fears of the wider world. "I'm obligated to create questions for my audience, to engage them, entangle them, puzzle them—all so that they can get drowned in the safe and infinite space of the art."

To this day, Khalil's childhood suffering and loss is what inspires his art—to an extent that one can imagine the little boy lying in the reed fields on the outskirts of Qasr-e Shirin.

He recites his favorite poem to me, by Rumi:

I'm a heavenly bird and not from this land,
who only for a few days has built a cage from my body,
Longing for the day to depart for the true friend
and fly in the air of the place I truly belong.

مرغ باغ ملکوتم نیم از عالم خاک
چند روزی قفسی ساخته ام از بدنم
ای خوش آن روز که پرواز کنم تا بر دوست
به هوای سر کویش پر و بالی بزنم

Mina

*I*T'S MURDER WHEN A CHILD—A YOUNG GIRL—is forced into marriage. It's as though you killed that girl."

She was only twelve when she married a thirty-year-old man. "My parents were illiterate and didn't know any better," she says. "Back then, a lot of poor and illiterate families would marry their girls off at that age." A decade later, when she asked her mother why she hadn't stopped the marriage, the older woman replied, through tears, that the decision had been up to her grandfather. "I had nothing to tell them; even when I got older," she says. Beneath her warm voice and kind smile lay years of pain. "There is nothing I can do now to change my past."

While it may be hard to imagine a twelve-year-old girl getting married, in the Middle East, Asia, Africa, Latin America, and even parts of Europe and the United States, it is still sadly commonplace. In the US, the minimum age for marriage is eighteen, but there are exemptions, the most common of which are when parents approve and a judge grants consent. In twenty-five states, there is no minimum marriage age when such exceptions are made. According to the US-based organization Unchained At Last, some 248,000 children as young as twelve were married in the country between 2000 and 2010.[1] Worldwide, over 700 million women were married while they were still children; if the current trend continues, by 2030, this number will reach nearly one

---

1. "Child Marriage—Shocking Statistics," *Unchained at Last*, accessed January 24, 2020, https://www.unchainedatlast.org/child-marriage-shocking-statistics/.

billion.[2] Six countries—South Sudan, Saudi Arabia, Equatorial Guinea, Gambia, Somalia and Yemen—have no legal minimum age for marriage. In these nations, a girl as young as one-month-old can be married off to a man as old as her grandfather.

In Iran, the legal age for marriage is thirteen for girls and fifteen for boys. However, many child marriages in Iran are not registered, as they happen in rural areas and among tribal and impoverished families. In most cases, financially insecure, illiterate, or addict fathers marry off

their daughters out of financial desperation.

"I was scared of him," Mina says of her late husband. "They (his mother and aunt) would put me to bed first, and once I'd fallen asleep, he'd come to the room." At the age of fourteen, she became pregnant with her first son. "One day I felt something moving in my stomach and I started crying and ran to my husband's aunt," Mina recalls. "I was screaming 'abji shirin, abji shirin (abji is another word for sister in

2. "Child Protection," UNICEF, accessed January 24, 2020, https://www.unicef. org/protection/files/UNFPA_UNICEF_Global_Programme_CM_Fact_Sheet.pdf.

Farsi), a mouse has gone into my stomach! See it's moving!'" It was that moment between childhood innocence and adolescent fear that turned Mina into a woman. Four years later, she gave birth to her second son. The following year, when Mina was only nineteen, her husband died in a car accident outside of Tehran.

One of Mina's main regrets as a young girl was that she was never allowed to study. Even before her marriage, Mina's family banned her from going to school. "My grandfather told my father that I couldn't go to school without a scarf—they were so backward," she shares. "It was still during the Shah's time, so girls were not yet forced to wear the scarf and my conservative grandfather thought it'll be shameful if I went to school without my hijab."

⊡

Mina's husband never held a steady job, and after his death, everything fell on her shoulders. Left alone with her husband's poverty and heartbroken by her poor parents' neglect, Mina had to learn to survive on her own while taking care of two young children. "I had to survive. I had no choice," she says bluntly. "I had no one and my husband's family also didn't want me. His parents were too old, and his family's financial situation was worse than my own."

"Hope" was the only thing Mina could hold on to during her early years as a single mother. "I don't know what it was, but I've always had hope," she says. "I swear to God, sometimes I think ten grown men could have not survived my life—but somehow I did, and I think it was all because of my never-ending belief in the power of hope." The only person who offered her any kind of support was her younger brother. Tragically, he too died a few years later in a car accident.

While Mina did have opportunities to remarry, most of the men wanted her to make a terrible choice. "So many people told me to get married, but I didn't want to rely on a man," she says. "Sure, my life could have become better, but almost all the men who wanted to marry me were forcing me to choose between marrying them or keeping my boys." This is a situation that many poor young women with children in Iran sadly face, as the men who are pursuing them know that by accepting their children, they will have more people to support, and more mouths to feed. Therefore, they try and make the women give their children up.

⌑

Before her husband's death, Mina had earned a small living cleaning people's homes, working as a janitor in a hospital, and taking care of a diabetic mother and her blind daughter. With her husband gone, she realized she needed a permanent job in order to support her sons. "My boys were my life; they were my everything," she shares emotionally. "All I wanted for them was to live a good life. I wanted them to grow up like other children—go to school, eat well, play well, learn well, be kind, and become good boys."

Her older son, Bijan, who was in second grade at the time, would help his illiterate mother go through the job postings in the newspaper. One day, in between the black-and-white scribbles on the page, Mina saw an ad that would change her life forever. "A recently divorced man was looking for a full-time nanny for his young daughter in Northern

Tehran," she says. "I thought that not only could I move my boys uptown and raise them in a safe neighborhood, but I could also help the man with his young daughter." While Mina's encounter with the divorced man did not result in her getting the nanny position, it did get her an introduction to a woman who referred Mina for a full-time job. "When the man met me, he smiled and said, 'Miss, you speak so well and are very professional,' and he told me that I deserved a better job than his!" Mina recalls with a laugh. That was perhaps one of the very few times that she felt genuine kindness—an authentic feeling of respect—especially from a man. He introduced Mina to a wealthy *haj khanoom*— a phrase that literally translates to for a woman who has come back from the religious Hajj pilgrimage, who also engages in philanthropy and community service. While the job the woman offered would save Mina and her two boys from poverty, it would also put her on the frontlines of a war that would kill so many other young boys.

It was 7:00 a.m. on a Tuesday morning during the early days of the Iran-Iraq War—a catastrophe that killed nearly one million Iranians and left hundreds of thousands of people injured. The haj khanoom had asked Mina to visit an army hospital in central Tehran. She gave Mina a box of pastries—a common custom when you're visiting someone and want to pay your respects—and asked her to deliver it to an army captain, along with a letter.

Mina went to the hospital, where she was forced to wait several hours until she was finally allowed to see the captain. "He didn't even look up," she remembers about entering his office. "I gave him the letter and said I was looking for a job. He still didn't look up—my legs were shaking. Suddenly, I pulled the box of pastries out from under my chador and told him that haj khanoom Nikkhah had sent this along with her regards for your newborn." It was then that the man finally looked at Mina. He was all smiles, and greeted her with a warm welcome, saying, "'Why didn't you tell me earlier that you were sent by haj khanoom?'"

The young mother was then hired by the army hospital. From washing patients, covering night shifts, and cleaning the floors, to assisting the surgeons and injecting syringes, Mina did it all over the next four years. "There was very little personnel at the time, and I was used for many tasks. I saw twelve-, thirteen-, fourteen-year-old boys who would join the army and die on the frontlines," she recalls, still feeling the horror of those years.

Her job soon sent her to the 77th Infantry Division near the Karkheh River in Iran's Khuzestan Province, which borders Iraq and the Persian Gulf. During the Iran-Iraq War, Khuzestan was frequently under fire, as many of its cities were attacked by Saddam's forces. For many Iranians, the worst tragedy of the war was Saddam's use of chemical weapons. Nearly 8,000 Iranian civilians and military forces died by Iraqi nerve agents and mustard gas; today, thousands of victims still receive treatment for "chronic chemical weapons injuries." Iraq's main Western ally in the war was the United States, which according to CIA files, was aware of Saddam's use of chemical weapons against Iran.

Mina's memories of the war are gloomy and sad. In addition to the violence and carnage she witnessed, she also missed her two boys terribly. Fortunately, her sister helped her get through this trying time. "I left my boys with my younger sister who was now married," she says. "You know, if I had to pay for two people, I would pay her for six, she took such good care of my boys."

⚏

After the war, Mina continued to work at the army hospital overnight, while by day she'd clean homes and babysit for upper class families in Northern Tehran—the affluent part of the capital where she had once dreamt of raising her boys. "Nobody believes I lived in Niavaran (a district in Northern Tehran)," she says with her usual kind laughter. "If I made 500 toman a month, I would spend 400 for the rent on the apartment, and the rest on the kids."

Her sons, Bijan and Hooshang, are older now. While they never went to university as she had hoped, at least—as Mina says with pride—

they are "healthy boys." One works for the army, while the other is a music instructor, teaching violin, piano, and keyboard. "I didn't get my wish, which was for them to get a university degree, but I'm still proud of the men they have become," she shares. "You know how hard it is to raise good boys, good men, in abject poverty. It would have been so easy for them to swerve in the wrong direction."

If there is one thing that distinguishes Mina from other women who have struggled with poverty and getting married at such a young age, it is her exuberant love for life, for others, and hope. "I still think I can learn things, educate myself," she says confidently. "My dream is to leave Iran and maybe live in another country. There is still so much I can do, so much I haven't done."

It's hard to imagine Mina spending her entire life working to provide a bright future for her boys—a future that at the raw age of twelve was stolen from her. "I could not afford to not work around the clock. I could not afford to take a break, a breath, a pause," she says with an evident weariness in her eyes. As a result, she has never had the chance to do anything just for herself, something fun. I ask her if she can remember one moment when she didn't feel the weight of the world on her shoulders—one moment when she truly felt like a twelve-year-old. With excitement, she recalls a Friday afternoon when her late younger brother took her and the boys to Tehran's Shahr-e Bazi, which for the longest time was the only open door amusement park in the city—that unfortunately due to lack of inspection and malfunctions was forced to shut down. It was there in the old-time fun fair, with its giant metal rides, that Mina spent hours laughing with a brother she lost too soon. "It was still early on in the revolution, and they were strict about letting men and women get in the same carts together," she recalls. "I so badly wanted to ride the sky train, and my sweet brother finally convinced the guy to let him ride with me. I still remember." For Mina, this thirty-year-old memory is one of the few worth reliving.

Laleh Seddigh

SHE LOOKS LIKE A MIDDLE EASTERN MODEL. Her cheery smile is vivacious, her childlike energy contagious, and her feminine allure resembles that of an elegant version of a "Real Housewife." Through the mischievous confidence she exudes, you can sense her passion for control and her undeniable desire to be in charge. "I always ordered my siblings around. Sometimes they'd get me in trouble, but mostly they'd obey. The house was huge, and no one could tell what we were up to. I was in charge and they followed."

By the age of nine, she was beating the other neighborhood boys in bicycle races; by twelve, she had already mastered "Surgery 101" by killing little sparrows in her backyard and dissecting the pool frogs to learn about anatomy. "I wanted to be a surgeon when I was a kid," she laughs. By the age of fourteen, she was driving her brothers and sisters around the family garage. "I would throw my three siblings in the back of my dad's white Buick and drive back and forth in our L-shaped driveway," she remembers. She named the Buick *Nahang*—Farsi for *whale*.

Her favorite memory of that American car—which in early 1990s Iran was considered a luxury—was the day she invited her best friend Maryam over, under the pretense of doing homework. Her actual mission was to steal the whale for a ride on Jordan Street. "At first she cried and said she wasn't coming, but how could she say no to me," she says with a smile. "I would always protect her from the bullies in school."

Jordan Street (officially known as Nelson Mandela Boulevard, though many refer to it simply as Jordan) is one of the most crowded, fashionable, and popular streets in Tehran—a combination of the traffic of New York's Fifth Avenue and the luxuriousness of Rodeo Drive in Beverly Hills. Jordan begins and ends in two of Tehran's chicest neighborhoods. Clusters of coffee shops, clothing boutiques, flower stores, and office buildings line the sidewalks, enthralling hustling pedestrians and drivers in expensive cars. Flocks of young men and women flirt through open car windows while blasting their latest American and Euro playlists. Driving on Jordan is your ticket to mingle, exchange numbers, and spot your next date—all under the watchful eyes of the government's "morality police." (Although compared to twenty years ago, youthful escapades on Jordan and other streets are no longer a secret nor cracked down upon as heavily—depending on the mood of the government and how conservative the president is.)

This glamorous boulevard was no place for a fourteen-year-old to go joyriding in a stolen Buick. "It was so darn hard driving *Nahang* out of our alley and onto the main street," she recalls. "I was short and couldn't see well. Maryam would constantly get out of the car to show me the way." After an hour of struggle—and only two blocks of travel—the two teenagers successfully made it to Jordan Street. But the adventure quickly went south after an accident with a Zamyar van in the middle of an intersection. "The driver was shocked when I got out of the car," she says. "I had no driver's license, my parents didn't know what I was doing, Maryam was crying, so the only thing I could do was to beg the man to let me go. I had no choice but to tell him that we were rushing to the hospital because my grandma was dying!"

Such is the daring and chutzpah of Laleh Seddigh, one of the few Muslim female race car champion in the world. In 2005, before she turned thirty, she claimed the title of "Little Schumacher," because of her petite frame and incredible driving skills. In a field long dominated by men, she has paved the way for other Iranian women to compete professionally in motorsports.

Born into an affluent family, Laleh's obsession with speed was visible to her family from a young age. "They knew I loved to compete—whatever it was, I wanted to win the competition," she says. When she was just thirteen, her father taught her how to drive at the family's country villa in Karaj—about 100 miles outside of Tehran. She remembers how her family would stay in the villa during the Iran-Iraq War in the 1980s and she'd drive the village kids around in a mini-truck. "Dad loved my ambition and passion for speed. In my life, Mom was the brake, and Dad was the gas. He let me push forward and she put me in check."

In 1995, eighteen-year-old Laleh was accepted to study industrial engineering at a private university in Tehran. To this day, Iranian high school students have little choice in their preferred field of study. Instead, millions of twelfth graders—known as "pre-university" students—cram for a year to pass an excruciating exam called *konkoor*. Based on their scores, they can apply for available majors; the higher the score, the better chance of getting something you actually want to study.

Upon starting her first term in college, Laleh's father bought her a Peugeot 405—one of the only cars directly imported from France into Iran. Back then, American cars were not easily available in Iran—and they still aren't. Most luxury cars were basic European or Asian imports; but these days, as a result of years of sanctions, Iran's automotive

industry has become self-reliant, assembling much of its needs inside the country. As for luxury imports, occasionally, a few Maseratis, Ferraris, or Lamborghinis electrify the cracked asphalt of Jordan and other streets. The majority of these cars are bought by the ayatollah's kids, regime insiders, or those connected with the government.

Unlike her failed driving attempt when she was fourteen, Laleh drove the Peugeot like a pro, racing through the turbulent streets of Tehran. "The city was my track," she says with a proud smile. "I tinted the windows, lowered the car, changed the exhaust to boost the engine's roar, and raced around Tehran like there was no finish line."

At a time when joint outings for boys and girls in Iran were limited to coffee shop meetings and occasional private parties, Laleh's driving helped to bring together her female and male classmates. "I would pump up the girls against the boys in college, and we would bet on who'd win the car race that day—it would be me against a guy," she remembers. When one of her classmates encouraged her to look into professional racing, Laleh asked him, "Are girls allowed to race?" The answer back then was no.

⌗

When Laleh was twenty-two, she went to the Motorcycle and Automobile Federation of Iran to ask about getting involved in rally racing. She vividly recalls the director telling her, "Girls don't race, they only read maps. They may do rallies, but definitely don't speed race." A month later, she went back, this time carrying a gift: a painting she had done of a forest with beaming rays shining through the darkness of the woods. "I was trying so hard to convince the director and the only thing that came to my mind was to paint something for him," she says with a laugh. The man had three daughters, and Laleh is not sure if it was his fatherly emotions or frustration with her persistence, but he gave her the green light to take part in the rallies.

Even after being allowed to rally, Laleh was still unsatisfied. "I was so irritated with the girls who would sit next to me in rally (the map readers) and freak out every time I'd drive fast. They would cry—I mean seriously!" One morning, fed up with her rally partner, Laleh went over to talk to the male drivers. "As soon as he got out of his car," she says about the driver she approached, "I jumped in front of him and said, 'I want to race, sir, what should I do?'" The driver, who turned out to be Alireza Tabatabaei—Iran's then-race car champion—rebuffed her. However, a few weeks later, she was out driving in Tehran: "As usual, I was driving like a maniac, and this guy stopped next to me, pulled down the window, and looked at me in awe." It was Tabatabaei, who now understood that the young driver could not be ignored.

Laleh was still not allowed to race professionally nor register for a team, because she was a woman. At the time, under Islamic law, women were not permitted to race; rules about dress codes and interaction between the sexes also prevented them from competing. "As soon as I heard that I couldn't race, I went home crying to my dad and told him they wouldn't allow me to race because I was a girl," she says. Her father took her to see a religious cleric—an ayatollah—who wrote a letter on her behalf, known as a fatwa. The "fatwa" in Laleh's case was equivalent to a religious "doctor's note," "excusing" her for being "a woman" and justifying that it was not forbidden for her to race—provided she didn't forego wearing her hijab under any circumstances, dressed appropriately, and abided by the federations' "moral and Islamic" rules and guidance.

Equipped with religious permission, her father's unconditional financial and emotional support, and her own fervor, Laleh was now free to compete with the boys. Despite her triumph, it was still a very trying time for her. "It wasn't easy at all," she shares with a bit of anger. "There were so many obstacles thrown my way, simply because they didn't want to see a woman succeed in an all-male field." From loosening the tires of her car and accusations of cheating, to banning her from taking

the stage due to her hijab, Laleh's path to stardom was tumultuous. "I don't want to talk about it and remind myself of all the hardships and bad memories," she says with some bitterness, "but let me put it this way, there were so many people—mainly men—who wanted me to fail rather than see me succeed." Even her first victory was tainted by the fact she was a woman: "The funny yet sad thing is that the first time I won a race, they didn't even show my face on television!" The struggles that Laleh experienced are not unique to her, or her profession, but are a sad reality for many Iranian women who want to succeed in their fields, but to do so, must overcome societal barriers, governmental regulations, and deeply rooted prejudice toward women.

Instead of breaking under the pressure, Laleh became a warrior. "I became a fighter," she declares defiantly, "and thought I could get back at all those haters and bullying men by working extra hard." She was able to weaponize her anger into a fire that fumed out of her race car, growing the sport for herself and other women. "This sentence that you can't do it because you're a woman needs to be eliminated," Laleh remarks. Since the start of her professional career, she has simultaneously had to fight two battles: excelling in the sport, and dodging, ignoring, and maneuvering through constant jealousies, accusations, and harassment by men—and on occasion, women—in the field. As a matter of fact, what torments her most is the jealousy she has faced from other women. "I knew what it was, but I couldn't do anything about it," she says sadly. "When you choke a group and prevent them from thriving and doing what they want, they grow hateful and self-conscious."

Over the past two decades, Laleh has traveled across the Middle East, Europe, Canada, and the United States. Despite her worldwide success, she never left Iran, and has no intention of doing so. "I've had every opportunity to leave," she says, "but I wanted to stay and succeed here. You know, the loneliness I'd face elsewhere would suffocate me. My entire family, failures, successes, struggles, wins, are all here."

While many Iranian women, especially young athletes, look up to her, for Laleh, defining a goal is the only sign she wants to leave on the road behind her. "Many young girls in Iran don't envision a target for themselves," she says. "I pray that more and more young girls set goals in their lives. It's the goal and mission that'll push you to survive, to fight, and to thrive."

For Laleh, both her professional and personal life continue to be a "mission to accomplish." Though she's not married yet, she knows the right man will still come along. However, he would have to be someone who can accept her as she is. "I can't have someone in my life that would make me choose between him or my sport," she says. She owes much of that independence to the strong character she's carved out through her two-decade-long professional career. "Life is about achieving," she asserts. "It's an experience, like a stroll in a beautiful garden. You see every flower, get stung by bees, but you savor it all. You achieve that experience, and then move on to another garden."

At the end of our conversation, we talked about role models, and I asked Laleh which female leader she'd like to meet. "I'd love to meet Hillary Clinton or Margaret Thatcher—if she was still alive, of course," she answered. "I want to learn how they maneuvered through a male-dominated world, how they chose their male friends, their part- ners. I'd ask Mrs. Clinton how she handled men in a world that's so

Mohammad Reza Soltani

*I*STILL TEAR UP WHENEVER I WATCH Anthony Bourdain's Iran episode from his hit series *Parts Unknown*; it is perhaps the single most human story to come out of the country since the Islamic Revolution. Bourdain may be gone, but the humanity he captured through his "food adventures" will live on forever—highlighted by one of the jewels of Iran: its cuisine.

There is nothing more tempting than its smell. It is hard to believe that something with so few ingredient is regarded as one of the most delicious Iranian dishes. Minced calf (veal) sirloin meat is mixed with salt and pepper, turmeric, and ground saffron; it's then laid on long thin metal skewers by hand and cooked over flaming charcoal, to make a national dish that's unlike any other kabob in the world. It's traditionally paired with fluffy long-grain saffron rice and a few charcoal-grilled tomatoes on the side. *Chelow* (a more traditional word for rice) *Kabob-e Koobideh* is a mouthwatering masterpiece of Persian cuisine. It is often paired with *doogh*, a cold, yogurt-based drink mixed with mint and salt. Iranian rice "polo" is like no other rice, and "tahdig"—the crispy crust in the bottom of the pan—is a culinary sensation that stuns anyone who takes a bite into this crunchy goodness. Sometimes, before digging into their chelow kabob, old school Iranians will mix a raw egg yoke into their rice and add some sumac for a subtle tangy flavor.

In Iran, side dishes are a show of their own. Sweet basil, red turnips cut into small rosettes, tarragon, mint, cilantro and scallion all make up the "herb platter" on each lunch table, which next to the small bowl of strained yogurt mixed with cucumber and dried mint or minced Persian shallots, make you feel as if you're sitting in a fragrant garden. The extravagance and complexity of Iranian food are part of the daily lives of Iranians, for whom food serves as an integral part of their millennia-old culture and history.

While Iranian food may be unrivaled in taste and color, its secret sauce is the time-consuming process of cooking that reflects a love and passion that transcends generations. Rare is the Iranian mother who doesn't know how to cook; it's like reading, writing, and breathing—it's part of life. Eating together around the table, patiently waiting for the elderly to begin first, and over-entertaining guests with an excess of dishes are among the niceties you learn as a child growing up in Iran. The essence of Persian hospitality is demonstrated through the host's "killing of guests" with kindness and abundance. For Iranians, the importance of the homemade meal is second to none, as it amplifies the significance of family life. Food is somewhat sacred; people respect food, respect eating it together and scruple to waste—especially rice and bread. There's something so reverent about the two that perhaps underscores the intensity of labor in farming an ounce of rice or wheat—an agricultural practice common in Iran's rainy provinces of Gilan and Mazandaran in the north.

"Purchasing products for the restaurant is the hardest task; it's perhaps the hardest responsibility these days," says the young man who

owns one of Tehran's oldest "chelow kabobi(s)"—the common name used for restaurants that primarily serve authentic Persian kabobs among other traditional rices and stews.

⊡

Bordering the potent waters of the Caspian Sea, Gilan and Mazandaran are two of Iran's most fecund provinces, producing most of the nation's fruit, vegetable, poultry, fish, and agricultural exports. The area's lush forests date back thousands of years, and some of the country's most notable poets, artists, and political figures have hailed from the region.

The Caspian Sea is a rich asset that until recently was split between Iran and the former Soviet Union. For centuries, the entire body of water belonged to Iran, but the country lost control of the north coast to Russia in 1820. Today, due to a 2018 treaty signed by Russia, Iran, and four other former Soviet-dominated neighboring countries, Iran controls less than 13 percent of these fertile inland waters.

According to the US Energy Information Administration, the Caspian Sea is estimated to hold some "forty-eight billion barrels of oil and 292 trillion cubic feet of natural gas." But that's not all; the Beluga fish, which produces the priciest of all caviars, also lives in these waters. The caviar is harvested from a rare albino sturgeon that swims in the southern waters of the Caspian Sea. *The Guinness Book of World Records* calls *Almas* (diamond in Farsi) the most expensive caviar in the world; a pound can sell for $17,000.[1]

Long before the revolution, caviar was harvested in Iran and shipped across Europe and the United States. While the delicacy became an indulgence of the rich and the famous worldwide, it was never popular among ordinary Iranians. After oil, caviar was Iran's second "black gold." Reportedly, the country's ousted monarch, Mohammad Reza

---

1. "Most Expensive Caviar," *Guinness World Records*, https://www.guinnessworldre-cords.com/world-records/most-expensive-caviar.

Shah Pahlavi, served more than 300 pounds of the tiny black beluga eggs during a 1971 soirée that marked the 2500 year anniversary of the Iranian civilization. Today, Iran's fishing industry is controlled by the government. Due to years of economic sanctions imposed by the United States and its allies, the glory days of caviar production and exports to the West have significantly dwindled.

The southern coast of the Caspian Sea is covered with lush paddy fields used for farming rice. Here, in the wet fields of Gilan and Mazandaran, female farmers plant rice with their bare, often swollen hands, for less than a dollar per day. While much of Iran's rice farming has been mechanized, there are still thousands of women whose livelihood depends on their manual labor in the fields—women who at times must carry their newborns on their backs. "I directly buy rice from farmers in the north," the young restauranteur says. "I talk to them in advance, ask them to put some good rice aside for me for winter and tell them everything I need. You just have to be involved and know what you're doing. You have to trust the people you're working with; otherwise there's so much corruption and cheating that for sure you'll end up losing."

From dates, nuts, exotic fruits, abundant arrays of vegetables, to poultry and meat, you can find everything and anything in Iran. However, since the early days of the revolution, followed by an eight-year-long war, and years of international sanctions, internal mismanagement, and corruption, Iran's economy has endured massive inflation, exponential depreciation of its currency, and sky-rocketing price hikes, which have prevented the country from seeing the commercial and economic growth it deserves.

"When you buy rice, even if you go to the most trusted sellers, you will find out that with each ton you buy, there's at least two to three hundred kilos of bad quality rice that's mixed in with your purchase," the young man shares. "The same goes for meat. There are four or five old-timers in Tehran who you can trust. We buy our meat and poultry from them, but if you don't pay attention to what you're buying, you'll find that in every hundred kilos of meat, at least 10 percent of it is useless fat or other things they add to the meat that make it unusable." There is an undeniable exhaustion in his voice. "You see, quality and trust are all you have in the restaurant business—I can't lose that. I can't lose people's trust."

Mohammad Reza Soltani was born one year before the 1979 Revolution into what he calls a "religious" family. It was in that tumultuous time that his father managed to buy the top floor of his basement kabob shop and expand his business into its current form—the Soltani Chelow Kabobi. "Before the revolution, the top floor was a hair salon," Mohammad Reza says, "but a year later, Dad was able to buy it and turn it into the dining area that we have today. The layout of the restaurant is still the same; we haven't changed anything."

The Soltani Chelow Kabobi is located in the southern end of Sohrevardi Street—a bustling commercial neighborhood in central Tehran filled with home-goods and appliance stores. Like many other kabob houses in Iran, the Soltani Chelow Kabobi serves a broad range of kabobs, along with traditional stews, appetizers, and fish dishes.

Every day at noon, a flood of working men and women stop by the restaurant on their lunch break. Sometimes, the phone doesn't stop ringing during lunchtime, as many local companies and offices have their food delivered. "I have about thirty personnel working at the restaurant," says Mohammad Reza. "I usually hire younger guys from smaller cities and rural areas who are seeking work in Tehran. They're less entitled than the university students who grow up in Tehran and are looking for part-time jobs. Those who work hard are the ones who will be loyal to the job."

In early 2019, more than one-quarter of Tehran's seven hundred registered restaurants filed for bankruptcy or shut down due to sky-rocketing inflation and price hikes. "It's just hard," Mohammad Reza says dejectedly. "Having integrity and trying to make good food doesn't cut it. We need support from the government. The restaurant industry is not supported, and the daily price hikes are just breaking our backs.

Every morning, you wake up and there are new prices for everything."

Mohammad Reza recalls the many times he thought of closing. "There were so many times that I thought I should just rent the place out or just sell it all together and put the money in the bank and just live off of the bank interest. There's a system that makes you tired of working."

But for the young man, the Soltani Chelow Kabobi, is more than just a business— it's personal.

⊡

Like many others both before and after the revolution, Mohammad Reza's father saw Tehran as place of progress and growth where he could make a better life for himself and, ultimately, his family. "He moved to Tehran from Khansar when he was only fifteen years old," his son remembers. "He wanted to find work. His two brothers then followed in his footsteps and moved from their village into the big city for jobs." Mohammad Reza remembers his father, Akbar Soltani, with pride—a man who was born and raised in a small village in northwest of Isfahan only to establish one of Tehran's oldest and still standing chelow kabob restaurants.

It was the early 1950s, and Akbar was hired as a laborer at Shamshiri, one of Iran's most prominent chelow kabob restaurants, located in the bustling Tehran Bazaar at the southern end of the capital. The restaurant's owner, Mohammad Hassan Shamshiri, first opened the place as a coffee house, or *ghahveh khaneh*. In 1941, at as Anglo-Soviet forces were marching their armies into Iran, Shamshiri turned his cafe into the eponymous kabob house that would disrupt the Iranian restaurant industry for the years to come. Shamshiri was regarded as a "man of the people" and a "patriot"—whose support for the late Iranian Prime Minister, Mohammad Mosaddegh, cost him a great deal of money, as well as political imprisonment.

Akbar learned the restaurant trade in Shamshiri's kitchen. "The first few years, he was just working nonstop and sleeping in the basement of the restaurant," Muhammad Reza recalls. Akbar eventually became the lead *takhte kar* (the person who makes the barg kabob that consists of lamb or beef cut into strips, which are then marinated and grilled). According to his son, "he was so good at his work that other restaurants wanted to steal him from Shamshiri."

One of the restaurants that wanted to steal Akbar was Sorento, which was one of Tehran's hot spots back in the 1960s and 1970s, up until the revolution. It was located on the corner of Jame-Jam Street and Vali-e-Asr—a wide and long boulevard where century-old plane trees continue to transform this streetscape into a green tunnel. Sorento was one of the first eateries in Iran to be regarded as posh, upscale, and Western. The menu featured a wide range of international food— making it a favorite destination for Tehran's elite. "Sorento desperately wanted him, and Shamshiri was not letting him go," Mohammad Reza says. "He was earning a good salary making barg kabob at Shamshiri, but Sorento was also going to pay him well, so he decided to work at both places." Once he was employed by both restaurants, Akbar literally had to work around the clock. "Dad told me how he would work until midnight in Shamshiri and would then ride his bicycle all the way up from the bazaar to Vali-e-Asr to prepare Sorento's barg kabobs for the following day," his son shares. "Sometimes, he would go back to Shamshiri straight from an overnight shift at Sorento, but here and there he'd come back home to rest for a few hours in between." There's an evident sense of admiration in Mohammad Reza's voice for his father's vigor and work ethic.

Sorento was shut down during the Islamic Revolution. It reopened a few years later, but its golden years were long gone, alive only in the memories of the many Iranian expats. Today, Shamshiri's doors remain open, not so much for its food, but for those who flock downtown for a taste of old Tehran in one of the city's most iconic locations.

Despite the country's broken economy, there are expensive, modern and luxurious restaurants that have popped up all over Tehran in recent years. The majority of them opened in the past two decades; but a few like the famous Indian restaurant, Taj Mahal, the classic PAPA steakhouse in the glamorous Fereshteh neighborhood, or the charming Swiss Restaurant in central Tehran have stood the test of time and political turmoil.

These days in Iran, restaurants and cafés are more than just places to satisfy the appetite; they are also the only public spots where teenage age boys and girls can hang out and eye one another, young couples can enjoy each other's company, and groups of friends can spend hours eating, drinking, and laughing, like others do elsewhere in the world. For every cool spot in world-class cities like New York, London, or

Dubai, you can find an equivalent in Tehran. Of course it all comes with a premium price tag sans alcohol. From frozen yogurt, "fake" Starbucks, and rebranded KFC to sushi restaurants on par with Zuma and Nobu, French restaurants as high quality as those in Paris, and old-school teahouses in historic buildings, Iranians love spending their time in the many dining establishments they may or may not be able to afford.

"Back then, workers, laborers, in fact anyone, could save up money," explains Mohammad Reza. "People were able live and also put money away on the side, enough to be able to buy something like a car or a property somewhere. These days, that's absolutely impossible. I have workers who come to me after two weeks and ask for the next month's salary in advance."

Eventually, Akbar was able to save up enough to start his own restaurant. "After a couple of years of working nonstop, Dad was able to buy a small basement in Salsabeel and turn it into a kabobi," Mohammad Reza reminiscences. "We've been here since." Fifty years to be exact.

Imagine one of the oldest neighborhoods in the south of Tehran. It was once filled with lush gardens, farms and springs—nothing like the new Salsabeel that's now home to clothing wholesalers and cluttered shops in the neighborhood's narrowly built streets. You no longer see signs of old pomegranate gardens and crystal clear streams that were once the only source of water for the entire neighborhood.

"Half a century is no joke. Whenever I walk in the restaurant, I feel my dad is here. He built fifty years of reputation, trust, and credibility; that's no easy thing to accomplish."

Mohammad Reza is the youngest child and only son of the Soltani family. If you look at it through a traditional lens, it's not difficult to see why he was chosen as the heir apparent to the restaurant his father built from scratch. However, the restaurant business was not Mohammad Reza's first love. Instead, science and technology were his initial passions, so much so that he attended the university to pursue a degree in industrial engineering: "I loved science and technology; I always have. It was my passion." But where he was needed most was in his father's restaurant.

As a little boy, Mohammad Reza would often find himself by his father's side at the restaurant, helping with small chores and other tasks.

By the time he was in university, he was taking on more of his father's responsibilities, especially as the hard-working man's health deteriorated over time. "Dad worked until he no longer could. He worked all his life and in his final years, it was hard for him to accept that he could no longer work." After working for almost six decades, Akbar Soltani passed away in 2007 after a short battle with cancer—leaving a legacy for his only son to follow.

As much as the young restaurateur tries to remain positive, he isn't optimistic about what lies ahead. "One morning you wake up and the prices of produce and meat have gone up five- to ten-fold," he says. "There are months that we make no money—especially during religious holidays or the month of Ramadan. This is not an industry you can count on." Each time he thinks of giving up the business, however, the memory of his father shines through. "Dad worked so hard. I could only imagine what it took to build this place. That's why I'm not selling it. I just can't."

Though he inherited the restaurant from his father, Mohammad Reza has no desire to pass the business on to his own children. "My kids are everything to me. But you know what, I'd never introduce my sons to the restaurant, to the chelow kabob business. I don't want them to get into this field," he says with utmost sincerity. "I want them to pursue what makes them happy, not like me, who was excited about electronics and science but ended up in the restaurant. I don't care what they do as long as they're happy, as long as they have chosen their profession themselves, as long as they are passionate about what they do every day."

And that's the thing. For Iranian families, from one generation to the next, people change, habits evolve, but at the end of the day, a fervent love, endearment and care for their offspring remains. A man or woman works around the clock to give their family a better life, only to miss seeing their children grow up. The next generation will then work hard to prevent this from happening again, only to be left with the same question: did they do enough? Just like Iranian food, the answer is loving, but complicated.

Nikoo Cheheltani

*I*t was a turning point in my life. It made me into the woman I am today—it changed my life forever."

Her curly blonde highlights amplify her energetic smile, which appears even brighter against the blue backdrop of the sea behind her. The calm foamy water and gentle waves belie the fact that she operates her businesses in one of the most hotly contested bodies of water in the world—the Persian Gulf.

The Persian Gulf is home to two major islands—Kish and Qeshm. A little over 100 miles from Dubai, Kish attracts millions of Iranian tourists to its high-end hotels and shopping malls. Less than 140 miles from Kish is Qeshm, Iran's largest island, with a free zone that covers a little over half its land mass. While Qeshm is less glitzy than Kish, its strategic location in the Strait of Hormuz serves as an important commercial port that links Iran to the rest of the world.

The Strait is a narrow water passage that connects the Persian Gulf to the Gulf of Oman. Given that 90 percent of the Gulf's oil exports go through the Strait of Hormuz, any impasse here can affect global energy markets and the world economy. According to the US Department of Energy, each day, nearly 20 percent of the world's liquid natural gas and 20 to 30 percent of its oil pass through the Strait. Most crude oil is exported from Iran, its archrival Saudi Arabia, as well as the United Arab Emirates, Kuwait, and Iraq. It is also the route for nearly all the liquefied natural gas from its leading exporter, Qatar—home to the largest US military base in the Middle East.

In addition to the many geopolitical disputes, the historically accurate name of the Persian Gulf has long been a point of conflict, with many Gulf Cooperation Council (GCC) countries, as well as the US, preferring to call it the Arabian Gulf. Back in a 1974 interview, American journalist Mike Wallace was schooled by Iran's then monarch, Mohammad Reza Pahlavi. In a possible attempt to stir controversy, Wallace raised the ambiguity of the "Gulf's" name, to which the Shah responded, "what was the name that you read [learned] during your school days?" With a nervous chuckle Wallace replied, "The Persian Gulf." The ever present murmur over the name only amplifies the fact that, independent of governments and political beliefs, the "Persian Gulf" is a nonnegotiable for all Iranians—especially its people, who take strong pride in this crystalline body of water.

Tucked away about a mile from Qeshm is Hengam. The small island is comparable in size to St. Barts, but with none of the glamour of the

French-speaking colony. Instead, Hengam is a humble place—a dry stretch of land with few inhabitants and nearly nonexistent commerce. "Up until a few years ago, if you told me, 'Oh, you'll be living here one day,' I would have laughed and thought you're crazy," says the young woman.

One of the few female divers in Iran, Nikoo Cheheltani was born into a highly educated middle-class family in Tehran. Her father was a mechanical engineer, while her mother taught high school physics. Because of their parents' jobs, academics were important for Nikoo and her two sisters when they were growing up. However, far from the typical fields of medicine and engineering that often interest many young Iranians, it was in the underwater world that Nikoo found her true calling. "I never imagined to be where I am today, or getting into this field," she says with a sense of happy surprise. "It was all so unexpected, but I would not change it for the world."

What's striking about Nikoo is not just how she has managed to build a life as a professional diver and expert marine biologist, but that she has done it in partnership with her husband—a rare relationship in today's Iran, where so many youths marry for money or superficial values. "How can you not fall in love with someone who is so passionate about his goals?" Nikoo says of her husband, Mohammad. "It's that passion that inspires you to also do what you love and follow your dreams—no matter how elusive they may appear at first."

The diving community in Iran is small, so it's easy to connect with fellow divers—especially on social media. That was how the young power couple met. "Mohammad told me he wanted to talk to me about coral reefs," Nikoo says with a cute laugh, "but I think it was just an excuse. He reached out to me on a Facebook diving group and that's how we initially got to connect."

Today, the couple own a diving center on Hengam called Dive Persia. "It's our baby," Nikoo says. "Mohammad built it with his bare hands. There was nothing he didn't do for the center. If there was an issue with the air conditioning, Mohammad would learn how to fix it;

if the place needed painting Mohammad would figure out how to paint. Whatever the center needed, Mohammad did it on his own."

What's so special about Mohammad, as Nikoo confirms, is how he built the business out of nothing. "He wasn't this rich kid who was bored or had nothing else to do and decided to start a business," she says. "He worked so hard on everything without any support from anyone. You know, starting and growing this business from scratch was ridiculously hard, but it was his dream and soon it became mine." Nikoo goes on to explain how they couldn't survive by merely working as diving instructors, so they also opened a diving equipment shop in Kish in order to make ends meet.

Nikoo's independence and strength as a young Iranian woman is enhanced by her support for her husband, and the confidence and hard work she puts into their joint ventures. "When you feel you need to take care of yourself as a responsible adult, your dreams and mission become a reality of life, an incentive to push you forward through all potential challenges." The tone of her voice, like that of many other young Iranians when discussing professional obstacles, is oddly calm— as if it's natural to face, and overcome, so many hurdles.

With Dive Persia in Hengam and their equipment store in Kish, the couple have become leaders in the diving industry in the Persian Gulf— especially when it comes to high-quality professional instruction. "We're both IDC (Instructor Development Course) staff instructors trained under the PADI (Professional Association of Diving Instructors) system," Nikoo explains with a vigor similar to that of a business manager or an American professional athlete. "None of this training exists in Iran because of the sanctions. Our goal was not just to set up a business. We wanted to do it right. We want to be as professional as the centers in the US, or Southeast Asia, or even those in the Middle East." She's referring to the global diving centers that are licensed under PADI, a world-class American diving organization headquartered in Southern California.

It's mind boggling to see the challenges they face in an environment that could easily become of the world's finest diving destinations. The couple had myriad issues getting training certificates from centers that operate under the PADI system due to US sanctions, which won't allow American organizations and companies to do business or have an official presence in Iran. "Like many other businesses, we have difficulty signing contracts with American companies to buy diving equipment for our store," says Nikoo. "American companies get so nervous when you mention Iran, so we work with the Italians, Japanese, Polish, and others. But it's hard—here, everything is double or triple the difficulty of everywhere else."

Despite these obstacles, the couple has pushed ahead. "We're very

proud of ourselves," Nikoo says confidently. "We recently launched the first professional Iranian diving magazine, called *Persian Divers*— we share stories both in print and online and have it available in English and Farsi." The couple is so devoted to their work that for their honeymoon they went to Bali so that Nikoo could pass her Instructor Development Course. "Southeast Asia is one of those places where it's easier to participate in these tests; they run it quite a few times per year," she says. "Obviously, we don't have access to this test in Iran, so we decided why not, let's do this on our honeymoon."

In a country where most students are desperate to get into prominent, high-paying fields like medicine or engineering, how did Nikoo wind up in marine biology? "It's so crazy. I didn't even swim well when I was a kid," she says with a laugh. "I was once thrown in the pool when I was a kid by the swimming instructor and the fear of water stuck, so the idea of getting into this field was beyond my imagination."

When Nikoo was taking her university entry examination, her aunt suggested she look into marine biology. At the time, Nikoo knew nothing about it, but her aunt helped her to become interested. "You know, it's a running joke in Iran among students and their families when applying to university: 'Oh, you're applying for the bachelors in the gardening of underwater plants.' No one took this field seriously— it was the field people would assume you apply for when you don't have high enough grades for anything else."

Nikoo attended Shahid Beheshti University, one of the most prestigious public universities in Iran, and majored in marine biology. While there, she came to realize that there were precious few resources devoted to the discipline. "No field trips, no diving camps, no practical work," she recalls. After receiving her bachelor's degree, Nikoo decided to leave Iran to pursue her graduate studies. "My family was so supportive. I could have not done it without them," she says. After applying to programs in Southeast Asia and Australia, in 2007, Nikoo was admitted to the University of Malaya, in Malaysia. The then-twenty-three-year-old became the first of her three sisters to leave Iran. "I was the first to leave; my sisters later left. One of them is married now and the younger one went off to study not too long ago."

Nikoo's time in Malaysia was filled with the thrill of independence, exploration and adventure—a new sense of adulthood that cannot not be achieved in Iran by many young women. "I was so excited to leave and explore this independence—to live by myself." While in countries such as the United Kingdom, France, Germany, Sweden, the UAE, Canada, and the US—especially in larger states like California, New York, and Washington—you can find many Iranian immigrants, that was not the case in Malaysia. "There were no Iranians there," Nikoo shares. "Can you imagine? I knew no one, so my only task was to work hard in school, focus on my thesis, and learn as much as I could."

With a laugh, she recalls the early days of her education at the University of Malaya, when she would shadow different groups and her program supervisor to learn the ins and outs of diving. "The first six months I was stuck to my supervisor," she says with a smile, "but the first time I went by myself I felt one of the most incredible sensations in my life. It was there that I fell in love. I could not believe it."

While the rush of excitement in diving captivated Nikoo, more than anything, the young student wanted to make it work on a practical level. "I wanted to succeed. There was no other option," she says, the determination apparent in her voice. "I remember as soon as I was granted a full scholarship, I called my dad and told him not send me money anymore. I was so proud of myself—of my ability to support myself—of course in the minimal way that I could back then."

That sense of independence is one of the most precious feelings for any Iranian girl. Unlike in the US and other Western countries, Iranian parents (especially the father) support their children well into young adulthood. In Iran, there is no expectation of moving out at the age of eighteen to get a job or go to college. Of course, many young people do work from a young age—especially if they come from a financially-challenged family—but in general, Iranian parents do their best to take care of their children financially for as long as necessary. "I remember this Iranian girl who came to our university," Nikoo recalls. "She was ten years older than me and was incredibly homesick. Seeing her frustration and loneliness somehow made me more eager to fight through my journey there and come out strong."

Three years later, armed with a graduate degree and a strong set of diving skills, Nikoo returned home to Tehran to find work. "In my first attempt to find a job. I went to the Iranian National Institute for Oceanography and Atmospheric Science (INIOAS). I thought, I have this degree and all these experiences, so they'll naturally be welcoming of someone like me."

But Nikoo did not receive the warm welcome she had anticipated. Had she not met Mohammad, Nikoo would likely have become one of the thousands of young Iranian students and recent graduates that leave the country. She'd probably be somewhere in California now, near her sisters, either teaching in one of the PADI centers or working on a research project. "I'd already visited my sister once; they both left with student visas and I was hoping to work on my PhD application and visa that year—until of course I met Mohammad."

It was around the same time that she got a full scholarship to attend a one month intensive course in Bermuda to work on coral reefs, eco-diving, and ecology. "I needed a British visa and God knows how long that took." In Bermuda, she completed yet another advance course in eco-diving alongside European, American, Latin American and Asian divers. "The astonishment I see on the face of foreigners when I meet them during my diving travels is beyond fascinating. They are always shocked; kind, but shocked. It's as if an Iranian woman cannot be a diver."

In recent years, countries like Australia and New Zealand have become popular hubs for young Iranian immigrants. However, Nikoo and Mohammad have no desire to leave their home country. "We've had the opportunity to leave Iran," she says, "but we've put all our energy and all that we've had in this, so leaving it all behind doesn't make any sense. We can't leave what we have built unless we get so desperate, disillusioned, and disheartened that we can't see any future here. We're not there yet," says Nikoo whose only "baby" other than the center is her fluffy Shitzu puppy Noris.

Many in the West who are bemused by the hijab may wonder what

Nikoo's diving outfit looks like. "Same as everywhere," she says with a chuckle. "Obviously, the diving suit or the wetsuit covers my body. With the goggles and everything, there's nothing to see—I sometimes also wear a bandana." While diving in Hengam is not as restricted, in Kish and Qeshm, there are morality police and security personnel who monitor diving centers and other recreational activities so that women and men dive separately and that there is no "misconduct." As for the beaches, the beautiful sandy grounds of the Persian Gulf are gender-segregated.

For Nikoo and Mohammad, the diving center is more than a business; it's also a place where they can demonstrate Iranian hospitality at its best. Nikoo tells me about the time they met a Canadian tourist in Qeshm. "He was like a bag-packer. We randomly met him and told him about our center in Hengam." The couple ended up inviting the young man to lunch, and they all spent the rest of the day diving together. "It was an amazing day," Nikoo remembers. "We then invited him to dinner with our friends, and afterward he looked at us and said he had never expected to have such an incredible experience in Iran."

However, there was still one more surprise in store for this tourist. "It was so funny—at the end of the day, he asked how much he had to pay for everything, and when we told him twenty-five dollars, he was so shocked." Nikoo explains that he had expected to pay for the ride to Hengam, as well as the food and drinks. "We only charged him for the dive; I mean, he was our guest. A Canadian—we rarely have people from North America, so it's of course our duty to receive the guest as best as we can."

When I asked Nikoo about her dreams for the future, she paused. "Dreams? I don't know. Maybe one day to have the president of PADI visit us and see what we have, what we're capable of, and how good we are at what we do. That would be amazing."

Aren Barkhordarian

OUR FIRST YEAR, WHEN PEOPLE WOULD call us to make a reservation, my partner and I would just laugh quietly and tell them, 'Sure, we've got a table for you.'" He still laughs when he recalls the early struggles of the restaurant. "The first winter was horrible, but we're in much better shape now and business is slowly picking up. This season we've barely had any empty tables at night. Even in freezing temperatures, we have customers sitting outside and enjoying themselves."

It's one of those ice-cold February evenings in Tehran (pre-COVID) when the temperature is in the single digits, but laughter, loud voices and chatter warm up the joint. The aroma of cooking burgers and French fries fill the air inside the restaurant and in the alley and adjacent street. The place is packed with couples, families, and young men and women gathered around tables awash in baked pizzas, meaty burgers, and sandwiches. It's hilarious how many people are secretly drinking. These days in Iran, no matter which restaurant you walk into, you'll most likely find people stealthy sipping alcohol from water bottles and small flasks. Despite the supposed ban on alcohol, Iran has one of the highest levels of alcohol consumption in the Middle East.

The scene reminds you of a cozy café in one of the narrow dead ends of Mar Mikhael in Beirut, or the small hipster establishments tucked away in the dark alleys of Karaköy in Istanbul. "You know, when I was signing the contract to rent this place, everyone told me that I was crazy for choosing this quiet alley, but it was the best decision I ever made," he says. "Sure, we may not be in front of everyone's eyes, but once we got our regulars, they became super loyal and brought their friends, and our clientele grew. It's as if we have our own little private space."

It is hard to believe that this jovial space is meters away from Tehran's Grand Mosalla. Foreigners—Americans and Israelis in particular—will recognize the interiors of the mosque as the main stage for regime devotees to gather for Friday prayers and chant their

infamous "Death to America" and "Death to Israel" slogans. Such seemingly irreconcilable contrarieties exist in every single corner of the country—especially in larger and more populous cities. In one spot, you can find yourself immersed in some of the latest American hip hop music while rubbing shoulders with fashionable boys and girls whose perfume and cologne intoxicates until you find yourself taking a puff of their joint and falling further into a haze. Moments later, you may be stopped by the morality police, asked to fix your hijab or turn down your music.

He is charming and genial, and his semi-bald head draws attention to his kind green eyes, which are striking against his five-o'clock shadow. "There are so many variations of burgers and sandwiches all over this city," he explains, "and people are trying so hard to be innovative and come up with unique sauces and recipes to make their food stand out.

But I wanted to stay true to the classic taste of a hamburger. I wanted to make sure that I'm creating an authentic burger, similar to what people used to have back in the day."

From the meat to the buns and vegetables, the young chef uses high-end—and highly priced—ingredients. "People tell me how my menu pricing is far too low for the quality that I serve, but I don't want to raise my prices too high," he reveals. "It's not fair to people. I sure am using the best ingredients, though. Why? Because you don't know what garbage is mixed in with the cheaper meat." To show how transparent he is about his food, he tells his customers that they are welcome to tag along when he goes shopping for the restaurant. "I always tell people who our buyers are and invite them to shadow me whenever they like. Anyone is welcome to join and see where I get my meat, how I marinate the patty, what spices I use, what goes into the sauce, and so forth. Honesty is the most important ingredient, and I want to remain honest with my customers."

The modest restaurant has an open kitchen, so that the customers can see everything that is going on behind the scenes. "I have dads who tell me that they never allow their kids to eat out, but our hamburgers are the only exceptions they make for their children," he shares happily. "That's a big deal for me. I want to be known for quality and I want to make sure that I never lower my standards."

Quality and honesty are indeed two of the main traits of this community, and it's no surprise that the young man keeps both values close to his heart.

They are known for their delicious pastries, coffee, cold cuts, sandwich shops and quality service and food. They introduced the French cafe' scene to Iran, started producing some of the best hot dogs, sausages, and deli meats in the country, setting an unprecedented standard for high quality products starting all the way back in the 1950s.

Among their many specialties, they continue to be known as the country's safest winemakers, who would often help their Muslim friends, neighbors, and "clients" get their hands on the latest bottles of liquor or homemade wines. For them, in contrast with the majority Muslim population, alcohol consumption is not illegal. However, it can't be consumed publicly, and one must always be respectful of the overall "rules and regulations" of the land.

They are the Armenian community of Iran—the Christians of the Islamic Republic—a minority group that for centuries has peacefully lived in a majority Muslim country. One of the beauties of their culture is how they consider themselves as Iranian as they are ethnically Armenian and Christian in faith.

Aren Barkhordarian is one of the thousands of Iranian Armenians living in Tehran. His family migrated from Armenia well over 100 years ago. At first, he picked one of the most popular colloquialisms used by Muslim Iranians when addressing Armenians, for his restaurant. "I wanted to name the restaurant Monsieur," he chuckles. "Even though it's a French word, we have historically been referred to as 'monsieur.' It was just a perfect word, as it would immediately take people back to the 1950s and the beautiful cafés and restaurants owned and operated by these sweet old men who'd speak with a thick Armenian accent." Unfortunately, the government authorities in Iran have banned the use of non-Farsi words when naming brands and restaurants. "It was hilarious, we tried everything to make it work. A friend of mine had an uncle whose name was Monsieur on his birth certificate, so I asked him to go in and say how we're naming the place after 'our uncle,'" he explains with laughter. "We were like, yeah, we love him so much that we want to name the place after him, but nope, that didn't work either." Eventually, he came up with Yerevan (pronounced Eeravan in Farsi), after the Armenian capital.

Aren and his wife live in Majidieh—one of the main Armenian neighborhoods in Tehran. Surrounded by three highways, the central enclave of the area still has an old-world vibe to it, despite the numerous developments and residential buildings that have sprung up over the years. The neighborhood's main Armenian school, Ararat, is up the street from the Saint Grigor Lusavorich Church, which was built in

1982. A ten-minute walk from the church will find you engrossed in the sound of the Adhan blasting from the Al-Mahdi Mosque. During your walk, you can stop in to get some food for your pet at the Ted Pet Shop, as well as some incredible coffee at George Café—pronounced *Jorge* in Farsi.

Armenians, who make up the largest population of Christians in Iran, have long lived peacefully among the country's Muslim majority. While there are many contradictory statistics, at its peak, there were several hundred thousand Armenians living in Iran; today, that number has reduced to approximately 100,000 to 120,000. The vast majority of Iranian Armenians are members of the traditional Gregorian Church of Armenia. In a region where some of the older Christian minorities such as those in Iraq, Kurdistan, and Syria have been forcefully displaced by the flames of sectarian wars and barbaric terrorism, the Christian minority of Iran has remained untouched.

Iran and Armenia have a long and intertwined history. As Europe was slowly emerging out of the Middle Ages in the late sixteenth century, Armenian migration to Iran was rapidly growing under the reign of the Safavid king, Shah Abbas I. The king was wary of his two archenemies—the Ottomans to the west and the Uzbeks to the east—who were making gains into Iranian territory. The king moved the nation's capital from Qazvin to the more centrally located Isfahan, and spent years building a standing army. In the interim, he sought the opportunity to create a diversified and lucrative capital with the help of his new Christian friends. Soon, the Safavid king transformed his newly designated capital of Isfahan into a grand cultural, architectural, educational, artistic and most importantly trade hub, which was chiefly ran by the Armenian community. Named in honor of their once-homeland of Julfa in today's Azerbaijan, Shah Abbas I gave a large territory to the Armenian community, who soon became some of the wealthiest and most notable merchants in the entire region, with an expansive influence that stretched all the way to India, China, and Europe.

Today, within the nearly 200 acres of New Julfa on the southern banks of the Zayandeh Rood River, you'll find reminders of the golden days of the silk trade, rich miniature paintings, and many examples of the masterful architecture of seventeenth-century Iran. However, what's most striking about the European-looking streets—adorned with clay houses, domed buildings, and cozy coffeehouses—is the reminder of how two distinctly different cultures and religions have managed to coexistent peacefully for several centuries, building an enduring piece of Iranian history in the process.

Over the years, the Armenian community has also produced some of Iran's greatest musicians, artists, photographers, filmmakers, and songwriters. One of the nation's first photographers was an Armenian named Antoin Sevruguin, who captured thousands of images in the late nineteenth and early twentieth century, documenting the lives of regular Iranians, as well as the royal court of the Qajar kings. Marcos Grigorian was an artist and actor who made a name for himself in the 1950s and eventually became known as the father of modern art in Iran. In the sciences, Alenush Terian was the first Iranian female astronomer and physicist, regarded as the "Solar Mother of Iran." A feminist at heart, she strove to prove that Iranian women were not solely meant to bear children and care for their husbands. Dr. Terian was the founder of the first solar telescopic observatory in Iran and was also the first person to teach astrophysics in the country. She had no children and remained unmarried until her death in 2011; but in a final act of utter kindness, she donated her residence to the Armenian community of Isfahan, to be used for underprivileged students.

Musically, Loris Tjeknavorian is regarded as one of the most revered Iranian-Armenian musicians and composers of all time. With an inherent passion for Iranian culture, his opera, *Rostam and Sohrab*, remains a brilliant treasure. In addition to the many pop Iranian Armenian singers, one remains a crown jewel. Vigen Derderian was a charming musician who gained the title of Iran's king of pop in the 1950s, and introduced Iranians to Latin rhythms, jazz, and European influences that had a long-lasting impact on the country's music. "Music was and is part of our blood," Aren says. "There is no Armenian family that doesn't have at least one or two musicians in them. A few of my dad's cousins were musicians. It's just part of who we are." Aren himself is an ardent fan of Elvis Presley and other American classics.

While it's hard to do to justice to capturing the entirety of the Armenian community's impact in just a few sentences, one man's vision at the young age of twenty-two is perhaps a perpetual example of the Armenian community's strong roots within Iranian society. In 1961, an aspiring Iranian Armenian architect named Edward Zohrabian won a national contest by drawing a simple yet elegant sketch of the Huma, a mythical Iranian bird that's said to bring prosperity and good fortune to whoever falls beneath its shadow. Zohrabian's sketch became the logo of Iran Air, the nation's flag carrier, and he went on to become one of the leading architectural authorities in Iran.

Nine miles to the north of where he currently lives in an apartment in Majidieh—an hour or so drive in traffic—young Aren grew up on an estate that would have fit perfectly in the English countryside. Except this calm and plush property was the residence of the German ambassador to Iran and his staff. In a city where many old villas have been knocked down and rebuilt into upscale high-rises and condominiums, the residence, which is located in Fereshteh, one of the most luxurious neighborhoods in the capital, is a reminder of the opulence of the prerevolutionary era.

Aren's father was a hardworking man in his own right. He initially built a strong reputation as a trustworthy driver who worked with a prestigious furniture company; in the years leading up to the Islamic Revolution, he started driving American diplomats. "One of our family friends who worked at the German embassy at the time told my dad that the situation may not be stable with the Americans, and it may be good if he looked elsewhere for work," Aren recalls. "He introduced my dad to the German embassy, and soon Dad transitioned to become the driver of the German ambassador."

Within the ambassador's large estate, there were several smaller homes that were allocated for his staff. "We lived in one of those houses next to other members of his team," Aren says. "Every few years we'd have a new ambassador, but most of the staff remained the same over the years." Iran's relationship with Germany dates to the late nineteenth century. By the 1940s, Iran-German relations were strong, but they disintegrated at the behest of the allies—mainly the United States and Great Britain—during the Second World War. In the aftermath of the war, relations picked up between the Pahlavi Monarch and West Germany, continuing until 1979. Following the Iran-Iraq War, Germany and the Islamic Republic re-established relations. Today, Germany is the largest European Union exporter to Iran. With over 100 years of diplomatic engagement—despite some setbacks in the 1990s and the early 2000s—Germany has always been Iran's strongest European ally.

Along with his two sisters and brother, Aren had a happy childhood living on the estate. "I mean, it was just beautiful," he recalls fondly. "Every house had their own little garden and you'd wake up to flowers and greenery. When we were young, we'd play with the kids of other staff members. We also became friends with other kids in the neighborhood." (Many other foreign embassies were located nearby.) Being surrounded by foreigners exposed Aren to a diverse range of cultures: "I had neighbors and friends who were Afghan, Italian, Filipino, Pakistani; we were all friends. I was lucky to be exposed to so many things from early on. It was a great time."

Those heady days were filled with parties and gatherings that would last until the early hours of the morning. "There was an exceptional level of security at the residence, so you can just imagine the comfort we had living there," Aren says with a wink. "When we were teenagers, we'd have parties quite a lot. Usually around midnight, the second round of guests would be arriving and would stay until morning." He laughs. "Loud music, hookah, nothing was an issue. I remember my mom always telling us her biggest fear was that we were not going to be able to cope with life outside of the residence once Dad retired."

Like other Armenian Christian students, Aren and his siblings attended an Armenian public school named Mariam, after the holy Mary. "For the girls, they had elementary, middle school, and high school, but for the guys, they only offered up until middle school, so I had to go somewhere else for high school," Aren says. "The other Armenian schools were quite far from us, so I ended up just finishing middle school there and then switched out." In Iran, Armenians have their own schools that, in addition to the public curriculum, teach the Armenian language as well as Christian and biblical studies. Attending such schools is not mandatory; however, for the sake of learning about their religion and language, most Armenian families enroll their children in these schools.

After completing middle school, Aren decided to get his high school diploma from a vocational training institute, or *honarestan*. These institutes were originally geared toward students who wanted to pursue higher education in the fine arts. Today, in addition to the arts, they focus on a variety of disciples including childcare, mechanics, farming, information technology, management, and graphic design. The purpose of a honarestan is to prepare students for practical jobs; they are generally attended by students who want to enter the workforce quickly instead of going to a university. "I wanted to study industrial design at first," Aren says, "but the honarestan that had that field was already full; it was actually really close to our home, but I couldn't get in. I also didn't really have super high grades, so I decided to go with another school that offered a more general technical and occupational degree."

A sharp and puckish boy, Aren's first job was at the age of ten, working at the estate during the annual Octoberfest. "It was crazy busy, but so much fun," he remembers. "Usually we would have two to three thousand people attending the ambassador's festivities. I'm sure you can just imagine the amount of work required to host that party. Instead of hiring outside help, the ambassadors would often ask the staff's kids to help out. The idea was for us to take part in the event, learn something, and also to make some cash."

It was during these events that Aren discovered his vocation in life. "None of the kids were allowed to work in the kitchen," he recalls. "I guess they were worried that it would get too messy. It was super intense in there." During one of the parties, the then-nineteen-year-old met the ambassador's personal chef—an Iranian-born, German-raised, meticulous "koch" named Ali. "He seemed really cool," Aren remembers. "We started talking and he asked me what I usually did and when I told him about my random tasks, he asked me if I wanted to start working with him in the kitchen. I immediately said yes! I was always interested to work in the kitchen and learn from the chef, and this was the perfect opportunity. I later found out that he had also heard that I was Armenian, so he was even more keen on working with me." By the time Aren began his apprenticeship with Ali, he was already done with honarestan.

Aren soon learnt all about the culinary world from the master chef: "The first few months it was just peeling potatoes and learning how to do some of the basic tasks to perfection—or at least as best as I could. Ali was so generous in teaching me everything he knew. The second thing I learned was how to make sauces. That was a whole other chapter in and of itself. After a while, I gradually began to actually help with the food preparation."

Things were going well, until the arrival of a new German ambassador—and his wife. "Ali was not too warm and fuzzy, but he was great at what he did, so everyone liked him," Aren remembers. "But that changed when the new ambassador arrived with his wife. Ali and her did not get along. She was just super bossy and wanted to change everything, and Ali wasn't buying her crap. One day, he packed everything and told me 'Let's go, we're leaving.'"

Luckily, Ali had set up a boutique catering company during his time at the embassy, working with foreign companies and delegations. Along with Aren, Ali expanded his team and after some well paid contracts, he started a new chapter. "He made the changes and got us going fast," Aren shares. "He got a deal with the French, British, and German schools, so that we'd provide their daily lunches. We split up the team and along with three other people I started working at the French school while the rest were spread out in the other two." Aren worked for Ali for almost two years, until he decided it was time to move on. "It just wasn't working anymore," he shares. "He was great, but I wasn't happy with the pay and wanted to try something different."

⌗

A longtime car enthusiast, Aren decided to open a shop with a friend: "It was a small shop adjacent to a gas station, but what we did was quite good. We would bring in American parts and work on old cars." Armenians have long been know for their work in mechanical and electrical work, and everything in between. "They're just great. They've always been," Aren says in a proud yet gentle tone. "It is one of those fields that we were always known for. Today, even though we are a small minority, if let's say there are ten official Hyundai dealers in Iran, at least three of them are ran by Armenians. I can easily say more than ten Saipa and Iran Khodro official dealers belong to Armenian folks."

In the years following the revolution, American cars, which had been popular before the overthrow of the Shah, became unavailable in Iran. The regime then began partnering with French, German, Japanese and Korean automakers. In the early 2000s, luxury cars began to slowly make their way into Iran. While by then the country had established its automotive monopolies—Saipda and Iran Khodro— it didn't take long for brands like Lexus, Mercedes, and BMW to start entering the mainstream market—with much higher price tags in comparison to Europe and North America. "We were doing really good, until about 2012," Aren says, "when suddenly the dollar went up and people who bought luxury cars instantly lost a lot of money on their cars." It was time for Aren to shift his career yet again.

By then, his father had retired, so the family had to move out of the German ambassador's residence. "When Dad retired, we had to move to our home in Majidieh," Aren says, joking about how how depressed he was to leave the glorious Fereshteh gardens for their humble Majidieh apartment. "I was so sad. My mom constantly told us about the change and was always concerned how we were going to deal with it when the time finally came for us to leave."

Around the same time, Aren's younger brother left Iran for the United States—settling in Glendale, California, home to one of the largest concentrations of Iranian-Armenians in the US. Aren was not surprised. "In the last fifteen to twenty years, an immigration fever has grown among the Armenian community in Iran," he says. "People want to leave for better education and job opportunities." Aren's brother was one of the many young Iranians who left the country with the help of an American agency called HIAS (the Hebrew Immigrant Aid Society).

Originally founded in the nineteenth century to assist the Jewish people fleeing Russia and Eastern Europe, over the past few decades, the US government-funded nonprofit has expanded its mission to also help non-Jewish people resettle in the United States. Since the Islamic Revolution, the organization has enabled many Iranian Jews and other religious minorities in the country to migrate to the United States as refugees or asylum-seekers.

There is a long-standing belief among many Americans and Westerners that Christians and Jews are persecuted in Iran. The reality is that the regime's handling of religious minorities is quite complicated and not as black and white as people imagine it to be in the West. Historically, Iran has always grappled with the tenuous mix of religion and politics. In the sixteenth century, when the Safavid leaders fought their way to the throne, they did so by using the support of the "Shia" clergy—and consequently declared then Persia to be a Shia state. Rather than a devotional declaration, their support for Shiism was strictly a political strategy that strengthened the Safavid interests of the time.

In the mid-nineteenth century, with the ascension of the Baha'i faith during the Qajar dynasty, out of fears of national unrest due to the rise of the religion, Qajar forces began to persecute the "Baab" leadership and its followers. Ousted and imprisoned with the support of the Ottomans, in the early 1890s the Baha'i found a safe ground in Haifa—atop Mount Carmel, in today's Israel. In the early years of Reza Shah's reign, tensions against the Baha'i initially subsided. However, intimidated by their growth, and fearful of losing his absolutist grip, Reza Shah eventually ordered the closure of all Baha'i schools nationwide. Years later and in the aftermath of the 1979 revolution, the newly formed Shia clergy—whose fundamental principle of supporting the coming of the twelfth Imam Mahdi is contradicted by the Baha'i faith—began to heavily denounce and persecute the followers of the late Abdu'l Baha. Tragically, the Baha'i community remains ostracized in Iran, with the government pushing the narrative that they are aligned with Israel and the United States.

As opposed to the Baha'i community, Armenian Christians have never posed a direct political threat to the powers that be in Iran. On the contrary, they were great assets against the British and the Russians in the nineteenth century, and later, the Turks. With strained relations with two of its neighbors, Turkey and Azerbaijan, Iran remains a major political and commercial ally to Armenia—an alliance that's mutually beneficial to both nations. With two seats in parliament, the Christian Armenian community has long been accepted by the Islamic regime. On the other hand, the current government opposes the so-called pop-up "house churches" and newly converted "priests." While converting from Islam is considered apostasy, the government also deems it criminal to promote conversion campaigns among Muslims. Such hardline attitudes have even affected the peaceful Sufi Dervishes, who in many instances have been harassed and persecuted by hardliners in Iran.

"In Iran, they respect the Armenian community a lot," Aren says. "I think even compared to the rest of the people, we have more social liberties."

Aren's brother is far from the only member of his family to have left the country. "A lot of our family members, aunts and uncles are spread out in the US and Europe," Aren shares, "but I always wanted to stay in Iran." This attitude made him determined to build something permanent in his homeland for himself and his wife.

The year was 2015, and the young man needed money to launch his vision. "I didn't have all the money and my dad couldn't help me back then. As much as he wanted to, his hands were a bit tight at that time." Aren decided to team up with his brother's former roommate, Patrick, and his younger sister's husband, Jora. The three young men put their money together and opened up Yerevan. "It was so much hard work to get everything off the ground," Aren recalls. "You know, I always wanted to work for myself; even when I was working for Ali, I always had this dream that I wanted to be my own boss, and wanted to feel that what I'm doing was for myself. A few months after we started Patrick wasn't too happy, so we bought him out and he left the business. Our friendship was so much more important. So now, it's just me and Jora."

While his family couldn't help him financially, they are supportive in other, equally important ways. "Dad is great," Aren says with a big smile. "He helps me with the shopping, fixing whatever needs to be fixed in the kitchen and just being that extra hand that you always need in work." And as for his mom, she has always offered strong "emotional support."

These days, there are many people in Iran who want to make a buck without knowing much about the industry they are getting involved in. This "get rich quick" attitude has also affected the restaurant business. "Listen, I'm not saying that I'm the best chef out there or know everything; not at all," Aren says humbly. "But at least I know what I'm doing and I try to do it as best as I possibly can. There are people out there working in kitchens and cooking at restaurants who don't even know the name of the food they're making or are not familiar with the ingredients. I think one of the reasons that we grew strong was because I knew the right techniques—all of which I learned from Ali."

Each day, Aren leaves for the restaurant late in the morning, and gets home around 1:00am. Together with his wife, they have turned the second room off their cozy apartment into a hair and makeup studio so that she can work on her own. "She's great at what she does," Aren says with pride. "For a while she was working for a salon, but she had a great client list who'd go there just for her. So, we decided why not, let's just use this room, so she could do her own thing without the need of anyone else." His wife is also Armenian. After dating for five years, Aren finally popped the question. They were married right around the time he was opening the restaurant. "We're just chill people. Sometimes I call her up right around the time I'm closing the shop on a Thursday night and ask her if she wants to go on a late night ride to Kordan to our little country house. It's a cozy place but has a small pool that makes for a great escape during the hot months of summer."

While he's now a proud burger master, Aren's motor fever has never completely cooled. "I have two cars now. One that Dad helped me buy, a very practical, just easy to use Peugeot Persia, and another one that's my baby. It's an old Russian Lada that I bought and fixed up myself." In an effort to manage Tehran's insane traffic, the city imposed a law that only permits cars with even numbered license plates to drive on "even days" and cars with odd license plates on "odd" days. This long imposed regulation covers the central parts of the capital, and those who don't comply can be easily caught by the many police cameras on the streets, and fined with a ticket "On even days, I take the Persia that Dad got me, and then on odd days I take out my Lada," Aren says with a laugh.

His love for cars is also reflected in his restaurant. "You know TGI Fridays in the US? I tried to kind of emulate the theme with cars and automobile motifs. I just loved decorating the place. It's not complete yet, but you know what, that car fever never went away, so nowadays I try to express my passion for cars in my restaurant."

Just close your eyes and imagine a thirty something year old jamming to Elvis in his old Russian Lada on Tehran's busy streets. Like many other young men around the world, all Aren wants is to earn a living for his family, be a good son for his hardworking father and loving mother, and live a happy life. "I was never too ambitious. I'm happy and content with my life, but I guess my biggest dream is to open up other branches. Make no mistake, I'm not going to open up for the sake of expanding. I'm never going to do it unless I know I can maintain the same level of quality and service. I want to stay as honest and good as I am today."

Hamed Sabet

*H*E HAS A CALM YET STRONG VOICE that commands attention, a fully bearded face, and long curly hair. "I was around five or six years old, and we lived in the central part of Tehran. I remember the street was not too wide and was divided by a narrow ditch; also, there was no gap or garden between the wall of the house and the street. Every time I would walk by, I'd feel as if my name was being called. I'd hear this voice saying, 'Hamed, Hamed, Hamed.' I was terrified, and in my little mind, I thought it might be God or the angels who were trying to communicate with me. I was keen to find out about the origin of those voices."

Eventually, he learned that "those voices" came from a house that was playing the movement "Amen" from Giovanni Pergolesi's *Stabat Mater*—sacred music written by the eighteenth-century Italian composer who died shortly after creating his last masterpiece at the young age of twenty-six. "For the longest time, I kept that a secret between God and myself, thinking that it's him calling me. I never told anyone about it." He laughs about his first encounter with classical music.

"My second encounter with classical music was a day when I sneaked into my dad's office. We used to draw and paint together and I was in search of charcoals in his drawer to finish my sketch. Instead, I found a few cassettes with funny names written all over them." Those funny names were Bach, Beethoven, Mozart, Vivaldi, and Tchaikovsky. "The first tape I listened to was Beethoven by Wilhelm Kempff. It shocked me to my core. I thought to myself, 'How can music be like this or sound like this?' It was that pure moment of curiosity that made me want to listen to the rest of the tapes." These trembling sensations and childhood musical encounters would ultimately shape his future path. "Becoming a musician is lunacy. A sane person would never become a musician, but you know what, I never made my decisions based on logic. I'm not the most rational person. I think with love. I live with love."

Hamed Sabet is a musician and composer who was born into a middle-class family on the brink of the Iran-Iraq War in 1980. Like many other Iranian children, he was groomed by his mother—an elementary

school teacher—to become a doctor. Luckily, his father supported him in his pursuit of music. "In our family, my dad is the artist," Hamed says. "He is an engineer, but also a talented painter and a sculpture. I grew up learning painting and drawing from him; I still paint sometimes."

When Hamed was eleven, his father bought him a piano on credit. "A piano was very expensive at the time, it still is, and dad couldn't afford to buy me one right then and there. So he managed to get one after the owner agreed to get paid in installments." For the next few years, Hamed was his own teacher. The boy relied on his ear—listening to those old cassettes and trying to decipher whatever he'd pick up. "In those days, it was difficult to find note sheets," he remembers. "I didn't have a teacher and wasn't familiar with notes. I didn't even know what notes were or that we could actually write music down on paper. Up until then, I thought music was something you only recorded. I was thirteen, and for the first time, I understood that music was a language in and of itself." A language that he taught himself in the most unconventional way at that young age.

In high school, Hamed became friends with a classmate who played the flute and taught him about notes. Still, he continued teaching himself and writing down whatever he could figure out on his own. "After a while, my friend asked me if I wanted to show my work to his teacher. I accepted the offer and for the first time ever, sat before a music instructor. With utmost kindness, he took the time to look at my scrappy sheets, asked if I wanted to hear what I had put together, and started playing what I had written down." Hamed recalls all of this with a boyish sense of gratitude that he still feels today. "It was such an incredible experience listening to a real musician play my silly work—especially since I didn't even know what I'd written. He could have easily ignored me or dismissed my childish scribbles, but he took the time to see it and hear my music. I'm forever indebted to his kindness."

Soon after that meeting, Hamed decided to find an instructor who could guide him along on his musical journey. "I loved contemporary and expressionist art, so I wanted to find someone who also knew contemporary piano," he says. "I searched, asked around, and finally found the telephone number of one of the best piano masters in Tehran. You probably know him too, but you know what, it's not worth mentioning his name." Unlike the other instructor's humility in acknowledging Hamed's enthusiasm for music, the piano teacher was arrogant and dismissive of the young man's self-taught efforts. "I remember I called him to ask if I could attend any of his classes. He told me to talk to his assistant to see what kind of arrangement could be made, but before hanging up, I asked if I could show him some of my work. He raised his voice and said I should trash whatever I had written so far, and that none of it meant anything."

Rather than discouraging Hamed, the instructor's hurtful words empowered him. "I was sad, lost, and disappointed, but that didn't last long. I couldn't let him stop me. I remember going to my dad and asking him for some money, and then rushing to Enghelab Street to buy whatever book I could get my hands on that could teach me music and harmony." By then, Hamed was already playing Beethoven and Mozart; by using books by Walter Piston, Theodore Dubois, and other musical authorities, he began to teach himself music theory, form, and harmony. "It's extremely difficult to learn harmony by yourself, without the help or guidance of an instructor," he points out. "It was an excruciating task, but somehow, I did it."

During his formative years, Hamed's father was his only source of musical encouragement, as his mother opposed anything other than academics. "My mom didn't really let me experience childhood. I was incredibly studious, but I failed to be a child." For Hamed, music was the only thing that allowed him to keep his childhood alive. "There is absolutely no doubt that music and art enable one to maintain their childhood or stay close to as many childlike elements as possible," he says. "Art is like child's play. Even in its darkest and most radical of forms, it's still child's play. My music and my art continue to keep my childhood alive."

In Iran, the attitude of Hamed's mother is not uncommon. "You know, in Iran, people look at an artist from afar and say, 'Oh wow, what a talented person,' but when it comes to having one in their immediate family, they get terrified," Hamed says with a laugh. "I think it's this fear of instability—this fear that the person will be wasting his or her time, and thus life. Iranians love artists, so long as the artist is not their child." Much of that fear is rooted in the instability that the nation has endured, particularly over the last forty years, which has created an inherent need for financial security and social safety among much of the populace. "I also think a lot of it goes back to this image that artists and musicians are a bunch of unprincipled people who are either going to die of an overdose or commit suicide," Hamed adds. "I guess much of it is based on this general belief that artists are somehow detached from any level of moral and ethical obligation. I don't know what it's like elsewhere in the world, but in Iran people like artists and their art from afar."

To his mother's initial delight—and later dismay—Hamed got into medical school as a teenager. But instead of going, he decided to get a degree in music. "My entire childhood and teenage years, my mom wanted me to be a doctor. That was the plan all along. Except one day, Dad intervened; I guess, just like myself, he could no longer cope with the pressure. I'll never forget the day he stood by me and said, 'Hamed will do whatever he wants. Whether he wants to be a doctor or whatever else is up to him, and all we need to do is to support him and whatever decision he makes.' And that was it. From then on, my mom let it go; she knew she couldn't force me anymore."

However, it didn't take long for the young musician to realize that school was not the right place for him. "I realized and to this day believe that one's musical and artistic scope and abilities cannot be measured by the degrees that are given out by universities," Hamed says. "For me, the university is a mass-producing platform that teaches some disciplines while factoring out the essence of the craft. It's like a factory—they create a copy-and-paste version of what they have decided to teach the masses."

Hamed's anti-establishment attitude led him to quit school, thus ending his formal music training. Nevertheless, he was still able to build a successful career as a pianist, composer, and musician who has worked on dozens of feature films, shorts, and animation projects in Iran and neighboring countries, as well as in Europe.

However, Hamed would soon meet a man who would forever change the young musician's life trajectory.

⁛

"I was twenty-five when I decided to show my entire body of work to a music master and hear an honest assessment and critique," Hamed says. That master was none other than the great Mohammad-Reza Darvishi, an Iranian maestro and ethnomusicologist, and author of the *Encyclopedia of the Musical Instruments of Iran,* who has spent his life working to preserve classical Persian music. The critique Darvishi offered Hamed was both confusing and sobering to the young man. "I was happy but also extremely muddled," Hamed recalls. "I wasn't sure what he was trying to tell me until he looked me in the eye and said, 'You're a great musician and know the classics, but so what? Sure, you know music and have created something along the lines of Luigi Nono and Pierre Boulez, but do you know who you are? Do you know where you come from?'"

This was a genuine eye-opener for Hamed. "He asked me if I knew where I lived, and I remember telling him, 'A third-world country.'"

That was enough for Darvishi to challenge the young man even further. "He told me 'No, you live in a place that is the culmination of a vast assortment of layers of culture and knowledge—all of which exist behind the mountains, streets, villages, and valleys of this land. All of which are a treasure—a book in and of themselves. What does Europe have to do with you? You need to find your own journey, your own story.'" And with that, he played Hamed some musical tunes from Kurdistan. "As soon as he did that, I was thrown back into my dad's office—to that same day when I stole the charcoals from his drawer and stumbled upon Beethoven and Mozart," Hamed shares. "I was feeling the same trembles, the same rush of light and emotions that tickled me back when I was only nine years old. I was hearing the most magical and exotic notes—a sort of unconfined music that was filled with form, yet devoid of any logic and structure."

The encounter with Darvishi would lead Hamed in a whole new musical direction. "I packed everything and hit the road. From the shores of the Persian Gulf to the Caspian seaside in the north, to the mountainous regions of the west and the dry lands of the east, I saw it all. Before that experience, I only thought you could learn music in its classical form, but as I journeyed through the country and researched the rich music history of Iran, I realized that music lives in anything and everything. It was then that I learned that music exists in distant villages, among farmers, nomads, and rivers and trees—places we fail to see."

For Hamed, this journey wasn't concerned so much on learning about his homeland, but rather appreciating and understanding its musical gifts. "This experience was not about being a nationalist, but about discovering a treasure that I would have otherwise never known. I'm going to be honest with you, I'm not big on flag-waving; my country and my homeland is my room, this small room where I write, work, and create music. More than anything, this was about learning a profound culture with a significant role in music." And so, unlike many other contemporary Iranian musicians who choose to emigrate, Hamed stayed in Iran.

⊡

Today, the award-winning pianist and composer lives in a small village on the outskirts of Shiraz, one of the oldest cities in Iran, which dates to the Achaemenid Empire (550–330 BC). Little is known about Persian music during that ancient era. The development of what is considered modern Persian music occurred during the Sassanid era (226–642 AD). Of particular importance during that period was Barbad, a minstrel-poet in the court of Khosrow II, the last king of the Sassanian Empire. Barbad developed the *khosravani*, believed to be the oldest system of modal music in the Middle East, and one that is still used by contemporary musicians in Iran. Nearly 200 years later, during the Samanid Empire, lived Rudaki, who is regarded as the first Iranian lyricist. Of his nearly 100,000 couplets, only about 1000 have survived—these are regarded as the blueprint for modern Persian poetry.

The diversity of classical Persian music is revealed in the mélange of the country's ethnicities, cultures, and tribal traditions. Persian poetry, especially that of luminaries such as Gorgani, Nizami, Rumi, Saadi, Ferdowsi, Khayam, and of course Hafez, remain the backbone of the Persian ballads and epics that were recited by musicians of their era and beyond. Of some of the greatest Persian instruments that have weathered the test of time, the Setar, Tar, and Oud may be among those most recognized by the Western world. But other classical instruments such as the Ghanun, Nay (the vertical reed flute), Robab, Tanbur, Santoor, Kamancheh, Dayereh, Dutar, and Tombak are among the centuries' old musical instruments that create the unique tapestry of classical Persian music.

In the sixteenth century, the Safavid Empire took power and proclaimed Shia Islam as the official religion of the country. As a result, the religion's mournful requiems crept into the musical landscape of the country, which are still visible today in the yearly Ashura and Tasua ceremonies. The Safavid dynasty also began a wave of musical exchange with Europe that grew under the succeeding Qajar dynasty, introducing Western instruments and musical disciplines to Iran.

The popularity of classical Iranian music dwindled among the nation's masses as European and American influence grew in the mid-twentieth century. The country then entered a musical dark age in the aftermath of the Islamic Revolution, as the new regime deemed music to be *haram* (forbidden), and began promoting a narrative that associated music, dancing, and any sort of joyous celebration with "paganism," and against "Islamic" values. Western music was regarded as a divisive tool used by the United States and its allies to tempt Muslims and promote sinful behavior. In the blink of an eye, foreign and prerevolution music were banned, women could no longer sing in public, and instruments like the violin and piano were considered "anti-revolutionary." The country essentially went musically mute— except for Islamic music that was approved by the newly established government and its Ministry of Culture and Islamic Guidance.

In the years following the revolution, musicians found different ways to dodge the censorship of the regime. Some left the country, while others tailored their music and its message to be acceptable to the hardline government. Many simply forged ahead on their own path. One such group was Arian, the first pop group since the revolution to be comprised of male and female members. Their debut album in 2000 was an instant smash smash—not so much for its profound musical quality, but because it was the first time since the revolution that the music scene seemed to be coming out of the "dark ages." The group's success set the precedent for the creation of a new wave of "government approved" pop singers and artists.

Despite incremental progress over the past few decades, the bottom line is that music and art are not appreciated by the ruling authorities in Iran—creating a tumultuous environment for musicians and other artists to produce their work. "Creating good music and quality films in Iran is like creating a miracle," states Hamed. "Those who you see who have created amazing work have done it with closed hands. I'm confident and can fully guarantee that if you brought an American or European musician or filmmaker to Iran, he or she wouldn't believe the conditions that we're working under. None of them could do one percent of what we have under such circumstances."

While some artists and musicians have chosen to leave to Iran, the many who have stayed created some of the most popular music of the new generation, which is listened to by millions of Iranians inside the country, as well as in the diaspora. Such music is now a dominant part of

modern Iranian culture—music that's not necessarily popular due to its high quality, but because it reflects a much desired change.

Like many other artists who have remained in Iran, Hamed has had to dance around the margins of what is considered acceptable. In spite of these limitations, he has managed to create unforgettable music for the cinema and other mediums, while working with some of the greatest Iranian filmmakers, writers, and actors. And while he has received multiple awards for his work, there is one in particular that he considers to be a lifetime achievement—his wife. "I was in Baku working on a project when I got news that I'd won the Simorgh Bolourin at the Fajr Film Festival," he says with a smile. "So many people reached out to me on Facebook and congratulated me for the win, including her. When

I saw her message, I immediately responded and asked her to marry me."

His wife was not just an ordinary fan, but an old childhood friend with whom he had lost touch. "We used to be distant family friends and I would see her here and there at family gathering and parties when we were four, five years old. I remember I always liked to just look at her. To this day, I recall the patterns of her dresses, the colors of her ribbons, and the way she talked. Even at that young age, she somehow carried herself with such elegance and poise." When Hamed found out that the young woman on Facebook was his childhood friend, he couldn't let her go. "The feelings and experiences of childhood are all real. They are the most innocent and pure forms of thought, emotions, and being. I trust my childhood; I will trust it forever. The beauty of it is that my wife is also a child at heart—she too has not forgotten her childhood." His wife, who works as a dentist, accompanied her husband to their new home on the outskirts of Shiraz. "I don't know how she puts up with me," Hamed jokes. "I'm not the easiest person to be with, but she somehow loves me."

Much like the manner in which he found his wife, Hamed's musical adventure has not followed a conventional path. Instead, his "fabric" is made of a noncommercial love for the craft, and the greatness it can create. "My dream has always been to complete a project that has taken me years to compose and shape. It's just impossible to explain and only musicians understand what I'm talking about. Producers here don't know anything about music; finding investment is pretty much impossible."

When Hamed speaks, you sense his utter disillusionment with the world, its decision-makers, and people at large—as if everyone has forgotten that life has an expiration date." "What are we after in this world? What do we want?" he asks plaintively. "I think we have forgotten what we are really after in this life." For this, he blames politics. "I think politics is the singular element that has separated our world from love, and it absolutely doesn't matter which country we're talking about. Politicians have created a controlling culture that promotes a monotonous and unvarying way of life, way of thinking, and behaving." Sadly, he doesn't believe that artists can change this state of affairs. "Throughout history, artists have always tried to make this world a more beautiful place, but we've always been the losers," he says. "I've always lived and worked with the belief that I want to create love and beauty, but as one of the losers of this game, I've decided to live on the sidelines and leave the battlegrounds of the city life. I'd rather think about life, culture, and love from this small corner." Fortunately, his small corner is filled with light and love. "Love is an all-encompassing thing," he says brightly. "My music, my wife, my parents, these are all inside this space called love. You don't create love or fall in love. Life itself is love."

Pedram Safarzadeh

*T*hink of Tehran as a large circle, then draw a line down the middle from the northern tip to the southern end. The one-and-a-half to two-hour drive (depending on traffic) along that line from north to south is like going from Beverly Hills to skid row.

Halfway through the trip, you'll hit the Grand Bazaar—a city in and of itself where carpet shops, clothing stores, wholesalers, jewelers, banks, mosques, kabob houses, and sandwich stalls merge together to create a frozen frame that's caught between the old and the new Tehran. As you leave the Bazaar and pass through Molavi Street, the vibrant sites, smells, and surroundings give way to an uncertain fear and an unexplainable melancholy. The luxurious high-rises and modern restaurants of the north slowly turn into colorless roads and lifeless buildings that are worn down by the heavy weight of financial insecurity and poverty. Upon reaching the southern tip of the city, you enter a rundown neighborhood of small tattered houses and narrow streets that look as if they belong on the set of an old Farsi film. Here and there, you'll spot shabby shops, but what's most striking are the green public areas that instead of children are home to drug addicts, shooting up by themselves or in small groups.

This is Tehran. On one end, you can have your ice cream served with gold flakes, your housekeeper flown in from Dubai, and your black-market champagne delivered to your door. On the other end, you'll see hundreds of drug addicts in small neighborhoods, teenage mothers who sell their newly born babies for less than one hundred dollars, and child laborers who are often victims of sexual abuse and violence. "How can it be?" the handsome middle-aged man asks with incredulity. "How can people sell their own children to complete strangers? Would anything other than abject poverty lead them to do so?"

Unlike the Columbian city of Medellín during the reign of drug

kingpin Pablo Escobar, or Los Angeles's Compton in the 1980s, this small yet dense neighborhood in the south of Tehran, known as Darvazeh Ghar, is not terrorized by guns and gangs—in fact, gun violence and mass shootings are almost nonexistent in Iran. Rather, the horror here exists inside the quiet houses that beyond their rusting doors and broken windows are "home" to addicts, prostitutes, and child laborers who use, abuse, and coexist together. The ones not lucky enough to have a roof over their heads sleep between cardboard sheets or on the bare asphalt of the streets. "When you go to these neighborhoods at night, it's as if it's the middle of the day—people are up and about doing their business. It's an incredibly mind-boggling sight," the man says. It's much bigger and more complex than imagined. In each crack hides a child—a story—a still-life.

Their "business" is drugs. It's a universal plague, with heroin, crack, meth, and opium on the menu. According to Iran's Drug Control

Headquarters, as of 2017, there were nearly three million drug addicts in the country. One out of ten addicts are women; nearly 7500 babies are born addicted to drugs each year. Many experts believe that the numbers are much higher due to the challenges of accounting for users and their dependents. "Hopelessness is the root cause of all this misery," the man says sharply. "I mean, you ask the guy, 'Hey man, why are you doing this—why are you ruining yourself?' and he responds, 'Why shouldn't I? To do what? To live for what?' If there was an inkling of hope, an inkling of support, an inkling of light, they'd get help, but for the majority of them, there's no hope."

One of the most destitute communities in Tehran was Khake e Sefid, an isolated island for drug addicts, felons and traffickers. Around the time of the revolution, many "gypsies" and villagers moved in and settled in the barren lands of this northeast quarter of Tehran. They stacked building upon building, and with no title, occupied a cluster that was soon largely avoided, even by the police.

In the early 2000s, the city's then police chief, Mohammad Bagher Ghalibaf—a conservative politician and former commander of the Revolutionary Guard's Air Force, who later became Tehran's mayor— ordered the bulldozing of Khak-e Sefid. While this forceful facelift managed to clean up the neighborhood, many of the area's residents dispersed to other poor clusters of the city. One of those clusters was Darvazeh Ghar, which literally translates to "the cave's gateway." Darvazeh Ghar is an old neighborhood that was built during the reign of Naser Al Din Shah Qajar as one of the "gateways" surrounding the capital. Little did they know back then that, a century and a half later, this gateway would be a refuge for drug users, traffickers, and prostitutes.

"I lost my youth, and I'll never be able to get that back," the man says bluntly. "I'm not saying I'm old or feel like an old man, but I lost some of the best years of my life—the best years in any person's life." His fit physique, full silky black hair and soft tone make it hard to believe that he was once of one of the many lost souls of Darvazeh Ghar.

Pedram Safarzadeh was born into a middle-class family five years before the revolution. His father was an entry level bank clerk, while his mother worked in a hospital. Growing up, his father's side of the family were all heavy users of the most popular drug in Iran—opium (*taryak* in Farsi.) "As a child, I'd watch my uncles, my dad, and their friends consume regularly," Pedram remembers. "The way they treated opium was as if it was a normal thing to do. It was part of their everyday life; not because of poverty, my uncles were educated, they all had university degrees and good jobs, but they used it with no shame."

In Pedram's father's family, drug use was something that was passed down from generation to generation. "My dad's father worked at the Iran Post (the country's postal service) and was a government employee," he says. "He died right before I was born, but he was a user for a very long time. Even my dad's mom would smoke."

A little less than 4000 years ago, in what's now known as the "cradle of civilization," opium poppy was first used to relieve pain. Nearly 1000 years later, the legendary Greek author Homer wrote about the drug's healing powers in the *Odyssey*. From the sixteenth century on, opium use and trade soared across Europe and Asia thanks to the monopoly of Britain's East India Company. This eventually led to the opium wars between China and England, which resulted in the annexation of Hong Kong by the British in the nineteenth century.

During the Safavid dynasty in the sixteenth century, opium became a popular recreational substance among the royals and elites of Persia. During the Qajar dynasty, the concept of "drug addiction" was first introduced in its modern form. However, by then, opium had already become interwoven into Iranian society and culture. Heroin—a direct derivative of opium—is the second-most used illicit substance in Iran.

Pedram's parents constantly fought over his father's addiction to heroin—which eventually led to a heartbreaking divorce for the then eight-year-old and his younger sister. "They fought and they yelled; it was a never-ending mess," Pedram recalls sadly. "It was painful to watch for a day—let alone your entire childhood. Can you imagine watching your parents scream at each other, fight every day, and push and pull nonstop?" While the marriage lasted nine years, the divorce process took up nearly half that time. "My mom wanted a divorce, but my dad didn't want her to leave," Pedram says. "He wasn't granting the divorce. Also, people would tell my mom to stay in her marriage and help my dad quit, but every time she tried, no matter what she did, he'd go back to square one."

In Iran, getting a divorce is no easy task for a woman. Often, the immediate family wants to step in to mediate, while friends and neighbors scrutinize the drama from afar. On top of that, the country's archaic divorce laws almost invariably favor the man. In fact, in many cases, prior to the wedding, the bride-to-be's father asks for the groom's signature so that she can have the legal right to divorce, if need be.

After the divorce, Pedram was given to his father, while his sister went with his mother. "It was so hard. I would visit her once a week, but nothing was the same anymore," he says, the pain in his voice showing how much it still hurts even after all these years. "At that young age, I kept asking myself, 'What is this thing that has encompassed my entire life? That made my parents divorce? What is this thing that my dad uses or does that has made my mom this angry? What is this thing that has shattered our life—my childhood?'"

Following the divorce, Pedram fell into a deep depression. "It took about a year after my parent's divorce for me to break my ice," he says. "It took me even longer to come out of my shell and accept everything that had happened to me, to my mom and dad, and to my family." During this time, Pedram's father changed jobs and went to work for the Telecom Communication Company of Iran. Despite his stable employment, Pedram's father's heroin addiction constantly endangered their living arrangements, as once a landlord found out about his drug use, father and son would be kicked out of their home and forced to find another place to live. "There are few hotels and motels across town that Dad and I didn't stay in," Pedram says. "We were constantly on the move. As soon as they'd find out about my dad, they'd throw us out." With nowhere to hide his addiction, Pedram's father would sometimes shoot up right in front of his son: "It was bad; sometimes he would inject in front of me."

Eventually, the two of them ran out of options. Luckily, one of his father's associates from work came to their rescue. "One of my dad's colleagues let us stay at his home," Pedram remembers. "He had a place in Narmak and rented us a bedroom on the second floor of his house. It was our last resort." By that time, the instability of constantly moving, combined with his father's addiction, had taken a heavy toll on Pedram. "I felt a heavy emptiness all the time," he shares. "I mean, it's only natural for a child that age to be affected by all his surrounding mess. I was not immune to any of that pain."

For a time, his only escape was school. "I had nothing else. All I could do was to make myself busy in school and do good in my studies." Pedram's school was in one of the most centrally located neighborhoods in Tehran. Everyday after school, the young boy had to take the bus all the way downtown toward the Grand Bazaar to get to his dad's workplace in "Toop Khaneh" Square, which literally translates to Artillery Barracks. Back then, double-decker buses were still running in Tehran. "I remember how I would go on the second floor and look down at the people and the busy streets until I'd fall asleep. Sometimes, the bus would go back and forth a few times and I'd still be sleeping. That was my daily routine." Pedram recalls.

Then, one day, Pedram found a new friend, and with her, came renewed hope. "She worked with my dad and noticed my frequent visits," he says. "I'm sure she got curious as to why I didn't go home and came to my dad straight from school. She might have just felt sad for me and wanted to help." Her name was Simin. She was a conservative, religious woman who was a few years older than Pedram's father. "She and I became close—she'd help me with my homework," he recalls. "Soon after, she started talking to my dad, found out more about our life, and turned into a friend for us both."

At first, Simin was unaware of Pedram's father's addiction, as he had told her that his drug use was all in the past. "She was somewhat reluctant to marry my dad—her family was against it," Pedram recalls, "but I could sense the sadness she felt for me. She even told me at some point that I was the only reason she married my dad." Following the marriage, Simin moved in with Pedram and his father in their small room in Narmak. But it only took six months for this newly found calm to collapse, as one day, Pedram's father went missing. "He was lost for about a week and a half, until one day he called my uncle to tell him that he had gotten in some sort of trouble in Mashhad and he was under arrest. By then, Simin had figured out everything."

Simin and Pedram flew to Mashhad to find Pedram's father in jail for heroin possession. "That was the first time I walked into a prison environment," Pedram says tensely. "It was then and there that we realized that my dad's addiction had worsened. I remember Simin was afraid to tell her family, but as soon as her brothers found out, they threatened to kill my father if he returned to their house with Simin. It was then that it all ended for Simin and us; she got her divorce and was free." Simin was six months pregnant when she got her divorce in absentia from Pedram's father. "I later found out that she gave birth to a son," Pedram says wistfully. "I heard he has gotten a good education and is successful. I'm happy for him." For Pedram, Simin was a small flicker of hope that had passed too quickly. "It all ended too soon," he says. "She was like a quick breeze that swiftly passed by."

⊡

After his father's release from prison, the two of them stayed with various relatives. "My dad was deep into drugs and was not willing to change—he just couldn't," Pedram remarks. "No matter which uncle or aunt we'd stay with, it was obvious that we were not welcome." Eventually, the two of them ran out of options, and for the first time in his life, the fifth grader, along with his father, became *karton khaab*—a term used for homeless people in Iran that translates to "those who sleep on cardboard."

As of 2019, semi-official government reports state that there are nearly 15,000 homeless people in Tehran and surrounding areas. While the accuracy of these statistics is subject to dispute, the reality on the ground nevertheless reflects a dismal condition for many—especially drug addicts, who often choose the streets verses rehab and shelters. Homelessness particularly affects children, who are often forced into labor. If you walk the streets of Tehran, you can't help but notice the children trying to earn a few cents cleaning car windows or selling flowers and gum to passersby. While in Iran it's technically illegal to employ children under the age of fifteen, the reality is quite different. Official government reports suggest that there are about two million street children and child laborers across the country; many experts say that the number may be as high as seven million, with the majority being refugees from neighboring Afghanistan.[1] These are little boys and girls as young as six or seven, who are also susceptible to rape, violence, and early marriage; and in a country faced with a high number

---

1. SH, "Seven million working children in Iran," *Deutsche Welle*, February 24, 2014, accessed January 24, 2020, https://www.dw.com/fa-ir/فه‌ت-میلیون-کودک-کار-در-ایران/ a-17453277.

of HIV positive people among its addict and homeless population, these children are easy targets of infection.

By night, Pedram and his father slept on cardboard boxes; during the day, they would roam the streets in search of food, some sort of a "job"— and, of course, drugs. Eventually, the crushing pain of homelessness forced Pedram to question, and ultimately sever, his only lifeline. "It was around noon, and my dad wasn't around," he recalls quietly. "I went to a phone booth and called my mom, crying—telling her that I'm coming. I couldn't take it anymore. I went back to where my dad and I were staying, took my backpack and my notebooks and left for my mom's workplace. I never said goodbye to my dad; I knew if I told him, he'd try to persuade me to stay—he'd always tell me he would find a job and get better—but nothing would ever get better, nothing would ever change."

After the divorce, Pedram's mother had remarried one of her coworkers from the hospital and had given birth to a son. While his mother knew about Simin, her ex-husband's continuing addiction, and everything else in Pedram's life, she was initially unable to help her first-born child. "She had gotten married under the condition that she would only bring my sister with her and that I would never live with them," Pedram says. "She told me that her husband didn't want me there and that she couldn't bring me into her new life. I always wanted to be with her, and I would see her here and there, but I knew that living with her was not an option."

Since she couldn't take him in herself, Pedram's mother initially sent her son to her live with her father. However, the old man was unable to take care of the now eleven-year-old boy: "I was about to start middle school, but my grandpa told my mom he couldn't take care of me either." Pedram's mother was thus forced to talk with her husband about taking the boy in. "My dad called my mom at some point to inquire about my whereabouts. She told him that I'd be staying with her and not going back."

While Pedram had finally found a place to call home, he still struggled to cope with everything he had witnessed and endured in his young life. "I was fully depressed," he says bluntly. "I looked normal, but deep down I was completely shattered. I guess back then I didn't even know what depression really was, but it was there. It still is. You can't erase the past. It follows you." While he kept himself busy with school and playing sports, Pedram found his real solace in the profound yet melancholy words of Sadegh Hedayat.

Hedayat was one of modern Iran's most brilliant literary figures. An atheist intellectual and admirer of surrealist and existentialist writers like Jean-Paul Sartre, Edgar Allen Poe, Franz Kafka, and Rainer Maria Rilke, Hedayat long suffered depression, which was reflected in much of his work—especially *Boofe Koor*, his 1937 masterpiece which he wrote while traveling in India. *Boofe Koor,* or *The Blind Owl*, is an absurd, pessimistic, and Kafkaesque story that takes the reader inside the unsettled mind of a narrator who's lost between two worlds. Most of the story is a turbulent journey in the dream-like state of a mind that's comforted by "opium and alcohol." Hedayat was a fixture among Iran's high-profile literati and anti-monarchy intellectuals of his time; but in 1951, the young genius committed suicide in his Paris apartment.

"I lived with Hedayat," Pedram says passionately. "I was obsessed with his words, his work. I would read *Boofe Koor, Zende Be Goor* (*Buried Alive*), and his other works over and over. I found them very powerful. I also loved Shamloo and Sepehri's poetry. I found an escape in their work as well. At that time, I was always thinking to myself; 'What's going to happen to me? What does the future have in store for me?'"

Unfortunately, that future soon became tainted by alcohol. "I didn't have a correct definition of life—I still don't. I didn't know what I wanted. I would drink and drink and just empty my rage, my emotions, and everything I was feeling in that moment." While even at that young age he clearly understood the dangers of drinking and addiction, for Pedram, it was the only way for him to alleviate the pain of his past. "It was an easy way to be happy and to forget all the pain I had endured in my childhood and life with my dad. Drinking filled my voids. It was that moment of high and forgetting the pain that made me drink."

Though alcohol has been banned by the government since the 1979 Islamic Revolution, like most other illegal products in Iran, it's readily available via the black market. Those who can afford it often buy marked-up champagne and whiskey, while others purchase homemade spirits. (The poor frequently have to make do with *aragh sagi*, a homemade vodka-like drink that's made from distilled raisins.) Each year, due to the irregularities of the black market, thousands of Iranians are rushed to hospitals due to alcohol poisoning or die after drinking poorly distilled and impure liquor. Lower quality alcohol is often sold in smaller cities, low-income communities, and rural areas, but even the European or American "products" that come in their original packaging can be knockoffs. The general belief in Iran is that the Islamic regime's ban on alcohol has created a more corrupt, dangerous, and unhealthy environment than if it were legal.

With the little allowance he got from his mother and a deeply rooted depression, Pedram drank his way through high school, until it was time to go to college. "I got accepted to an Azad university in Yazd," he says. "It was an incredible feeling. It was as if I had finally become independent. I was suddenly my own person and that made me excited. Until then, my mom was supporting me, but you can only imagine how limited she was in her spending ability. In addition to me and my sister, she now had two other sons, and with her basic salary, there was only so much she could do."

Pedram's uncle (his mother's brother) was in the watch business and ended up paying for his nephew's tuition and living costs. "When I first got to Yazd, I was doing great at university; I was studying hard and really trying to be good." However, Pedram soon fell in with a group who were into drugs and alcohol. "It didn't take long for me to get immersed in that crowd," he reveals. "The first few times I refused, but after the fifth time, I couldn't resist—I couldn't say no. I guess I wanted to see what was this thing that destroyed my entire childhood? What was this drug that consumed people's lives?" It wasn't long until Pedram had become an opium addict. "The first time I used opium, I overdid it and really felt sick afterward, but that didn't stop me. I became a heavy user, and nothing could stop me." He eventually got kicked out of school, which led to his mother cutting him out of her life. "I got kicked out of university after my second year and that was when my mom completely cut me out of her life. She was suspicious for a while, but by then everything had become too obvious to hide—the way I looked, the way I talked. I was broke; my uncle and mom stopped their minimal support, so much that my mom told me she was erasing me out of her birth certificate. I was dead for her."

Soon after, Pedram was arrested for the first time. "I was still living in Yazd. My friend and I needed money, so we went to this big house that we'd been monitoring for a few days. We knew the residents were not home, so one night we went in. I was an amateur; it was my first time. I went straight for the carpets and started to fold them. I didn't realize how quick I had to be and how heavy and hard it was to move carpets. By the time I had figured out my way, the neighbors had called the police. My friend managed to escape, but I was arrested."

⧉

After he was released from prison, Pedram went to Tehran, where, after nearly nine years apart, he decided to reconnect with his estranged father. "I didn't know what to expect," he says. "I was actually surprised that he was even alive. I had been in touch with Simin. She gave me a number for a downtown motel that my dad used to stay at for while. I found him in an old motel in Naser Khosro." Despite all his father had put him through, Pedram still felt a bond with the man. "No matter what he did or what he had put me through, he was still my father. I had a sense of belonging to him." Pedram now found himself back in the same place he had escaped from as a boy. This time, he returned as an addicted young man in search of his addict father in a community that he had so fervently feared as a child.

Pedram recalls how his father started to cry the minute he saw his son. "We stayed up all night and just talked. Since I'd left, he'd spent most of his life in prison. He had aged so much. His tears were not only because he missed me or was happy to see me, but because I had turned into someone like him—a pathetic addict. At the time, there was no turning back—not for him, nor for myself."

Once again, father and son were united—except this time, it was in their shared addiction. "The first time I used heroin was with my dad," Pedram says with obvious regret in his voice. "I told him I'd used it before—I was lying. I couldn't buy opium and needed something desperately bad. After the first time, I got hooked. Nothing, simply nothing was important to me anymore." Things soon went from bad to worse for the two of them. "We did it all," Pedram remembers. "They'd arrest us and then we'd get out. That's the thing; it's a disgusting cycle. I remember one time, the police arrested me for heroin and my dad came to help from across the street and they arrested him too. It was a regular thing—sometimes I wanted to go to prison just to escape the winter cold."

Along with drugs, prison became a regular part of Pedram's existence. "Prison had become a part of my life. I too didn't want to leave," he says. "It was the most terrifying place—but at least there was a roof over my head. Out there, it was as terrifying, except I'd be sleeping on the streets, on cardboard, and God knows where." Pedram witnessed some of the most brutal things imaginable while in prison: "Seeing a twenty-five-year-old raping a seventy-year-old for just one cigarette; meeting a man who was imprisoned for raping his own daughter; witnessing the death of a few people right in front of my eyes." He recalled some of the darkest moments of his life in a calm voice, seemingly numbed by what he had seen. "How can you see these things and not break? How can these things even be? But they are real; they exist."

Pedram would lose track of his father whenever he was incarcerated, and then find him once he was released. Eventually, however, Pedram lost contact with his father, and was forced to take refuge at a friend's small apartment near Mehrabad airport. "He had a music degree from Florence and spent a lot of time in Italy working as a musician," Pedram recalls of his friend. "Somehow, he came back to Iran and ended up like me. He was my last resort, but even he kicked me out—he told me I needed help, and unless I got it, I was gonna die." Tragically, this fate instead befell his friend. "Later, I found out that my friend had died in his apartment; his neighbors found out because of the smell." By this time, Pedram had permanently lost touch with his father. "I had already lost contact with my dad while I was staying with my friend. I never heard from my dad again; I doubt he's alive."

Now at a crossroad, Pedram decided to call the only person he thought would not hang up on him—his mother's sister-in-law from her second husband. "I knew her well," he shares. "She was a good woman; she had been supportive of me a long time ago. I had nothing to lose." The woman took him in and gave him the option of trying rehab, and if that didn't work out, going back to the streets. "I think the fact that she gave me the option was encouraging—she didn't force me to go to rehab, she said, 'You've tried everything in your life; maybe you should try this, too.'" But rehab turned out to be a horrible experience for Pedram. "It was the most painful experience of my life, but I had to go through it. I had to do it. I had no choice—the other choice was to come out and die." And so he pushed through, and came out clean. He was now thirty-one years old.

After getting out of rebab, Pedram reached out again to his mother's brother. "My uncle—my mom's brother—was always the most philanthropic person. He had money and he would give a lot of it to the poor. I knew that if anyone was going to help me post-rehab, it was going to be him." Despite a great deal of initial reluctance, Pedram's uncle gave him a tiny room in the basement of an apartment he used for cooking and preparing food for the needy during Ramadan and other religious holidays. Pedram was put in charge of washing, cooking, and cleaning. "I hated doing all of it," he says with a quick laugh, "but I knew I had no choice. I had to stay clean. I had to prove myself, because I knew what the other end looked like. I didn't want to be there."

It took Pedram some time, but he ultimately passed the test. "It was quite liberating. My uncle slowly began to trust me, he tested me on so many occasions just to make sure I wouldn't slip. He even had people watch me and report back to him. He had helped other addicts before, so he'd go to them for advice—just to make sure I wasn't diverting."

After working for his uncle for a few years, Pedram got an overnight job with the city, painting lines on the streets. "It was the only way I could make money, and it wasn't fulfilling whatsoever," he says glumly. "I knew I don't want to do it long-term." At the same time, Pedram found himself getting interested in photography, and learning the ins and outs of the craft. "I started taking classes during the day and at night continued my work with the city. I also bought a small car so in between I worked as a taxi driver."

It took him a few years to get on his feet, but he eventually managed to rent a place with a roommate and fully focus on his photography. Today, he mainly shoots commercials and advertising. Pedram believes that photography has the power to change lives. "I wish I could capture everyday moments of life that could enable people to see their surroundings differently—to take pictures that would have a message, that could add a new perspective for someone. That's my passion; that's what I want to do with my craft."

As Pedram grew stronger in his new life, he managed to reconnect with his mother. "After I got clean, my mom finally agreed to see me," he recalls. "It was almost three years after I'd first gone to my uncle for a job post-rehab and almost ten years since I had last seen her." Their first encounter did not go well. "We didn't have that mother-son relationship," Pedram shares. "I knew I was guilty—it was all my own doing, but she later told me how she had also made a lot of mistakes, and that she felt quite guilty with regards to my upbringing and life."

By then, she had separated from her second husband, who also ended up becoming a recreational opium user. She had also become distant from her other three children. "I don't know what it was with her. She had become incredibly obsessed with money," Pedram says. "I would tell her 'Mom, you have enough money to travel, to go to places, and to just relax'—but somehow she was living a tainted life—a life that was stuck in the past and everything she thought she could have done differently."

It was not an easy relationship to mend, but the two did their best in the short time they had together. "I remember she'd tell me, 'Pedram, please tell me what I can do for you? Just tell me and I'll do it.' And I'd tell her, 'Mom, nothing; you've done enough!' What could she do for a forty-year old at that stage? No matter what she'd do, she couldn't change the past."

And then suddenly, it was all over.

"I still can't believe she committed suicide," Pedram says calmly. "Two nights prior to her killing herself, she was at my place. She went to my room and came back with a will. She came downstairs and asked me for some ink to stamp her fingerprint on the paper. At first, I didn't realize what she was doing. I asked her, 'What are you doing, Mom? Why are you doing this now?' She didn't say anything. Maybe I should have guessed, or maybe I should have asked. I don't know. She had gone to Mecca a few months prior and had brought back with her this notebook that people write their wills in."

Pedram's mother died from aluminum phosphide poisoning after taking what is known as a rice tablet, or pesticide. "After she committed suicide, I realized religion is not going to save anybody; how can someone who'd gone to see the house of God in Mecca come back and kill herself? I do respect her decision though. Maybe she needed an escape; maybe she needed to let herself go—I think she needed peace."

Today, after an incredible and harrowing journey filled with unspeakable pain and tragedy, Pedram finds peace in his photography, instrumental music, and life as a clean and sober person. Before gaining his sobriety, he had never thought really about what would make him happy. When asked, he smiles quietly. "I don't know. I never thought of that—what makes me happy? To live without worry and to experience what freedom really means."

In the silence of his thoughts, the dark-haired photographer also reads and writes poetry.

> This cloud that took over my fortieth sky,
> was a souvenir of a bitter and brute battle
> And although its darkness gave way to light,
> it the result of my fight with destiny and faith.

"You know, I wonder if there will ever be a stupid person out there

ابری که بر پهنه اسمان چهل سالگیم درید
راه توشه ای بود از یک نبرد تلخ و سخت.
هرچند تیرگی‌های آن به روشنی رسید،
اما جدال من بود با سرنوشت و بخت.

who will fall in love with me? Maybe that's my only wish or dream. To find true love; to find someone who will truly, passionately, and genuinely love me back." And with that, he recites to me his favorite Shamloo poem—on finding love.

Hassan Rezania

*T*HERE ARE QUITE A FEW THINGS THAT are quintessentially Iranian—both in spirit and in form.

This is one of them.

It dates back several millennia. Cleopatra infused it in her bath as a sexual stimulant prior to her meetings with men; medieval nuns enjoyed it as a pick me up for their daily prayers, chores, and around the clock singing; Henry VIII used it to golden the color of the swans he served at his glorious feasts; during the Dark Ages, it was used as an antidote for the "Black Death"; and at times during history, its value has exceeded that of gold.

For centuries, Iranians have used it for culinary as well as medicinal purposes. They believe it to be a powerful antidepressant and an antioxidant that can weaponize their bodies against cancer, eye degradation, and Alzheimer's disease. "If I were to tell you all its benefits, it would take me until morning," the man says with a sweet laugh.

In the United States, Europe, and much of the world, it's known as an expensive spice that gives rice its silky yellow hue and adds an intoxicating aroma to everything from fish to risotto. However, in Iran, saffron is far more than just a spice. Thousands of years of history, family traditions, and a proud sense of nationalism are subsumed within this whimsical purple flower. Whether it be in the kitchen, the spice market, or on the farm, Iranians have a vast reservoir of respect for these tiny strands. At some point in their lives, most Persian woman are taught how to use this precious spice—don't lose a string; don't waste any while grinding it in the mortar; and don't add too much water while diluting it for use.

Saffron is also the pride and joy of Iranian farming, which produces approximately 90 percent of the world's "red gold." The spice is mainly cultivated on the vast farms of what used to be Iran's largest province— Khorasan. "Of course, Khorasan is its home, the place where it has been farmed for centuries," he says. "But in Iran, we are seeing it harvested even in some western provinces, as well as in the south."

Hassan Rezania is a young farmer whose family has been cultivating saffron from the now-dry lands of Khorasan for generations. "My grandfather, great grandfather, and his father were all farmers—this is what they all did, what we all know. It's in our blood."

In a stretch of land that once exceeded 800 miles, the state of Khorasan shared a border with Turkmenistan and Afghanistan. However, in 2004, the state was divided into three independent provinces—North Khorasan Province, Razavi Khorasan Province, and South Khorasan Province. Many objected to this division; those favoring the divide argued that it would be beneficial for the long-term economic growth and security of the region. Yet to this day, the opposition believes that political gain and corruption were the real underlying motives.

Hassan lives in Gonabad, a city of approximately 35,000 in the Razavi Khorasan Province. The capital of the province is one of the most historically important cities in Iran. It was once called Sanabad, but in the ninth century, after the murder of Imam Reza—the Eighth Imam of the Shia Muslims—the city was renamed Mashhad, which literally translates to "the place of martyrdom." Today, it is the second most populous city in Iran. Each year, millions of Iranian pilgrims flock to Mashhad, while others travel from all over the world to see the Imam Reza Shrine, and the city's glorious mosque, which is the largest by area in the world. The shrine was built several hundred years ago and has survived multiple Persian dynasties. In the mid-1970s, Iran's late Shah, Mohammad Reza Pahlavi, ordered the refurbishment of the main mosque, which added a fresh coat of gold plate to the shrine.

Beyond its religious significance, Mashhad was also home to the wealthiest "charitable" conglomerate in Iran. While it's supposedly a "endowment" for the poor and less fortunate, Astan-e Quds-e Razavi is a billion-dollar entity that owns the grounds of the Imam Reza Shrine, much of Mashhad, as well as numerous shares in the automotive, defense, and agricultural sectors—all feeding the Iranian revolutionary forces. The endowment has been around for centuries, but it evolved to what it is today after the 1979 revolution.

⬛

According to Hassan, it takes tens of thousands of the purple flowers and over 200,000 of their stigmata to make one kilogram of saffron. Now, imagine making 150 tons of these featherweight strands, and you have Iran's average yearly crop. "Some of the best products come from Gonabad," says Hassan. "My dad used to tell us that about fifty years ago they used to plant poppy here for opium—that's why the soil is so fertile in this region."

Hassan grew up in a small rural village called Zibad, which is twenty-five kilometers outside of Gonabad. To underscore the rich history

of Hassan's village, more than a 1000 years ago, the legendary tenth-century Persian poet and one of the greatest symbols of Iranian nationalism, Abu'l Qasem Ferdowsi, wrote about Zibad in his "Shahnameh," the world's longest epic, which single-handedly amplifies the depth, richness, and complexity of Persian poetry and culture. In the poem, Ferdowsi called Zibad the "triumphant land" where "twelve knights" fought the enemy's army. Today, Zibad is home to less than 5000 people—among them the remaining members of Hassan's family, who survive on their modest income from farming.

Hassan's two sisters left the village once they got married, which is typical for villagers in Iran. His older brother still works with Hassan in the family farming business, and his younger brother lives with their mother back in Zibad while he attends university in a nearby city. "When Dad died a few years ago, we all tried hard to keep the family farm. It's our blood, our roots," Hassan says with a humble sense of belonging. "It's not much—maybe one hectare—but it's enough to keep our roots alive, to keep us in the field and in the business. This is what we grew up with, and we're so proud of it."

⬚

Try to envision dozens of children holding metal lanterns and accompanying their parents, grandparents, aunts, and uncles to the saffron fields under the cloak of darkness. "Around four o'clock in the morning we would leave the house," Hassan remembers. "The sky would still be dark, so our lanterns would help guide us through the fields." As the black of night slowly faded into the dim light of the rising sun, Hassan and the other children would pluck the delicate florets from the ground. "The flowers have to be picked as soon as they bloom, otherwise the sun will weaken the petals and the flower will dwindle away—in that case they won't be of any use." Like a true saffron connoisseur, Hassan explains how the "red part of the stigma is what adds the color and the lower—more yellowy part—is what adds saffron's strong scent."

Saffron corms are planted and cultivated in the summer and are ready for harvest in November. "It was a family affair; everyone would help. Sometimes, the schools would close in the village during saffron-picking days," Hassan says, recalling those crisp autumn mornings. "After we would finish in the fields, everyone would go back home and gather around the korsi and start separating the thin stigmata from the flower." The planting and harvesting of saffron is incredibly labor intensive, yet for many like Hassan and his family, the fatigue of the farming was often eased by the love and intimacy of this type of collective effort.

One of the most delightful memories for many Iranian children—especially those from small villages—is their time spent beside the *korsi*, a short wooden table covered with thick blankets; underneath the table is a brazier with burning charcoal. (Modern ones are heated electrically.) People gather around the korsi and put their feet underneath the blankets so that the gentle heat can warm their bodies. In rural places where there is no gasoline or electricity, the korsi is often the only source of heat. However, this old-school square-shaped table is more than a "heater"; it is also a place for laughter, storytelling, and bonding for the entire family. "We would squeeze in between the adults, make ourselves comfortable, and start working like them," Hassan recalls.

"The whole family would come together."

Unfortunately, a lot has changed since those blissful days. "You know, it's different these days; it's not the same as it was when we were young," he says in a somber tone. "The labor is too hard and the money is too little. Young people move to the cities any chance they get. Things are not the same as they were twenty, twenty-five years ago—the intimacy of farming life is nowhere near what it was before."

Like many young farmers, Hassan understood the financial challenges of solely relying on farming, so he attended university, earning an engineering degree in agriculture and farming. While for many young men living in villages and farmlands the city bears the promise of stability and higher wages, Hassan never had any desire to leave his hometown. "I never wanted to leave," he says. "I wanted to grow and professionally build on what had existed in my family for generations." The result of this growth is the small shop he owns in Gonabad, which supports local saffron farmers and provides farming and agricultural services. "I'm proud of what I do. So many of the young village men want to leave, but why? At the end of the day, they're going to have a desk job or a government job. I'm glad to be here. This is where I belong."

Like most types of agriculture in Iran, saffron farmers have suffered in recent years as a result of cheap wholesale prices, uncontrolled markets, and economic sanctions. "Saffron has been conked on the head," Hassan says colorfully. "The sanctions are hurting exports and consequentially that's creating challenges within the Iranian market."

The challenges mainly have to do with the domestic devaluation of saffron. As wholesalers haggle for the lowest price, they pay the least amount possible to farmers—whose entire livelihood is based on their yearly crop. The wholesalers then sell for a much higher price to distributors, who in turn sell at an even higher price to shops and markets. "It's an unregulated industry, and so much of its value has been lost. Much of that is due to sanctions," Hassan explains. "Imagine, if we had a lucrative export industry worldwide; in that case there would be no reason for domestic haggling, corruption, and cheating. When you don't have a large international market, you try to make up for the loss elsewhere." This is one of the many ways that US and European sanctions affect the daily lives of Iranians. "The main countries of export are the UAE, the Gulf region, and China—but you know, these days China is producing saffron they grow in greenhouses," Hassan says with subtle agitation.

In addition to the sanctions and domestic corruption, Iran is also in the midst of a catastrophic water crisis that's drying up once-fertile farmland. "There's not enough water anymore and the region is facing a huge water crisis," Hassan states. The crisis is not unique to Hassan's region, as the entire country is facing one of the worst water shortages in its history. Sadly, little is being done to manage the problem. While climate change and minimal rainfall are contributing factors, poor irrigation systems, excessive damming of rivers, government mismanagement, and problematic trade deals in environmentally

vulnerable areas are among the other reasons making Iran's water crisis an issue of national security. And there are, of course, still the sanctions. "When there are sanctions, people overproduce in order to make up for the money they lose in the absence of export sales," Hassan explains. "Over the years, the pressure to produce more crops has led to a massive abuse of waterlines and underground water sources in farming regions."

Hassan tells me that if he had one wish, it would be to see a day when Iranian saffron receives the respect, appreciation, and value that it truly deserves. "You know, with all these challenges, water chaos, financial instability, I'm still grateful for my craft, for my field," Hassan says with a gentle sense of gratitude.

I ask him what he would say to a fellow farmer in the US or Europe. In a timid yet excited voice, he replies, "All I have to tell them is that farming saffron is the most beautiful and valuable craft out there. There is no field more beautiful and delicate than saffron fields. When you work with saffron, its beauty, color, aroma, gives you all the energy you need in life. I just wish the world could also see what we have to offer and realize the value of what we produce."

Much like the crop he harvests, Hassan's personal life is bright and valuable. He is married to a beautiful young woman named Fatemeh, who also spent her childhood in the dreamy fields of saffron. The couple have a young son. "Every Thursday, Friday (the Iranian weekend), we go to our village. I take my wife and son and we go to see our family. Any time we go to big cities, we get suffocated," Hassan says with a laugh. "This is where we belong; we still try to revive the old family gatherings and the intimacy of the past—at least during saffron season."

As for his little son, Hassan wants him to pursue whatever professional path his heart desires. "You know, when dad was dying he asked us to continue the business. It's a sense of duty, a sense of belonging for me, for my family. Saffron has taught us so much, to honor life, to appreciate water, to love the earth, and to be our own man —standing on our own feet," he says with pride.

Sima Raisi

HER COLORFUL OUTFIT, ADORNED WITH BEADS and the traditional Baluchi needlework, make her look like a beautiful fish that's somehow able to walk on land. Her petite frame resembles that of a teenager, but when she speaks, you can hear the depth of her heart and the maturity of her mind in her voice. "Our house is ten minutes away from the Big Sea," she begins. "I grew up next to the water. It's all part of who I am. To this day, I think of the sea as the most calming thing in nature. The water here is so different from the Persian Gulf or the Caspian Sea; it's untouched. We have the Pink Lake, the Crab Sea, the Big Sea, the Small Sea; every corner is different from the other."

She's talking about Chabahar, a strategic port city at Iran's southern end. Nestled in the historic yet vulnerable Sistan and Baluchestan Province that borders Pakistan and Afghanistan, Chabahar acts as a critical regional transit point for India and Afghanistan, both of which are keen to bypass the city's sister port in Pakistan. In the northwest part of the province lies the mysterious Lut Desert (*Dasht-e Lut*), which stretches more than 200 miles long and 100 miles wide. In the summer, Lut experiences some of the hottest temperatures on the planet; in the less-brutally oppressive months of the year, the desert's complex geology is a destination for adventure-seeking tourists and environmental professionals. A few dozen miles toward the east is Iran's famous semi-active volcano, located atop the 4000-meter high Taftan Mountain.

Chabahar's Martian Mountains, magical sunrises, and crystal blue skies instill the city with an unrivaled natural glow. In fact, the entire

Sistan and Baluchestan Province—considered Iran's poorest state— is home to a rich cultural and natural tapestry that dates back several millennia. "During the reign of the Shah, they wanted to turn this place into a tourist destination, but then the revolution happened and immediately after we had the war," she says. "So things didn't change much around here, but now we're slowly seeing a shake-up. Still, so much remains untapped and quaint—that's the beauty of this place."

While Sistan and Baluchestan is often regarded as a haven for heroin and opium smugglers from neighboring Afghanistan, as well as being home to a small group of Sunni militants with alleged ties to Al-Qaeda and foreign governments who occasionally cause isolated unrest in opposition to the country's Shia government, the diversity of its natural landscape, and the hospitality and culture of the Baluchi

people who live there, cancel out any negative political preconceptions of the region.

Over 5000 years ago, in the then fertile lands of Sistan and Baluchestan, some of the first complex societies were formed around Lake Hamoun—the third largest lake in Iran, that sadly, in the years since the revolution, has rapidly dried up. While continuous drought has been a contributor to Hamoun's demise, the Iranian government's mismanagement of the state's water resources, water diversion for irrigation, as well as dykes on the Iran-Afghan border, are partially responsible for what has become a quietly kept natural disaster. A skip and a hop into Afghanistan's arid state of Helmand, the dams and canals built with the backing of foreign aid are considered by some as another contributing factor to the drainage of Hamoun across the border. The crisis has caused thousands of fishermen to lose their jobs, families to leave their homes, and many animal species to die in what was once a lush plain.

In the barren lands of Hamoun—less than an hour's drive from the Afghan border—you can still find the remains of *Shahr-e Sookhteh*, or the "Burnt City." Built in 3200 BC, Shahr-e Sookhteh was an ancient community comprised of clay-brick houses, monuments, and burial sites that is celebrated today by archeologists worldwide. In 2016, deep in one of the graves of the ancient city, scientists found what is regarded as the first-ever artificial eye, which dates back to 2900 to 2800 BC and belonged to a woman around the age of thirty. It's mind-boggling to imagine that nearly three thousand years ago, a blind woman went under the knife and received an artificial eyeball that was adorned with gold wires and paint.

About an eight-hour drive from Shahr-e Sookhteh are the shores of Chabahar. "It's the sea that made me fall in love with the environment," she claims passionately. "The sea made me realize that I shouldn't hurt the one place that I so deeply love—the water, the beach. I respect the sea. I respect the environment." The bright yellow color of her long tunic and shawl mirrors the glistening hues of the sun overlooking the Gulf of Oman. In certain parts of the country, especially the south, people often wear traditional clothes unique to the culture and customs of their region—a beautiful tradition that she proudly follows. Since she was a little girl, she has found great solace in the sonorous waves of the sea. "I remember my father would gather all my siblings—even sometimes our guests—to go to the beach and sit by the water so he could read to us," she says wistfully. "My dad was always an open-minded man; even though he came from a religiously conservative family, he was always pushing boundaries for his children, breaking taboos, and wanting the best for his family and community."

⊡

Sima Raisi is a young Baluch girl whose father's broad outlook helped her to engage in the natural world around her. "When I first started college, my friends and I were having ice cream while walking on the beach," she says with a smile. "Suddenly, I asked my friends to keep the wrappers and not throw them on the beach. They laughed at me and said, 'Sure, so long as you pick up the ones that we've already dropped.'" And so she did. "I picked up their trash and asked them to help me clean the rest of the garbage. I'll never forget their faces," she recalls with a laugh. Keeping the beach clean quickly became an important ritual for her. "After that day, whenever we'd have a family picnic, I would ask people to help me clean the trash and plastic on the beach. I still do. It just feels like the right thing to do. I believe—from the bottom of my heart—that if I can change the culture in my small community, I have done something good. I feel I've contributed to something bigger. I really believe it matters."

Unfortunately, what matters to the environment is not always a priority for the Iranian government and its people. Similar to many other Middle Eastern countries, Iran has long been at risk of a water crisis, which in recent years has grown even more dire than originally anticipated. The deadly threat to the country's wildlife and the nation's water scarcity are the result of decades of public and private mismanagement, deforestation, unregulated dam-building, farming, water irrigation, and extraction, as well as minimal planning by the authorities. For example, Lake Orumiyeh in northwestern Iran was once the largest saltwater lake in the region, as well as a vast ecosystem for various species of fish and birds, and a lifeline for millions of surrounding residents and farmers. Today, however, what is left is little more than a salty wasteland. Since 2000, Isfahan's once glorious Zayandeh Rood River and much of the farmlands of Southern Khorasan—as well as other southern and central provinces—have all eroded due to drought and the mismanagement of policymakers. The catastrophic environmental issues in Iran has even turned into a political showdown between the country's academics and its hardline forces, with many researchers having been detained and targeted by the country's Revolutionary Guard Corps—leaving the nation's dwindling wetlands, flora, and wildlife at further risk.

Sima's passion for the sea and the water are a reflection of her inherent connection to the earth. It's as if her heart is entwined with the surrounding environment. "People think someone else's trash is not for them, but they don't realize that we're all in this together, that the earth belongs to all of us and that we're all responsible for our world," she states with intense conviction. "I don't understand why people don't consider the forests, the deserts, the seas, and the mountains as their home—all of those places are our home; it's everyone's home."

Tragically, with all her fervor toward the environment, she will never again see any of it with her own eyes, as since the age of eighteen, Sima has been blind.

Born and raised into a conservative family in the Sistan and Baluchestan Province—home to the majority of Iran's Sunni population—Sima's parents got married when her mother was only thirteen years old. At the time, her father was in his early twenties, and keen for his new wife to continue her education—something that the young bride was not enthusiastic about, which led her to only study until fifth grade. Sima's parents are both from Nikshahr, a conservative city located between Chabahar and Zahedan—the province's capital, which is about a two-hour car drive from Shahr-e Sookhteh. The couple had four girls and four boys, with Sima being the second-oldest daughter. "My parents are first cousins," she says. "Here, it's quite common for family members to get married to one another." Consanguineous marriages are still a frequent occurrence in many developing countries around the world—especially in tribal and ethnic communities in parts of Africa, the Middle East, and Asia. In Iran, the more rural you go, the higher the chances of encountering couples who are first or second cousins.

As a result of her parent's genetic proximity, Sima was born with a condition that impaired one of her eyes. "None of the doctors were able to tell what was wrong," she recalls. "For years, they told my dad that I had mental retardation without linking anything to my eyes. My dad took me to all the hospitals and doctors in Baluchistan. He even took me to Tehran, but the eye doctors there weren't able to figure out what was wrong, either. It took a while until the doctors confirmed that I had severe glaucoma. I was in sixth grade when they finally figured out my condition; unfortunately, it was a bit late."

Because of her eye problems, Sima was initially unable to attend school. "No single public or private elementary school in Chabahar would admit me," she says with a barely concealed anger. To these schools, Sima was considered a burden, a powerless child with no capacity to learn. "They didn't even let me try; they didn't even bother to let me sit in the classroom."

One day, Sima's father met a man on the bus. They two began a casual conversation, and the stranger soon found out about the young father's distress about his daughter. "He told my dad that he could help me," Sima recalls. "The man's name was Mr. Abyaran, and he was a teacher at the special needs school in our city. He insisted that my dad let me attend that school while he privately worked with me." Sima's father hired Abyaran right on the spot.

In many parts of Iran, unlike regular schools, special needs schools are coed. "I always played with the boys; it was so much fun," Sima says in a sweet yet bashful tone. However, the fun ended for her in the fourth grade. "Every year, except for the first and second year, where Mr. Abyaran was our teacher, we would have a new teacher. When I was about to go to fourth grade, I found out that the teacher beat the boys. I told my parents I was not going to go to his class. I cried for days and insisted that they change my school. I just couldn't imagine being taught by someone who would beat children."

Sima's father then went to the regular public schools and the private schools in Chabahar, trying to gain admission for his daughter. (The special needs schools for girls only until went through the fourth grade.) Things got to a point that Sima's father and Mr. Abyaran decided to confront the teacher and the principal of one of the schools opposing the young girl's admittance. "My father asked the teacher why she was not willing to teach me or at least let me sit in her classroom. I was there and saw the whole exchange," Sima remembers. "She told my dad, 'Because she doesn't understand anything; she won't learn.'"

Right then and there, Sima was put to the test. "My dad looked the teacher in the eye and told her to ask me to solve any problem a student in my grade would need to solve," she recalls with nervous pride. "I remember her snide look. She asked me to do a math problem and answer what one-thousand minus one was equal to. I did it on the spot. I'll never forget her face; she couldn't believe it."

That answer got Sima admitted to public school, giving her the chance to study alongside other children. Still, she ended up feeling more marginalized than ever. "It was hard," she recalls with obvious pain. "I was always treated as a *nokhodi* (Farsi for a person who's sidelined and ignored)." This treatment continued when Sima reached middle school, where she was bullied and ignored by her fellow classmates. "Emotionally, it was exhausting," she remembers. "I was always treated as if I was different from the rest of the students, the rest of the people, and the rest of the girls. The teachers, the students, and so many of our family members, they all treated me as if I was a strange thing—a strange person."

Sima's ostracization wasn't limited to school, as she recalls a moment from her home life when she was in eighth grade. "It is quite common for Baluch girls to get engaged by the time they're in eighth grade," she shares. "My older sister was already married, so naturally, I was next." But what actually came next would further shatter her sense of well-being. "I'll never forget the day my uncle came to our house asking my father's permission for his son, but the permission wasn't for me, it was for my younger sister who was in the fifth grade." The eighth grader's heartache wasn't because of her desire to get married, but because she was made to feel like she was worthless, and somehow damaged. "It wasn't like I was desperate to get engaged; it had nothing to do with that," she says. "Instead, I truly felt as if I had a defect—as if I had a flaw and a shortcoming that made me less of a person than other girls. I truly felt like an outcast."

From that moment on, Sima's sense of inferiority only grew, turning her into a tense and self-conscious teenager who immersed herself in books and schoolwork in order to bury her feelings of inadequacy. "I remember reading all of Moadab Poor's novels and Fahimeh Rahimi's books," she says. Just like any young adult or teen would get drowned in a romance novels, millions of Iranian girls found comfort in the simple yet familiar prose of Moadabpoor and Rahimi's stories that so vividly drew in elements from the realities of life in Iran. "I also focused on school; somehow I thought by studying hard and doing well in class, I could compensate for the shortcomings I felt at the time."

One day, Sima decided to let her guard down and speak openly with her father—a moment that brought the two of them closer than ever before. "Until then, my father and I had never had a private father-daughter exchange, and I had no grasp of how much he had sacrificed for me," she remembers. "He just never talked to me about anything. It was then that, for the first time ever, we had a heart to heart. Suddenly, I realized how things could have been so different had I not had the support of my father. I recognized how much my dad wanted me to thrive, to grow, and to be comfortable."

There's nothing more powerful than when a stereotype is proven false. Sima's father is a Sunni Muslim and a culturally conservative man from a rural community bound to religious and traditional customs. However, beyond that superficial definition, he has been a champion for his blind daughter, an ideal father for all his children, and a committed husband. "My dad has always been a progressive man—always breaking boundaries, always supporting those who needed support," Sima says with obvious pride. "He believed in education, especially for girls. All of my siblings are educated."

Despite the common belief in the West that there are no Sunni Muslims in the majority Shia Muslim country, Iran is in fact home to a considerable population of Sunnis. While there are no official numbers, Iranian Sunnis mainly reside in the provinces of Sistan and Baluchestan, Khuzestan, and Hormozgan in the south; West Azerbaijan, Kurdistan, and Kermanshah in the west; and throughout Khorasan in the east.

With the invasion of Arab Muslims in the seventh century, Sunni Islam was imposed upon the Iranian people, and gradually became the dominant religion of the country. It wasn't until the sixteenth century that a group of strong militants and political leaders in the northwest formed the powerful Safavid Empire and recognized Shia Islam as the official religion of Iran. Unlike the United States's dominant narrative that Iran has had a long-lasting feud with Sunnis throughout the world—particularly those in Saudi Arabia—the contemporary regional rivalries are solely embedded in power politics that are played out in the name of religion. While there is no doubt that the Iranian government has used religion to expand its domestic and regional grip—and also uses it to marginalize groups it deems to be a political threat—none of that has anything to do with the millennia-old Battle of Karbala, a legendary battle which deepened the split between the Sunnis and the Shiites.

Power politics aside, like many other countries in the world, minorities—both ethnic and religious—are often marginalized in Iran. While on paper Sunnis are privy to all societal and political rights as stated in the constitution of the Islamic Republic, in reality there are few senior political leaders, ministers, and government officials from the Sunni community. There are many Sunni members of parliament and in local governments, but their power is limited. However, under the Rouhani administration, for the first time ever, two of the country's ambassadors were Sunni—one a Baluch female from Chabahar, the other a male diplomat from the Kurdistan Province.

⊡

It wasn't long after the conversation with her father that Sima discovered the American self-help guru Tony Robbins. "I came across *Awaken the Giant Within* and began to get interested in psychology," she remembers. "I was a junior in high school and was slowly regaining my self-confidence. I soon began to excel academically and even got the highest score in psychology and social sciences in my class."

By the time Sima finished high school, she had developed into a confident young woman, accepting of her physical limitations, with the unshakable belief that she could conquer anything. "Somehow, in an effort to fight against all the impediments of my childhood and early teenage years, I built up a delusive ego to serve as my shield and protection," she says. "It was my way to fight the prolonged pain I had endured as a younger girl and in my middle school years."

Toward the end of high school, Sima grew interested in the political and social sciences. She dreamt of studying political science in college, but the young girl's confidence was shaken when she was denied admission to the public university of her choice. In Iran, there are two types of universities—public and private. The public universities are called *Daneshgah Sarasari*, and are made up of a group of esteemed colleges that include Tehran University, Sharif University, and Shahid Beheshti, as well as others across the country. Among the private colleges is the popular Azad University, which has dozens of branches nationwide. It is more prestigious to get accepted to one of the Sarasari universities; often, those attending the private Azad colleges are the students whose entry exam scores did not qualify them for the Sarasari schools. "I completely lost it when I got the Sarasari results," Sima says. "I didn't get accepted and somehow I thought I had failed. I had a tremendously high expectation of myself that didn't bear fruit—a high expectation that was the result of a defense mechanism I had built up over the years."

After the rejection, Sima wanted nothing more than to escape her home and her life. "I just wanted to leave," she says. "I wanted to escape. I asked my parents to let me travel to the north to stay with a friend. Their answer was a big 'no.'" It was only natural for a conservative family in the south to object to their visually impaired daughter's wish to travel to the other end of the country to stay with a friend they barely knew. Sima was devastated. "That night, I cried and left my parent's room," she recalls. "I went to the other room and sat down in front of the TV. I always had this bad habit of sitting very close to the television screen—I knew I shouldn't be doing it, but I didn't care; I always had a hard time seeing properly anyway. Shortly after, my mom came to check on me, but soon left the room and turned off the lights."

The intensity of the television light in the darkened room would result in tragic consequences for Sima. "I didn't feel anything immediately, but a few hours later, I couldn't sleep because of a terrible pain—a pain I'd never felt before," she shares with anguish in her voice. "As the result of the television light against the darkness, my eye pressure had gone so high that it had fully damaged the nerves. It was then that I lost the sight in my other eye." Sima was now completely blind. "I was going crazy; I kept asking myself, 'What happened? Why did this happen to you, Sima?' It was as if my life was over."

What followed were some of the most difficult times in her life. "It took me a while to get out of my depression," Sima recalls. However, a bit of light would soon shine through. "My dad had asked everyone to hide the Azad University results soon after the incident, but my sister in India didn't know and called me as soon as she found out that I had gotten accepted to Zahedan's Azad University for my top choice—political science!"

Despite being heartened by her acceptance at Azad University, Sima was faced with yet another challenge—convincing her parents to let her move 400 miles away to Zahedan. Initial family conversations centered around the idea of Sima staying home and memorizing the Koran—a common practice among conservative families in cities and villages across the country. "My dad was not pressuring me to do this—in fact my dad never told me what to do; he always left it for me to decide. You see, my mom comes from an even more conservative family. It was so difficult

for her to let her daughter move to Zahedan by herself—especially in my condition. My mom and some of our close family members were keen on me staying at home and doing what almost all other blind people do—pretty much nothing, except memorizing the Koran."

During that time, Sima was sent to Tehran for medical treatment, and stayed with a family friend. While she was there, Sima decided to take a leap of faith and tell her parents that she wanted to go away to school. "It was my only chance to pursue the higher education I always dreamt of; my only chance to live a normal life—to feel independent," Sima says. "I told them that if I failed the first semester or got into any trouble, they could bring me back and I'd forget about university."

However, unbeknownst to Sima, her father had already asked one of her cousins to register his daughter for the winter semester. "I got really lucky," Sima says. "My cousin, who was the same age as me, was also planning to go to the same college. I was so happy to have her there; it gave me a sense of security and a strong peace of mind. I'll never forget what my dad told me upon my departure. He said I can always come back home without feeling defeated."

⊡

Sima soon found herself living with four other girls in a dorm room in Zahedan. She was the only blind person in the girl's dormitories—the only blind student in her entire class. "It was a strange feeling at first," she remembers. "I had told everyone to leave me alone and not help me with my daily tasks. I would wash my own clothes, make my own bed, walk to class by myself, and wash my own dishes. I felt that people's help would take away my sense of ability, my sense of independence, and would sideline me as an incompetent person; that was my biggest fear. I was desperately trying to prove that I was no different from the rest of my classmates."

Despite her valiant attempts at independence, the now nineteen-year-old was severely held back due to the university's lack of services for the blind and disabled. "The first few months of college were incredibly difficult," she shares. "It was mind-boggling to experience how the university had no facility and support system for the disabled and the blind students. More so, the professors were very dismissive toward me. It was as if I was back in my elementary and middle school days, where the teachers thought of a blind person as a mentally incapable individual. It was all incredibly humiliating."

Luckily, Sima's roommates, as well as her fellow classmates, came to her rescue. "The one thing that came out of those hard first few months was the close relationship I developed with my roommates—complete strangers who treated me like their very own family." During exams, her classmates and roommates would either record the texts, or reread them to her after finishing their own studies. "I'll never forget the kindness of my friends—especially the first year or so," she says with obvious affection. "I am not exaggerating when I say there were zero amenities for the disabled at our college. Without my friends I would have failed that first term."

By far the hardest activity during Sima's undergraduate years was when she had to take an exam. "The minute I would enter the busy examination room, I would feel as if no one cared about my dignity, my identity, and my feelings," she says, the hurt still evident. "It was as if I was irrelevant among the rest of the students. I needed the help of some sort of an aid, a teacher or a teacher's assistant; I needed to be in a quiet room, to focus on understanding the questions—but none of that was available."

With the help of her fellow classmates, her father, as well as her own inner strength, Sima gradually morphed during her college years into a young woman with a robust sense of self, as well as an authentic confidence that no longer served as a shield, but instead became a mirror to reflect her limitless capabilities. "I didn't change anyone; I couldn't," she shares. "The only thing I changed was myself. No one will ever change for your sake—change needs to come from your own being." There's an indisputable maturity in her tone, in the way she explains her thinking. "I changed myself for the better, so I could change my surroundings. The hardships I endured made me so strong."

Despite all the hardship, Sima graduated with a bachelor's degree in political science, and was then accepted for a masters in the same field. During her master's, she would travel back and forth to Zahedan once a week for classes, while the rest of time, she would study at home. "All I wanted to do was to study," she says. "My dad got me a laptop and I learned how to work with it. I began to obsessively write, take notes, draft articles and just put all my thoughts down. I no longer had the same sort of difficulties I had during my undergraduate years."

Sima also rediscovered her love of reading. "Once again, I immersed myself in books. I would listen to whatever audiobook I could find. I truly enjoyed studying, learning, writing, and taking part in the discussions that mattered to me—discussions that I knew could have an impact on issues that I cared deeply about, like the environment, women's issues, and the disabled community." Today, she has over 1000 audiobooks in her collection. Among her favorite thought leaders are Martin Luther King, Nelson Mandela, and Mahatma Gandhi. One of the elements that connect all these great figures was their ability to rise above marginalization and adversity—a trait mastered by the young Baluch girl. "There are so many parents are out there who don't support their disabled children," Sima shares. "I was blessed with my parents—especially my father who was there for me no matter what. You see, parents play the main role in a child's life. They are the one's who can truly help a disabled child to thrive or just end up as a marginalized. Sure, a lot of it is also based on their financial capability, but so much of it is cultural."

Sima's master's thesis was on the participation of Baluch women in politics. Dating back to the tenth century, the Baluch people were a nomadic tribe with their own unique culture and language. Today, the majority of the Baluch live in Pakistan, while the rest are spread out across Iran, Afghanistan, and parts of India. Sima explains how the Baluch people have a rich oral history in literature and poetry: "There are so many beautiful proverbs, stories, and lullabies in our language—I just wish I could one day turn all of them into a book. It would be beautiful, don't you think?"

Sima is also proud of the open and friendly nature of her people. "You know that the Baluch are some of the most welcoming people!" she says excitedly. "There is not one day that we don't have multiple guests in our home. It's just part of our life. The happiness of our guest is our own happiness. If we frown upon guests, it's as if we have broken one of the most important rules of the house. Every Baluch family is like that."

Sima is now a socially and environmentally conscious professional who can be called Doctor Raisi. During her master's and later PhD, Sima held many conferences at her university on the topics she was passionate about. "I was no longer afraid. I would challenge the professor, freely speak my mind, and feel confident with my voice." She chuckles. "I remember how my professors would ask me so many questions, challenge me, and the debate would go on for way longer than scheduled. It was all great fun."

Today, Sima's world extends beyond the borders of her small hometown, and her ambitious heart beats stronger than the centuries-old traditions of her tribe. She's a passionate advocate for the environment, women, and the disabled people of her community—areas that break through any political divide or physical impediment. "I suffered as a girl, but grew up with a loving dad who was passionate about our culture and my education," she shares. "I learned the value of hard work. I learned that disabled people are no less than the rest of the population, and I want to make sure that they are given a chance." Sima explains how nearly 90 percent of the blind people in Sistan and Baluchestan are uneducated. "Unfortunately, the way people treat the disabled is really sad—especially blind people," she says with a sigh. "You know, blindness is a common issue in my community and I simply can't fathom how horribly the visually challenged people—especially children—are being treated. People think of us as mentally incapable, and that's wrong." Problem solver and activist that she is, it is not surprising to hear that Sima has stepped up to try and change things. "I helped set up a nonprofit group to teach computer and other skills (to the blind)," she says proudly. She's also an advisor on disability issues in Chabahar and does various workshops on the state level.

One of her biggest beliefs is in the power of young role models—people whose stories can inspire change for others who may not realize that there are other ways of dealing with their challenges. "I got a bit of press because of my master's thesis and then my doctoral work on the role of women in politics, and of course my environmental work and beach cleaning," she says, "but you know, I want to reach a point where my research and writings can have a tangible, day to day effect on those who I care about the most. We need role models who can pave the way forward. When we don't have examples to point to, then progress is not easy."

Sima believes in the strength of human connections, as well as aiming high and dreaming big in life. "I always try to look at everything from a humanitarian and human lens," she shares. "Whatever I do, whatever I say, I like it to be respectful of others' rights, of others' feelings and boundaries." When she speaks, I can't help but to think of the Pakistani activist and Nobel Prize laureate Malala Yousafzai's dreams of education and equal rights for girls; except for Sima, it is a sophisticated call for women's rights, a passion for the disabled, and an unparalleled love for the environment. "Some people in my community say I shouldn't share my dreams, or that I shouldn't dream so big, but I don't believe that. My dad always tells me to look at my goal and then quietly work toward that goal—he tells me to have patience in everything I do."

And, while so many women her age are married with children, Sima has other dreams to follow. "Since the day when my uncle came for my sister, I don't want any man to make me feel like a lesser woman because of my disability."

Amir Saneei

ONE OF THE MOST WONDERFUL things about the Persian—or solar *hijri*—calendar, which is structured around the earth's movement around the sun, is that you can tell by the month when one season ends and the next one begins. (Unlike the Gregorian calendar, which follows a set of rules in order to remain in sync with the solar year.) Spring starts in the month of Farvardin; summer begins in Tir; fall with Mehr; and winter with Dey. These names date to the Zoroastrian period, and with their poetic meanings and anecdotal references, they're a modern day reflection of a culture that can be traced back nearly a millennium, to before the Muslim invasion of Persia.

The first of Mehr—*Avval e Mehr* in Farsi—falls between the 22nd and the 24th of September, coinciding with the start of autumn, when the sun still has its summer glow, but the crisp morning breeze is a reminder to all children that the first day of school has arrived. The emotions surrounding Avval e Mehr differ for children based on their age; but between the fear of attending school for the first time, the innocent and sometimes confused feeling of growing up, and the stress of another school year, an immeasurable rush pulses through all students on that first day of school.

I'll never forget my very first Avval e Mehr. I was dressed in a crisp white headscarf that my mother had hand-embroidered my name on, which was matched against a perfectly ironed dark green uniform. I vividly recall my dad's excitement as he insisted on filming my first day on our 1993 camcorder as my mother carried my oversize school bag to the car. I cried during the entire fifteen-minute ride to school in our black Renault, my mother trying her best to calm me down. Even though I had been enrolled in preschool since the age of two, wearing an official school uniform and a headscarf that resembled a white paper bag, mixed with the anxiety of meeting new teachers and being forced to make new friends, was terrifying.

The narrow street in the front of the school was packed with cars and hundreds of schoolgirls saying goodbye to their parents. My mom parked a few blocks away, as she wanted to walk me inside. On that cool autumn morning, she handed me off to my first-grade teacher, Miss Assadi, a slender young woman who ended up being one of the kindest teachers I ever had.

After my mother left, I stood in the morning assembly line with the other students, greeting the principal, listening to a few verses of the Koran, singing songs, and doing a few minutes of stretching. In celebration of the new school year, we were also given candies, and a flower reef to put around our heads. It was then that I heard, for the first time, the chants, "Death to America" and "Death to Israel." The six-year-old me was confused as to why I had to hate the birthplace of Disney princesses and Barbie dolls. By joining my classmates in the chants, I felt as if I were betraying the lessons my parents had taught me: "To love all and don't say bad things about anyone."

Chants aside, in that refurbished estate that had once belonged to the famed Farmanfarmayan family, adjacent to the gardens of the Italian embassy, I would make many life-long friends and learn priceless lessons taught by teachers who cared not only about rigorous academics, but also about instilling love and wisdom into their students.

He comes from a long line of educators and teachers, which includes his father and uncle, who were both trained before the revolution. His cousin has also followed their path; teaching seems to be the family business. "When I talk to my dad and uncle, they tell me how things have changed," he says with a hint of displeasure. "My uncle tells me that there wasn't a day that he'd go to class without having spent the previous night in preparation. Back then, the level of education, the level of preparation, the overall qualification of teachers, and so many

other things, were different." He speaks with an honesty that's tinged with a vague despair. "These days, we have highly qualified people, but more than anything, social and financial pressures are tainting teacher's satisfaction with the public schools across the country."

Part of that dissatisfaction stems from the poor pay teachers receive. "People like me, *sarbaz moalem*, make 100,000 toman per month— pretty much nothing," he states curtly. "The contracted teachers receive between six hundred thousand to one million toman, and the full-timers make anywhere between 1.5 to 4 million toman a month." One hundred thousand toman is the equivalent of approximately seven US dollars. One of the most important economic nuances in Iran is that people are paid in toman, but much of their daily costs and expenses are valued in dollars— which hurts the working and middle class, and further marginalizes the poor. "You can see the weight of financial hardship on the faces of the teachers. In the cities, kids have become more rebellious—young parents are not the same as they were before—and everyone is under an enormous amount of pressure. The teachers have also changed—you don't get the same quality as we used to back when I was in school."

⚏

Amir Saneei was still in his twenties when he became a *sarbaz moalem*— which literally translates to "soldier teacher." For Amir, teaching wasn't a job, but a calling—just like with his father, uncle, and cousin, it was a way for him to give something back to his community, and ultimately, his country. "When I was younger, I always thought that our societal challenges were the result of a cultural and educational deficit," he says, "but when I visited the villages and truly got to know the rural communities, I realized that no, the biggest problem we have is poverty."

Under the constitution, education is free in Iran, but this free education is not always of the best quality, or available. "You have to realize that the government budget for public schools is so low that it barely covers the food costs at some schools," Amir says. In certain parts of the country, especially in rural villages, education is considered a luxury for many young people, who often forego attending school in order to take jobs on farms, fields, and other similar places.

In addition to public schools, there are private schools in Iran that are high in both educational quality, and price. These schools are only affordable for elite and wealthy families. The latest official reports indicate that almost 13 percent of Iranian students— somewhere around 1.3 million pupils—attend private schools, which are mainly concentrated in large cities and affluent areas. While these schools operate independently—usually under a board of trustees or sole ownership—they are still obligated to obey the guidelines and curriculum of the Ministry of Education. To put things in financial perspective, the annual tuition for a private elementary school in Tehran can range from three to ten million toman, while public schools are free of charge—except for a three hundred thousand to five hundred thousand toman yearly fee.

In these two separate worlds—one, a crammed, often obstreperous, yet highly regulated public space, the other an expensive, high-quality, semi-regulated private institution—Iranian students study toward the identical dream of scoring high enough on the country's university entrance exam, known as *konkoor*, in order to be admitted to a top university. Unfortunately, the odds are against most students getting into the university of their choice. It's simple numbers. Imagine, for example, there are one million students studying for konkoor in a given year. Based on their focus in high school, these students are divided into five sub-groups of Math, Sciences, Humanities, Foreign Languages, and the Arts. Let's say that three hundred thousand are taking the math konkoor. Those ranked in the top hundred on the test get to choose any major they wish, with the guarantee of admission into the country's top universities. For the rest of the students with lesser rankings, their choices are limited. "Sure, it's quite factual to say that the level of education has risen in Iran, but you need to realize that simultaneously, the level of unemployment has also increased exponentially," Amir says. "As a result, there is a massive generational gap in the country. On one hand, you have highly educated people with master's degrees and PhDs who are unemployed, and on the other hand, you have young people who are tirelessly studying for jobs that don't exist." In 2019, official Iranian officials reported that more than 43 percent of the unemployed were college graduates.

Amir was born and raised in Khansar, a conservative city ninety miles northwest of Isfahan. He explains that, in the old days, the people of Khansar were known for their calligraphy and art of transcription. "Apparently back then, if someone wanted to publish a book, they'd come to Khansar and have the transcribers and calligraphers write them out however many manuscripts they needed."

From a young age, Amir was inspired by his teachers. "I'll never forget my fifth-grade teacher," he recalls. "The way he'd speak to us, the way he'd teach us new ideas and concepts, and simply the vast amount of knowledge this man had, were among the many reasons why he was a pivotal figure in my early education. There are those teachers who really leave a positive mark on you—he was that person for me." It was his fifth grade teacher who introduced Amir to one of his role models — Mohammad Mosaddegh, the democratically elected Prime Minister of Iran who was later overthrown by the CIA and the MI6. "He made me fall in love with Mr. Mosaddegh who became my role model and hero for years to come." Later, when Amir was finishing high school, another figure inspired the teen: "During President Khatami's time in office, he became a popular figure among the youth and those in support of progress and change; I was quite fond of him. We all believed that he'd bring about change—at least we thought he would."

Amir began his teaching career tutoring high school students for their konkoor while also teaching preparatory courses at private institutions. Upon completing his bachelor's degree at Isfahan Industrial University, he began serving as a sarbaz moalem. In Iran, in lieu of compulsory military service, qualified young teachers can opt for a two-year term teaching in vulnerable communities or villages. "The teachers who teach in villages have no other reason to come other than love, kindness, and an inherent compassion for those in need," Amir shares.

All across Iran, there are impoverished villages across where parents struggle to provide their children with a loaf of bread, let alone a piece of protein. "You need to understand that when someone is hungry, he or she cannot think of anything else other than filling their empty stomach," Amir says. Much of the rural population were supporters of Mahmoud Ahmadinejad, especially during his first presidential campaign in 2005, where his promises of providing government subsidies and aid to the poor turned him into a "people-loving" candidate. "These communities need to be empowered from within, be given grassroot support, and their economies need to be localized," Amir believes. "These are the only ways they can thrive; giving them false promises or short-term subsidies won't help anyone in the long-term—in some cases, it may even hurt them."

Based on the time he has spent in villages across the country, Amir suggests that "localizing the economies of rural areas and creating financial opportunities tailored to their communities" will inevitably fix the existing educational and cultural challenges in the long run. The main obstacle, as is the case with much in Iran, is political. "The problem here is that anytime you want to fix something, you get stamped with a political label," he says. "You want to help a village with its education and teaching infrastructure, they call you a reformist; you want to help build a student-run charity to support the poor, they call you anti-establishment. In Iran, no matter what you do, taking an action in and of itself is regarded as a 'political act.'"

When you speak with Amir, you sense a strong yet humble confidence that he can help any student thrive, despite their circumstances. This is especially true when it comes to his poor and rural students. "Based on my experiences teaching in vulnerable and distant villages, I've learned that those who have the least are often wealthiest in their hearts," he shares passionately. "In the villages and some of the poorest communities, you see things that shake you to the core. You see impoverished children who, despite living in abject poverty, will give their new pencil to their classmate. You see poor students taking off their shoes and giving them to a barefoot friend. You learn a lot from these kids, and you want to give them all that you can—because you see how quickly they absorb all the love and teachings you provide."

Ultimately, Amir compares his job as a teacher to that of a coach: "For me, teachers should act like coaches. When I work with students, no matter their age, I consider myself their coach, their friend, their counterpart. Their success is my success; if they do good, I'm doing good; if they do bad, I'm doing bad. I want to be their partner."

From Booker T. Washington and Eleanor Roosevelt in the United States, to Tatyana Velikanova in Russia and the Palestinian Hanan Al Hroub, teaching, educating, and fostering the minds of future generations has historically been a form of public service among many intellectuals and activists, born out of a desire to establish alternative ways of thinking for the poor and the oppressed.

One such figure in Iran was Samad Behrangi. He was born in 1939 in Tabriz—an ancient city in the Azerbaijan Province that was Iran's on and off again capital from the thirteenth through the sixteenth century. Today, Tabriz is the capital of the East Azerbaijan Province and is the sixth most populous city in the nation. Iranians of the Azerbaijan region speak Azeri Turkish, in addition to Farsi.

Given its proximity to neighboring countries and subsequently the West, Tabriz was a place of strategic importance—both for commercial as well as political reasons. In the early nineteenth century, as a result of years of conflict between Russia and Iran, the Qajar dynasty lost control over nearly half of the Azerbaijan Province, leading to the drawing of new borders that created the modern-day Azerbaijan Democratic Republic. During both World Wars, Tabriz was occupied by the Turks,

along with the Soviets, and later, the Allied Powers.

Tabriz has been the birthplace of many revolutionaries and national heroes. Two of the most prominent were Bagher Khaan and Sattar Khan—champions of the Iranian Constitutional Revolution of the early 1900s—whose leadership and patriotic zeal helped lead to the creation of Iran's parliament and constitution in 1911.

While many Azeri revolutionaries were armed with guns and bullets, some, like Behrangi, fought with their words, stories, and teachings. Behrangi only lived to the age of twenty-eight, but in his short life, he wrote some of the most powerful works of literature for children—timeless treasures such as *The Little Black Fish* and *Ulduz and the Talking Doll*, that are filled with the simple yet profound realities of life, and are often as touching for adults as they are meaningful for kids. Behrangi grew up in poverty and, similar to Amir, believed in empowering vulnerable children by giving them the tools they needed to think for themselves. His melancholy tales were inspired by the real-life stories of his students, many of whom were forced to work in factories, carpet-weaving workshops and on farms.

Behrangi was also an outspoken critic of the Iranian educational system of the time, which for the most part was built upon American and British curriculum and disciplines. Despite his young age, he recognized the devastating impact of marginalizing millions of rural children by teaching them "Americanized" values. His vehement critique of societal disparities and fearless stance against the authoritative forces of the time turned the young patriot into an enemy of the Pahlavi monarchy; as a result, many of his children's stories where banned. While never proven, it is widely believed that his drowning in the Aras River in the summer of 1967 was at the hands of government officials who feared his anti-establishment teachings.

Behrangi's stories captured the real-life agonies of poor children in his time—stories that are still part of the realities of life for many children in Iran. In some of his stories, Behrangi writes about the rural classrooms where he simultaneously taught multiple grades together under one roof. It's hard to believe that nearly six decades and one revolution later, Amir and many of his colleagues teach under the same conditions, in the same financially destitute communities, while witnessing the same heart- wrenching stories. "The first year at Khom Peech I had eleven students in one class," Amir remembers. "While they were all in third grade, their ages varied because some of them couldn't go to school at the right time and some did not pass the previous class the first time. In another village that was only five to ten minutes away, my colleague was the headmaster, the teacher, and the janitor of the school, and taught three classes at the same time."

Khom Peech is a small village nestled on the outskirts of Khansar County, within the Isfahan Province. The majority of the villagers are farmers and shepherds, who produce some of the best dairy and honey in the region. Many of the people who live in Khom Peech are illiterate, and thus struggle to contribute to their children's educational and professional growth. "I remember the first time I asked my students what they wanted to be when they grew up," Amir shares. "All the boys said farmers and shepherds. The girls actually surprised me. I'll never forget the little girl who said she wanted to be a doctor. These kids dream about what they know. The boys see their fathers and think that's all they can do and that's what they should aspire to. Somehow the girls think differently. I think it's because they are closer to their mothers and their mothers often have a wider outlook than the men." In addition to his regular work at the school, Amir added two extra hours each week to teach his third graders about professions like engineering, management, science, and medicine. "I started explaining how everyday people from smaller cities and villages can become mayors, members of the parliament, and even presidents. It was as if they had never heard of such opportunities—as if a person who is born and raised in a village could never reach beyond their village life."

Before starting his job in Khom Peech, Amir was warned that he'd be teaching a difficult group of students. "I had no idea what to expect," he recalls. "There was a student who didn't talk, another with severe ADHD, and the rest had other financial and emotional challenges." Amir explains that while there are fewer students in rural classrooms, their daily life struggles are exponentially more complex in comparison to those living in larger cities. "In villages, you have to handle so many additional challenges you don't face in the cities," he says. "In village schools, you're forced to deal with kids single-handedly and with no additional support."

Without any psychosocial support system in place, or sufficient government aid, teachers in villages have to also act as therapists, doctors, and any other kind of caretaking role that their students require. For example, Abolfazl, one of Amir's students in Khom Peech, had been stuck in the third grade for two years. "He had severe ADHD and was not able to pass his final exams," Amir says. "The teachers before me had pretty much given up on him, but the minute I arrived, I realized his condition, and I gave him more responsibilities. I added more activities for him, and among other things, asked him to be in charge of the classroom. It was astonishing to see his rapid improvement. His energy was being channeled in the right direction." Abolfazl came from an incredibly poor family, and both of his parents were illiterate. "He was super smart; you just had to acknowledge his condition and help him through," Amir shares. "You see, these children are all thirsty to thrive, hungry to learn, and ready to rise. It's our job to open their horizons and give them the tools to reach their full potential."

Unfortunately, the story didn't end well. The following year, after Amir was transferred out of Khom Peech to a neighboring village, he found out that Abolfazl had been expelled from school. "It broke my heart when I heard the news," he says sadly. "They kicked him out because they said he was too loud and didn't pay attention in class. I wish I could do something for him. You just had to give him a chance, be there for him, and guide him along. Some of these teachers don't know what ADHD or autism even are, so they don't know what to do. They think the students are just being lazy or naughty." You can hear the dismay in Amir's voice—it's as if he failed his young friend. "I've heard Abolfazl is now working somewhere on a farm or in a factory; I don't know."

In an effort to get closer to his students in Khom Peech, Amir created a little box called *harfhaye daregooshi* that literally translates to "words to whisper in the ear." "It was our little secret box," he says with a smile. "It was my way to see what was really hurting or bothering these kids. I thought the more I knew, the more I might be able to help." In that little cardboard box, Amir would find all sorts of notes from his students. "They were very honest and actually liked the idea of sharing their secrets with me—someone they could trust. I'd see everything from them asking for color markers to opening up about their emotions. I'll never forget the day when one of the girls wrote me a long letter explaining how she was forced to move to the village and live with her grandparents after her mother passed away in the city."

After being transferred out of Khom Peech, Amir went to another village further north called Rahmat Abaad. There, he taught two grades simultaneously. "I was teaching fourth grade and sixth grade at the same time," he remembers. "Each hour was divided into two sessions. I had forty-five minutes for the fourth graders and then another forty-five minutes for the sixth grade students." Eager to bring tangible change to his students, Amir decided to forego religious studies and teach English to his sixth graders instead. "Here's a simple fact," he declares bluntly, "the educational system that works in the cities does not work for kids in villages and rural areas. What I did was fully logical given the circumstances. You see, in seventh grade, all students are expected to know the basics of the English language. This is while English is not taught in sixth grade. So how can a sixth-grade student in a village who has no access to private tutors and English classes get prepared for what's ahead in seventh grade? The system just doesn't make sense." For this decision, the young teacher was disciplined by his higher ups. "I wish I could do more; I simply couldn't. It's a hard fight to fight."

Speaking of hard fights, back in his university days, Amir, along with some of his friends, launched a student-run nongovernmental charity organization to help the poor families living in the region. "That was our way to go that extra mile," he says. "We created it from scratch when we were still in university. We would collect donations to support vulnerable families, pay for emergency medical support, and also set up libraries in local hospitals and clinics." You can hear the pride in his voice when he speaks about Danesh Amookhtegan—the name of the NGO. However, his joy soon gave way to frustration, as after two years, the local authorities asked them to shut down. "Things would be so different if only good people could unite in an effort to contribute to their very own communities," he says with a hint of wariness.

Amir's students are like his family—a family that's built around a mutual desire to rise above the adversities of rural life. "The first time I stepped foot into my classroom in the village, I realized that these kids had never seen a school play, a ceremony, a field trip, or an award certificate," he recalls. "I promised myself that for as long as I was there, I would change that—even if it came out of my own pocket." One day, Amir took his students on a field trip to a friend's restaurant in Khansar. "None of these kids get to experience what millions of kids around the world experience on a regular basis. The following year, I asked the kids what their favorite memory had been from the previous year, and they all collectively said, 'Going to the restaurant, the restaurant.' I tried my best to bring fun and a sense of normalcy to the lives of some of the most deserving children I have ever met." He adds, simply, that "teaching is the greatest thing if done right."

Like so many young Iranians, Amir has contemplated leaving the country, but for now he's content to teach in the villages of Khansar. "I don't know, maybe if I could redo my life, I'd choose to leave," he says wistfully. "The hardest thing is to live in a society where you want to make a difference, but you simply can't." Amir wonders if the sacrifices he has to make as a public-school teacher in Iran are similar to what teachers have to go through in other countries, such as the United States. "In Iran, there are inherent redlines when it comes to politics, religion, sex, and other topics as such," he says. "I'm curious to know how teachers in the US maneuver through sensitive topics concerning religion, race, sex, and politics. I wonder if their Ministry of Education also has mandates on these topics as well. These were always challenging topics for myself—especially dealing with sexual education, my relationship with the student and their parents, as well as the financial insecurities of working as a teacher. I want to learn how they handle these issues."

In the end, all Amir wants is for other teachers—as well as the rest of the world—to see the "kindness and warmth" of his students. "I want them to see the sincerity and humility of these kids. Never have I seen such love, kindness, and unselfishness in anyone's eyes. There's an unparalleled warmth that exists in the eyes of our kids in Iran. That kindness and love is worth everything."

Hooshang Shahbazi

*H*e was nineteen years old when he first saw an airplane up close. The year was 1976, and he was at Mehrabad International Airport in Tehran—Iran's once bustling international airport that was also a weekend attraction for many blue-collar families in the 1950s and 1960s, who'd spread their picnic baskets on the surrounding grounds of to watch the planes takeoff and land.

Mehrabad opened in 1938 as an airfield for aviation club planes, and later became a military base for the Imperial Iranian Air Force. It wasn't until the late 1950s that Mehrabad began to operate commercial flights. The modern version of the airport was designed by renowned American architect William Pereira—whose futuristic Transamerica Pyramid in San Francisco was once the second tallest building in the world.

Located on the west side of Tehran, close to Azadi (Freedom) Square, Mehrabad held on to its global prestige until the revolution, when American carriers stopped flying to and from Iran—including the infamous nonstop "Iran Air" flight from Mehrabad to John F. Kennedy Airport in New York City. During the eight-year-long Iran-Iraq War in the 1980s, the influx of Western tourists into Iran dwindled, which was followed in the 1990s by the Clinton Administration's tough aviation sanctions against the country. As a result, fewer international airlines traveled to Iran; and over the years, old Russian planes slowly replaced the mighty Boeings and Airbus's that flew in and out of the airport during its heyday.

Today, Mehrabad Airport is used exclusively for domestic flights and by government officials, as well as for the annual pilgrimage of millions of

Iranians to Mecca, Medina, Syria and Iraq. In 2004, under the presidency of Mahmoud Ahmadinejad, and named after the leader of the revolution, Imam Khomeini, a new airport was scheduled to open outside of Tehran. But as often the case in Iran, internal conflict between government agencies caused severe delays ,and ultimately the new international airport didn't open until 2007.

⊡⊡

His voice exudes an authoritative sense of command, entwined with a gentle humility that often contrasts with his cogent personality. His demeanor is that of an old-school gentleman, something that is rare to find these days among men—whether in Iran or around the world. Deep beneath his prestige, expertise, and confidence, however, are the remnants of a hardworking childhood that prepared Hooshang Shahbazi for the day he would become a hero.

His father was a schoolteacher from a humble background whose only wish for his six children was a prosperous future. Hooshang was in eighth grade when, in 1970, his family left their hometown of Mianeh to move to Tehran. Mianeh is a small town located in the East Azerbaijan

Province, the largest province in northwestern Iran, where the majority of people speak Azeri (a variation of Turkish). "My dad thought that the highest achievement we could have in Mianeh would be to become a teacher like him. He wanted a better future for all of us," Hooshang says. "He wanted us to fly."

For Hooshang, who grew up only speaking Azeri, adjusting to a new language in Tehran was difficult. "I would buy two movie tickets—one for myself and the other for my cousin. I wanted him to come along so he could translate Farsi to Azeri, so I could practice my Farsi with him," he recalls with a laugh.

Hooshang also enrolled in a German high school, simultaneously learning German and English, and receiving diplomas in both languages. He then honed his German language skills with what many people today would consider a surprising group: Israeli soldiers. Despite the present-day hatred between the two governments, in an effort to strategically maintain robust relations with the United States, the Shah developed a strong alliance with Israel starting in the 1950s. Simultaneously, Israel—in search of legitimacy in a majority Sunni-Arab neighborhood—found an ally in Iran. "Back then there were no cable television or any foreign radio channels in Iran, so my classmates and I would practice our German with anyone who knew the language," Hooshang remembers. "There were a lot of Israeli soldiers just hanging out in the streets of Tehran. The Shah had given them permission to enter the country and they were just there, and every day we would use our lunch money to buy them *barbari* (a type of traditional Iranian bread) so we'd have a chance to speak with them in German. Isn't it funny—we'd make any excuse to practice our German, and for some reason, they spoke the language."

Because of his family's poverty, Hooshang was forced to start working at a young age. "We grew up very poor—I knew if my dad bought something for us, he had worked hard to make it happen, so replacing it would not be easy," he says in a modest, reflective tone. "I learned how to do everything." From cooking and sewing to doing mechanical and electrical work around the house, the young Hooshang was a renaissance man in the making. "When I was young, there was nothing in my parents' house that I did not fix or at least try to mend," he recalls. "There was nothing in our home that I would throw away or allow to be wasted—I revived everything." This aptitude has continued to the present. "If the washing machine, radio, heater, or anything mechanical breaks, I need to fix it, and I will. It bothers my wife, though," he says with a smile. "I grew up wanting to breathe life into broken things. To this day, things that live around me can't die."

Hooshang went on to obtain several engineering and aviation degrees in Iran and abroad, as well as mastering command of four languages. A mechanical engineer by craft, he finished his master's degree right around the time of the revolution. He then began his career as an aviation inspector, working his way up to aircraft maintenance engineer and, eventually, to flight engineer. After mastering the technical world of aviation, he became a commercial pilot in 2008.

Three years later, his need to "breathe life into broken things" would save 113 lives.

⊡

It was a cold October day in 2011. Iran Air Flight 742 was heading to Tehran from Moscow, captained by the then fifty-four-year-old Hooshang Shahbazi. In the midst of landing preparations, Hooshang noticed a mechanical malfunction—one that could not be rectified. The airplane's nose gear would not open; without that, there was no way to avoid a crash or a midair explosion. "I had three tons of gasoline that was about to explode," Hooshang remembers. "The plane's configurations were not normal. It was an old plane and its gears were uneven, and the front wheels were not opening. There were over a hundred innocent lives that I had to protect."

The plane was scheduled to land at Imam Khomeini International

Airport, but Captain Shahbazi decided instead to divert to Mehrabad. "I was not ready to give up on people's lives, on fixing the crisis, on life," he says nervously as he recalls that autumn day. "I asked Mehrabad to get ready for us. I knew that if I crashed at Imam Khomeini, it would turn into a political disaster for Iran, given that it would have halted all international flights. I also knew that it was rush hour and it would be impossible for ambulances and fire trucks to get to us from Tehran. Imagine three tons of gasoline burning—there was no way they'd be able to contain that at Imam Khomeini."

As the plane descended sharply toward the ground, all Hooshang could see before him was death. "I remember as I was looking down at Mehrabad, I could see our burnt corpses—I could imagine our bodies and ashes all over the runway. In a few seconds my entire life flashed before my eyes—my childhood, my parents, my wife, my children, the innocent passengers who were all loved by someone." Just as things looked hopeless, the thought that "things that live around me can't die" took hold in Hooshang's mind. "Thirty seconds before landing, I came to my senses. I was responsible for the lives of so many people. I was responsible for fixing the problem and couldn't let go without trying. I was not going to let them die."

Whether it was God's will, his profound technical knowledge, or a

combination of both, Captain Shahbazi landed the plane safely. "It was a 'kiss landing.' No one believed it—no one—not even myself," he says, the panic of the day still evident in his face and voice. As he had done in his childhood, but this time with 113 lives at stake, Hooshang had brought back life into a failed machine.

⊡

Hooshang gained international recognition following his heroics, with many in the aviation field in awe of his miraculous landing. "I remember right after, quite a few German, Canadian, and French aviation experts started commenting on the incident," he says. "They all concluded that it was solely because of the pilot's technical mastery that the plane had landed without crashing—there was no other explanation."

When the American pilot, Chesley "Sully" Sullenberger, landed US Airways Flight 1549 in the Hudson River on January 15, 2009, after engine failure due to a collision with a herd of Canadian geese, his country and government turned him into a national sensation. Then President George W. Bush and President-elect Barack Obama both personally thanked him for his service, and he remains a celebrated and revered hero in the United States to this day. While Captain Shahbazi's heroic landing brought him attention in Iran as well as around the world, unlike his American counterpart, his was not celebrated by his government, which instead forced him into an early retirement, as a result of his politics.

Former Iranian President Mahmoud Ahmadinejad once declared that foreign sanctions against his country were nothing more than "scraps of paper."[1] But after cheating death aboard Flight 742, Captain Shahbazi began to challenge that narrative by asserting that foreign

---

1. Christopher de Bellaigue, "Sanctions Have Crippled Iran's Economy, But They're Not Working," *New Republic*, November 12, 2012, https://newrepublic.com/article/109971/the-sanctions-have-crippled-irans-economy-theyre-not-working.

sanctions were, in truth, killing Iranians. "I became extremely vocal about the impact of sanctions on innocent Iranians—their lives were at stake," he says passionately. "The plane I was flying had undergone maintenance over one hundred times, and it was patched up with many unoriginal parts purchased from the black market." At the time, the government wanted to project the illusion that the American and European Union sanctions were not weakening the Islamic Republic of Iran. Thus, the regime had no interest in hearing a popular figure like Captain Shahbazi challenging their "anti-sanction" PR machine. "It was no longer about politics, it was about people, about humanity," Hooshang says bluntly. "It was no longer about foreign policy; it was about saving lives. The sanctions were killing people, and they had to be stopped."

Whether it is the inability to import medical machines, cancer medication, or airplane parts, sanctions have long had—and continue to have—a detrimental impact on the lives of ordinary Iranians. For example, over the past few decades, several hundred Iranians have died in plane crashes due to malfunctioning or poorly maintained aircraft. This is a result of the government's inability to update its planes or to buy standard parts or replace a fleet that dates back to before the 1979 revolution, all due to the crushing sanctions imposed by the United States and other Western nations. "That 727 Boeing was one of the many hundreds of fleets that over the past four decades have undergone alternative maintenance that was not on par with aviation standards, and that's categorically a direct result of aviation sanctions against Iran," says Hooshang who, despite his fight with the government, still reveres the aviation industry in his home country. "We have brilliant pilots, technicians, engineers—we have the human resources, but our planes are old. The United States is not allowed to sanction people's lives and no country is allowed to let its people die because of politics."

A few months after his critique about the impact of sanctions, with a monthly salary of 4 Million Toman—the equivalent of $200 USD in 2021, Captain Shahbazi was forced to end his flying career. "Flying is an addiction," he shares. "For those who fly, it's impossible to stop and let it go. I did. I was ready to let go of my personal desires to work on life, to push for the rights of the people." Since then, he has had multiple opportunities to leave Iran—but each time has rejected the offer in order to continue championing his cause. "It would not be honorable to leave."

Today, the hero captain does pro bono consulting for aviation and transportation companies, spends time with his wife and children, and advocates for civil rights, especially for those who have been stifled under decades of foreign sanctions against Iran. "Working for others brightens one's soul," he says with a smile. "When a little girl holds her mother's hand to go to Mashhad or Shiraz or Istanbul, that little girl's life should not be jeopardized because of a political tug of war."

Delaram Delafraz

H AND-PAINTED PLATES IN THE SHAPE of small pomegranates, colorful shawls, and handmade silver earrings adorned with Persian calligraphy and bejeweled with precious stones are just some of the items sold in this vibrant boutique. In one corner of the shop, there are several pairs of espadrilles; one shoe features a black and white image of the infamous Qajar king, Naser al-Din Shah, while the other is embellished with a vintage coin. *Eshgh* (love in Farsi), is a frequently used word in her designs. From clutches to tea trays and dainty bracelets, the word finds its way into many objects in the store— adding life to the pieces that the young owner makes with her hands.

Over the past few years, small boutiques have popped up all over Iran—especially in larger cities like Tehran. One of the reasons for this is, ironically, the government's conservative rules—in particular, its mandatory hijab policy. Since the Arab invasion that brought Islam to the Persian Empire in the late seventh century, wearing some variation of a head scarf, chador, abaya, or other traditional headdress has been part of Iranian life for women. The only exception was during the first part of the twentieth century, when the first Pahlavi king, Reza Shah Pahlavi, forced women to remove their hijabs as part of his "Westernization" of Iranian society.

While wearing the hijab again became mandatory following the 1979 revolution, in the forty years since then, Iranian women— especially the young—have found the most creative, fashionable, and stunning ways to express their individuality through the clothes they wear, while still complying with the restrictions of the regime. While you still have conservative revolutionaries who continue to obsess over women's long black veils, and the morality police whose sole mission is to impose their obligatory laws on the resentful masses, women's fashion in Iran has evolved out of a desperate need for color and an inherent desire for beauty.

This has in turn emboldened many talented seamstresses, young designers, and creatives to open their own ateliers, shops, and galleries to showcase their latest collections of manteau, scarves, shawls, and a host of accessories that are beautiful in design, colorful by choice, and at points quite pricey, depending on the clientele. It's remarkable how in the forty years since the ayatollah dimmed the light on the once fashionable crowds of the mid-twentieth century, Iranians have become some of the most stylish and fashion-loving people in the region.

One of the most revered fashion icons in modern Iran was the country's former *Shahbanu* (Empress), who along with her family, left the country just before Ayatollah Khomeini's arrival in 1979. A close friend of the designer Yves Saint Laurent, Farah Diba was featured in many fashion magazines of the 1960s and 1970s. Like many of her couture ensembles, her December 1959 *Life* magazine cover shot, in a custom-made Christian Dior creation, remains a classic representation of the elegance of Iranian women. But behind her iconic style was the vision of a man who captured the true Iranian essence of fashion.

Keyvan Khosrovani was born in 1938 into an elite family of generals and close allies of the Pahlavi monarchy. Educated in the United States, France, and Italy, he became a well-respected architect, artist, and designer who transformed ancient Persian patterns, themes and traditions into fabric and clothes. Khosrovani used these historically rich techniques to create some of the most exquisite brocade, embroidery, and needlework for Farah Diba. For over a decade, he was the designer of her official wardrobe. At a time when European fashion was in vogue, Khosrovani's Iranian-inspired clothing made waves throughout the world. He soon found himself managing a boutique called Number One on Soraya Street in Tehran, not far from the bustling Lalezar Street.

Today, many designers, artists, and illustrators are increasingly influenced by the same historical motifs that once inspired Khosrovani, finding their fashion muse in the ancient Persian ruins and the splendid artwork, architecture, and paintings of the past.

One of those artists is Delaram Delafraz, owner of a cozy boutique called Deltak. She is a small business owner, who, like many other young men and women in her country, decided to set up shop and market their own talent.

⧉

Standing tall above the old Yousef Abad neighborhood, the A.S.P. Towers are one of Tehran's most renowned high-rises. Among the country's first residential skyscrapers, the towers were completed a few years before the revolution. Today, while there is no shortage of towers and superstructures in Tehran, A.S.P is a reminder of the city's first attempts at urban modernization.

Inspired by Delaram's last name, Deltak (which stands for "unique heart") is located on the ground floor of the towers. Similar to many other boutiques and galleries in the capital, it stays open until ten o'clock at night. While Tehran technically doesn't have a "night life"—at least by American or European standards—many shops and restaurants stay open late, and there's still people and traffic on the streets even as midnight approaches.

Like many other modern Iranian girls, Delaram is well-dressed and has a keen eye for fashion. Her semi-covered thick black hair shines bright underneath her self-designed silk shawl. Not too heavily made up, she still looks perfectly put together and is as charming as any chic boutique owner in Dubai or Milan. Rows of handmade jewelry, shawls, ceramics, and home accessories are displayed all over her shop. "These days, I'm busy with special orders, but I try to take on as many projects as I can," she says with a smile. When Delaram opened her shop, her only other employee was an older man who helped with the gold and silver orders. Today, she employs a salesgirl, three artisans who assist with jewelry production, and three seamstresses who work on her manteau and shawl designs.

The young entrepreneur started out from scratch, but is now displaying works by other artists and designers in addition to her own work. "When I was first starting out, people would tell me to only display items from more famous designers, but I didn't want to do that," she explains. "I remember the days when I needed to support myself and would take my pieces to other galleries—I didn't want to be snubbed, and I'm not going to do that to others who come to me and want to show their work at my gallery." She currently has about fifty other designers whose work she displays in her shop. "Everyone deserves to have their work seen," she says with conviction. "I don't see any difference between myself and another girl who is just starting out. We all want to work, we all want to create something beautiful, and we all want to sell it. I never see myself better than others simply because it's my gallery."

Along with two younger brothers, Delaram grew up in a hardworking middle-class Jewish family. Her parents instilled a sense of independence and creativity in their children, especially their only daughter. "My mom was never like, 'Oh, a girl should stay at home and wait for her husband to provide for her,'" Delaram remembers. "Both Mom and Dad wanted us to grow independent and be successful individuals in our own right. You know, it wasn't so much about making money, but more about learning to do something, to create something, to go out there in society and know what's going on and be able to contribute." There's a profound sense of gratitude in her voice when she speaks about her father: "My dad was the biggest influence in my life."

In order to succeed in business or the arts in contemporary Iran, one needs to have ties to the government, or some level of personal investment, connection, or backing. Just like in many other parts of the world, creating something out of nothing is a tumultuous journey. "Of course, I could have not done it without the support of my family," Delaram shares. "In Iran, whatever you want to do, you need some sort of an investment, some sort of support to give you that initial jump start. Even if you're a super talented artist, you still can't start without support."

Before starting her business, Delaram attended college, where she earned a bachelor's degree in statistics. "I focused on math in high school, and later got my degree in statistics. You see how that turned out," she says with a laugh. "Dad always told us to make sure we get our college degrees. He'd say, 'Do whatever you want to do for work, but make sure you get your university education.'" Beyond their emphasis on education, her parent's passion for life was also a source of inspiration for Delaram. "They were never rigorous in anything. Both my parents would tell me to go out with friends or just go out and about to see what was going on in the world. My mom would tell me, 'It's okay if you don't get twenty (equivalent of an A+ in Iran), go out and see what the kids are doing.' They just wanted to make sure we were not one dimensional and bound to a singular perspective."

Despite her focus on statistics, Delaram's real interest was in the arts. "I was always passionate about art, painting, and just creating," she recalls excitedly. "I wanted to create something that I could see with my own eyes." While in college, Delaram took several jewelry-making workshops in addition to painting and drawing classes. "I knew I didn't want to work in statistics, so I did everything I could to prepare myself to start this business. I was always good in the arts. I started taking courses that would help me get better in my painting and teach me how to make jewelry and work with metals."

Delaram also discovered that she was skilled at sewing. As a result, she began to sew manteaux and hand-painted scarves, in addition to creating some of her first jewelry collections. "I had a super tiny workshop in the same building where I have the gallery now, and would sew my own items and take orders from clients," she says. "But after a while, Dad suggested that I get a larger space so that I could showcase all my work and be able to attract more customers." Delaram's father owned and operated a store of his own, which sold clothing, before switching to home décor and appliances after the revolution. Delaram recalls how, when she was young, her father would frequently take her and her brothers to his shop. "He wanted us to be exposed to the outside world, to society, and to learn by being around people."

About five miles south of Deltak, her father's store, now run by his two sons, is located in Vali-e-Asr Square, in one of the oldest and most densely populated neighborhoods in Tehran. In the 1950s and 1960s, the area was a popular destination for shoppers on nearby Lalezar Street, as well as a place for students to rendezvous—given its proximity to the University of Tehran—and frequent some of Tehran's classic cinemas. In the early 1970s, the "Theatre-e-Shahr" (City Theater of Tehran) was built five minutes away from the shop. Commissioned by Queen Farah and designed by renowned Iranian architect Ali Sardar Afkhami, the theater remains a magnificent fusion of modern design and traditional Iranian culture.

But what may come as a surprise to many foreigners are the synagogues that are quaintly located throughout the neighborhood. A ten-minute car ride from the shop down Hafez Street will leave you in front of the blue turquoise doors of the Haim Synagogue—one of Tehran's most prominent synagogues—which was built in 1913, right after the country's constitutional revolution.

With over a dozen synagogues that date back over 100 years, Tehran is one of the main locations for Iran's Jewish community. Just like Jewish people anywhere else in the world, Iranian Jews celebrate their religious holidays, fast, and go to temple. "In our synagogues, we have very special Torahs and books that are only pulled out during the holidays," Delaram shares, "but on Yom Kippur they make sure to bring out everything. It's such an important day for us."

A modern girl in appearance and mind, Delaram was nevertheless raised to be respectful of her Iranian heritage and her Jewish faith. "You know what I hate?" she asks. "The fact that some people instantly think of Israel when you say you're Jewish. One has nothing to do with the other. Being Jewish is following a beautiful religion that has nothing to do with Israel and its politics. I really get sad and upset when people don't have the understanding to differentiate between the two."

At a time when the didactic attitude of the government has driven many young Muslim Iranians away from religion, Delaram takes pride in her faith and is comforted by its teachings. "I feel Judaism is kind and flexible," she says. "I also love the importance that it places on the family and family life—that's an incredibly important aspect for me."

Raised by two open-minded parents, Delaram was never forced to date Jewish guys, but she still feels that it may be best if, one day when she does get married, it's to a Jew. "I personally don't care if I marry a Jew, Muslim, or whatever else," she says. "But at the end of the day, I was raised with certain values, traditions, and customs that I feel only a Jewish man would understand and be familiar with. I also want to pass on these traditions to my children and I feel that might be hard if my partner is from another background."

Delaram went to high school at Hadaf—one of the oldest private schools in Tehran. Despite attending a non-Jewish school, she never felt any type of pressure from the teachers because of her religion. "In school, our Koran teachers would ask me if I wanted to stay or leave; they were totally cool about it," she remembers. "We were not forced to take Koran or other Islamic studies. We just had to go to our Hebrew classes on Fridays, so I was pretty much at school every single day of the week." She laughs.

With the exception of the Baha'i community—which has historically been mistreated and continues to be ostracized by the current regime—Jews, Zoroastrians, Christians, Assyrians and Caledonians have parliamentary representation, can be employed by the government, and are "free" to practice their religion. While non-Muslim Iranians can't run for president or be hired by the military, they still have to complete military service, which in many cases can be bought out or exempted under exceptional circumstances. There are also specific divorce and inheritance regulations that often frustrate the non-Muslim community, and of course, the blinkered attitude of those who make bigoted or uninformed comments. "This is not just in Iran," Delaram says. "It's the idea that sometimes—not always—the majority sees the minority through an inferior lens. It's the same in many other parts of the world. It's just a reflection of the fact that society is not educated enough."

One of the questions that upsets Delaram most is when she is asked if she is really Iranian. "It's like, are you kidding me?" she says with exasperation. "Of course, we're Iranian—in fact we have been here since Cyrus the Great was King of Persia thousands of years ago. It's so annoying, but it's only because people are not exposed to other communities and minorities as much as they should be." There's an enormous sense of pride and nationalism in her voice—a strong sense of ownership of her homeland, as well as an ambassadorship for her faith. "But you know, it's only twenty percent of people who are like that. I feel you just have to be open with them and explain. It's so funny because I feel I often go overboard. My brothers always tell me, 'Oh my goodness, she or he got it,'" she says with a sweet laugh.

The presence of the Jewish community in Iran dates back over 2500 years, to the Persian Empire under the rule of Cyrus the Great, who released the Jews from captivity in Babylonia and helped them move back to Palestine. While some left for the holy land, many Jews remained in the empire. At the end of the 1700s, the first Qajar king moved the country's capital from Shiraz to Tehran. With that, the Jewish communities of Isfahan, Hamadan, Yazd, and Shiraz began to slowly find their way into the newly established capital. They mainly settled in Oudlajan, one of Tehran's oldest neighborhoods, a short walk from the opulent Golestan Palace—the seat of the Qajar monarchs and a masterpiece of nineteenth-century Iranian architecture.

Located in Oudlajan is the Ezra Yaghoub Synagogue, one of the oldest synagogues in Iran. In 1917, the Tehran Jewish Committee began there. Today, the committee continues its operation and manages all the affairs of Iranian Jews, though it has moved to another location not far from Vali-e-Asr Square. Less than a hundred meters from the small metal door of the synagogue is a perfectly homologous cloister called Akbarian Arcade that dates back nearly 250 years and was once a place where Jewish merchants and vendors did business. (It has since been turned into a classic eatery that serves an old-fashioned meat soup called *aab goosht*, and *kashke bademjan*, an eggplant-based delicacy.)

At the turn of the twentieth century, while there were Iranian Jews who were successful merchants, physicians, and shopkeepers, many lived in poverty and despair in the dark alleys of Oudaljan. It was only after the constitutional revolution in 1911 that Jews and other religious minorities acquired seats in Parliament and were officially accepted as rightful citizens with representation.

In 1942, a group of Iranian Jewish doctors came together to start a community health clinic next to another historic synagogue called

Mola Hanina—a five-minute walk from Ezra Yaghoub—so they could serve the impoverished residents of Oudlajan. At the time, there was an outbreak of typhus, and among the physicians attending to the sick was a young doctor named Ruhollah Sapir, who worked selflessly to care for his patients. A year later, after attending to many children, women, and families, the thirty-two-year-old contracted the disease himself, and died soon after.

The work of the community clinic eventually evolved into one of the largest private hospitals in Tehran, now called the Dr. Sapir Hospital and Charity Center, in honor of the young physician. In 1959, the former US first lady, Eleanor Roosevelt, visited the center. Nowadays, Dr. Sapir Hospital serves the medical needs of whoever walks through its doors, whether they be Jewish, Muslim, or other.

⌗

During the Second World War, thousands of Polish Jews fled the flames of Europe into Soviet Russia, eventually finding safe refuge in Iran. While World War II heroes are often depicted as French, British, or American, one young Iranian diplomat in occupied Paris played the role of savior for many Jews fleeing Nazi persecution. Known as the "Schindler of

Iran," Abdol Hossein Sardari used his connections, personal money, and whatever legal techniques and gimmicks he could figure out to save the lives of many at-risk Iranian Jews living in France.

Years later, as the Jewish communities dissolved within Muslim-majority neighborhoods, Oudlajan deteriorated into a slum. In the summer of 1977, Keyvan Khosrovani—artist, designer, and the former stylist of Farah Diba—set up a public art display on the worn down and partly ruined clay walls of Oudlajan. His street exhibition was a poetic attempt to raise awareness and pay homage to the deserted homes and alleyways of what had once been one of the most prominent residential neighborhoods in the capital. While today the old neighborhood is inhabited by the poor and is a destination for tourists, it will forever remain as evidence of the long history of coexistence between Muslimsand Jews in Iran.

With the creation of the state of Israel after the war, the first wave of Iranian Jews left the country for the new Jewish homeland. A second wave of Jewish migration occurred after the 1979 Islamic Revolution, when Ayatollah Khomeini claimed Israel as an arch-enemy, and Iranian Jews were uncertain of their future in Iran. Today, with the unemployment issues, financial insecurities, and general societal challenges that the country faces, many Jewish Iranians who can easily relocate have decided to leave their homeland in search of better opportunities. "A lot of people have left. Lots of my family members are now living in the US and outside of Iran," Delaram says. "You need to understand that we can all leave if we want to; it's not hard for us. There are US agencies that can help us relocate, but not all of us want to leave. So, if we have decided to stay, it is because we want to live here. It's our choice."

Delaram's parents were among the Jewish families who decided to stay in Iran. "Dad didn't want to leave because he had a good business, and Mom didn't really pressure him to leave, even though some of her family had left," Delaram says. "I always remember Dad would tell us, 'Why should I leave everything here for an unknown future in a foreign country? How do I know I can work or be able to make a living as comfortable as what we have here?' He was right. We had a good life here and there was no need to leave for the unknown."

Despite her father's feelings, at one point, the allure of the American Dream did tempt Delaram. "I'm not going to lie, for a second I thought it might be better work-wise and for my education, but I'm so glad I didn't go," she admits. "The idea of leaving my family behind and being away from them breaks my heart. I can't imagine living away from them." It was thus extremely hard for her when she lost her father to a stroke a few years ago. "I still get teared up. I can't believe he's gone. I learnt so much from him. Now that I think about it, I would have never forgiven myself if I had left Iran."

This painful guilt is not unique to Delaram. It's a throbbing anxiety felt by millions of Iranians who left their parents and loved ones for the promised land. After all, the only reason many of them had the opportunity to leave in the first place was because of the support and sacrifice of their loving parents. "It's a beautiful country here," Delaram says, "but like many other places in the world, nothing comes easy."

Ehsan Rasoulof

*I*RAN IS LIKE A VAST FARM THAT HASN'T been plowed for years. It's a magnificently rich and fertile land that can yield the greatest crops, but unfortunately, the farm hasn't had loving farmers to care for it in a while."

He's sitting in the basement of what looks like a residential apartment building from the outside, but inside is a special space that — for its owner and its many visitors—serves as a place to commemorate, to be, and, in particular, to create. "You just have to worry about loving it and nurturing it. That's what Iran needs," he continues. "It's a a field that needs to be looked after. If done so, it'll bear the greatest harvest imaginable."

It's ironic that he uses "farm" as a metaphor for Iran, as following the revolution, his father served in senior government positions in the Agricultural Ministry of Fars Province, as well as being Iran's Deputy Minister for Agriculture in the 1980s. Later on, he was appointed as the CEO of one of the nation's most prominent banks, Bank Keshavarzi, also known as Agribank, which was established in the 1930s as a national bank for the agriculture industry, and remains one of the strongest financial institutions in Iran. After the automotive industry and the oil and gas sector, banking is the most significant financial pillar of the government. Unfortunately in the recent years, as a result of the paralyzing sanctions imposed by the US and Europe, in addition to domestic political rivalries, and Iran's growing private banking sector—with interests in government-owned infrastructures—billions of dollars have been embezzled and laundered by government insiders, bankers, and wealthy middlemen.

After Mahmoud Ahmadinejad's election as president in 2005, his father quit working for the government and joined the lucrative private sector banking industry. "I look up to my dad a lot—he's my hero, a role model," he says with obvious admiration. "He's a man that has done everything he could for his family and his country. I will forever cherish our conversations and time we spend together." There's an undeniable sincerity in his voice. "The one point of contrast between us is that he's religious and I'm absolutely not," he says with a quiet laugh. "But you know, even his religious beliefs are his own—he doesn't go to any major religious events and has never imposed his beliefs on us. Whatever he does is for himself, in private, in his own world."

In addition to not being religious, the young man also doesn't believe in the traditional boundaries that define marriage. "I was once engaged when I was twenty-eight, but I soon realized that it's not for me—at least in the classic way it is set up and defined here in Iran," he shares. "Don't get me wrong, I like a healthy partnership, but being

bound to marriage, as it's done here, is not for me." He's not being arrogant or pretentious with his comments; in fact, there's a refreshing sense of authenticity in his tone. "I just feel that marriage in its classic form is for those people who want to have children. I don't want to have children, so I really don't see a point in getting married."

He is calm and collected—perhaps one of the biggest similarities he shares with his father. "I've always walked the middle ground," he says. "I've always tried to make the best decisions, decisions that are good for the collective. In my calmness, I find peace." His gentle, pragmatic, yet determined personality would make him the ideal banker. Instead, Ehsan Rasoulof is an art gallery owner, curator, music publisher, and movie producer—all professional areas that, to this day, still surprise him. "I never thought I'd be an art curator or have a gallery or do any of the things I've done," he says with a smile. "I had to learn a whole lot, research so much, and dig deep. You need to do all of that if you want to grow."

Ehsan was born in Shiraz ten months after the 1979 Islamic Revolution. At the age of four, along with his then six-month-old brother, Ehsan and his family moved to Tehran due to his father's new post at the Ministry of Agriculture. Even after leaving, the family still maintained close ties to their extended family in Shiraz, a city that is an important part of Iran's cultural heritage. In addition to being home to many beautiful and historic buildings, gardens, and palaces, the city is also the resting ground for several of the greatest Persian poets, including Saadi and Hafez. "I don't remember much about my time in Shiraz," Ehsan says. "It was during the war and I was quite young, but Iran is a cultural hub. Everywhere you look, there's an undeniable richness of culture."

While he doesn't remember the details of his life in Shiraz, Ehsan still vividly recalls childhood memories with his father: "He loved poetry and would write poetry himself. I remember reading poetry with him from a very young age." Ehsan's love of literature pushed him toward novels and short stories—to the extent that he would illustrate the stories that his mother read to him. "Jules Verne and Agatha Christie, they were exciting for me," he says. "Somehow, I become drawn to science fiction and writing short stories myself." He gently laughs as he recalls how much he wanted to be Robinson Crusoe, or to "just be with him on his voyage."

Despite what many in the West may believe, access to books is actually quite easy for kids in Iran. World literature is readily available in school libraries, bookstores, and of course, home libraries. And that's not just for the middle and upper classes; even for the working class, books are a common household item. "There was a bookstore in Tajrish called Arghavan," Ehsan says. "My mom and I would always go there after school so I could buy a book or to just look around. But I remember when the shop, the one next to it, and the whole place went under water during the horrific flood that destroyed everything there." He's referring to the 1987 flooding that killed more than 300 people in Tehran's Tajrish and Darband districts. "I cried so much when I found out that the bookstore had gone under water. I was sad for months."

Tajrish is known for its main square, the Grand Bazaar and surrounding shops. Today, both Tajrish and the Darband neighborhood that's a bit higher up in the hills make up a historic yet modern part of Tehran. The bustling square is as lively as Columbus Circle in Manhattan, and its traffic is as intense as the 405 freeway in Los Angeles during rush hour. Despite the deadly pollution of the capital, the air somehow feels quaint, homey, and simply Iranian.

While Ehsan's strong emotional bond to his father remains steadfast, he is incredibly close to his mother as well. "I grew up in the most loving family," he says with a smile. "My mom is the most beautiful woman— the kindest, most generous and loving person ever." He explains that she doesn't come from a religious family, and is therefore not religious like his father, but still respects her husband's personal beliefs.

Ehsan attended some of Tehran's best schools. However, he found himself disillusioned by the "one-dimensional ways of teaching" during his time at the University of Tehran. "I immediately became disappointed in the university system—I don't know, everything was linear," he says. "All the professors would talk about was the academic coursework; there were no open conversations about life, about politics, or all the social issues that went on back then. The university was just so mechanical. I didn't like it."

It was the early 2000s, and Mohammad Khatami—the man with the "chocolate-colored robe"—was Iran's president. It was the first time since the revolution that the country's government wasn't dominated by heavily conservative elements. Like him or not, during the presidency of Khatami, an unprecedented lightness swept across the nation, with many ordinary Iranians experiencing a newly found societal liberation. Women started to wear more colorful headscarves; nonreligious music and films emerged from the underground; and young men began westernizing their appearance. "It was during President Khatami's time that the press, entertainment, and just about everything was starting to look different," Ehsan recalls. "It was the first time that young people were talking about change, about things that they weren't talking about before. It was all exciting and I wanted to be part of that—part of the real society, part of the conversation. I wanted to see and learn about what people were saying and doing."

While the Khatami administration allowed a limited amount of freedom of expression and a more progressive cultural and artistic agenda, the hardliners reasserted their influence under the subsequent presidency of Mahmoud Ahmadinejad. In post-revolution Iran, the work of all writers, filmmakers, artists, musicians, and creatives needs to be approved by the Ministry of Culture and Islamic Guidance. Until it is approved, it is not permitted to go public.

That was the case for Mohammad Rasoulof, Ehsan's older cousin, whose internationally acclaimed films have never received permission to be shown in Iran. For Mohammad, filmmaking was about tackling social issues. In 2009, during the unrivaled protests against Ahmadinejad's re-election, Mohammad, along with Jafar Panahi—one of Iran's most talented and outspoken filmmakers—was detained and imprisoned. Mohammad has been in and out of prison since then, while Panahi remains under severe scrutiny by the regime. "Why has mendaciousness become systemized within the fabric of the society? These are the issues we need to question," asked Mohammad during an interview.

Mohammad wasn't the only artistic member of the Rasoulof family. "He was incredibly artistic and insanely creative," Ehsan says with a heavy sadness in his voice. "He was always out and about, and whenever he would be home, he was in his own room and in his own world." Eshan is talking about his younger brother, Mohsen, whose shyness and reserved nature were a testament to an inner passion and creativity.

Mohsen was initially sent to the United Kingdom to finish a degree in computer science, but he soon returned to Iran. "My mom had this obsession that all three of her sons should be engineers, but Mohsen didn't like it there. He came back soon after leaving." Unlike Ehsan, Mohsen was not fond of literature, but instead was a talented illustrator, caricaturist, and later on, photographer. "In all my creativity and love of literature, I was still pragmatic and calculative. I was never as free and spirited as he was. He lived life—he was as close to a living being as I can ever imagine anyone to be." Eshan's usually stern voice cracks when he talks about his brother.

Mohsen became a rising caricaturist at a time when young graffiti artists were popping up all around Tehran, painting controversial and thought-provoking artwork—only to see it quickly painted over by the authorities. "He was pretty good at doing caricatures, but I pushed him to focus on photography, and just go for it."

It was a hot summer day in August 2008, and Mohsen was flying back to

Tehran from Kyrgyzstan aboard a Boeing 737 that was operated by Itek Air (a Kyrgyz company) on a charter flight for Iran Aseman Airlines. The plane dated back to the early 1970s and had recently been banned from flying in Europe. "I still can't believe he's gone," Ehsan says, his grief still evident more than a decade after the tragedy. "He had so much life, so much love, so much talent. He was only twenty-five." Eighty-five passengers and five crew members were flying that Sunday afternoon when the old Boeing crashed near Manas International Airport in Bishkek, the capital city of Kyrgyzstan. Sixty-five of them were killed, including Mohsen. "He was the most liberated and highly spirited person I've ever met," Eshen says. "He was so full of passion—a passion for exploring, visiting places, seeing things and capturing it all. Mohsen was the most important and most significant friend I've ever had. All the imagination, looking at pictures, watching films, and everything creative was all because Mohsen and I were together, because he was next to me."

Mohsen's death wasn't the only significant loss that Ehsan faced that summer. "I've had two best friends in my entire life," he explains. "One was in the family and the other one was a schoolmate from my childhood. Mohsen was the first; when he died, he left a huge scar that has never healed. The other was my best friend from school, Amir Pooyan, who two weeks after Mohsen's passing, came to me to say goodbye. His graduate school admissions and visa request had gone through, and he was off to the US the next morning. In one month, I lost two of the most important and closest people in my life."

Mohsen's death made Ehsan reassess the meaning of his own life. "I realized it when he left—it was he who was living all along, it was Mohsen who was alive; I wasn't. Before I lost Mohsen, I would always safely plan things, ponder, and just analyze; but when Mohsen left, I realized that I needed to live, I needed to do, to act, to fly."

In the months leading up to his death, Mohsen had been planning to open a studio in the basement floor of the same building Ehsan was using as office space for his marketing work. While the young

photographer didn't live to see his studio come to fruition, his older brother made sure that not only would Mohsen's work continue to live on, but so would the work of many other young artists. "When you lose something in your life, you realize what you need to do with the time you have left," Ehsan shares sadly.

With the help of his father, Ehsan opened the Mohsen Gallery in January of 2010. "This way he'll always be alive, people will remember him, people will still talk about him," Ehsan says. "I remember going to so many art exhibitions and galleries when Mohsen was alive. After he passed, I had to keep on learning so much about the art world in order to do this gallery justice."

Over the past few years, there has been a major uptick in the number of art galleries and private theater spaces in Iran. Under the presidency of Mahmoud Ahmadinejad, most government funding to support the arts was severed. As a result, private donors, producers, and curators began to take up the slack, opening private galleries and performing art spaces. "Creating a theater, setting up art galleries, or a performing arts' space, do not require a lot of funds," Ehsan says. "It's still something that people with money can and will do, but regardless, you need government permits to actually be able to work. After Rouhani became president, a lot of doors opened up and his government began giving more permits to art galleries and theater spaces compared to previous years."

Since launching the Mohsen Gallery, Ehsan has displayed the work of some of Iran's most prominent up and coming artists, as well as artists from the wider Arab world. "Pop art, fusion art, and contemporary works are what I try to represent the most in the gallery," Ehsan says. "There was a lively boldness about Mohsen—and I'm trying to keep that alive in the type of artists and art we represent." Ehsan also started Tehran's annual Digital Art Exhibition, the first digital art show in the Middle East. "I'm trying so hard to do things that have not been done before in Iran and the region." In addition to art, Ehsan also supports many young musicians, whose work has been loved not just by those inside the country, but by many Iranians living elsewhere in the world. Pallett, Damahi, and Kamakan are among the fusion bands that he has helped produce. "Music is the most powerful and influential form of art in Iran among people. After that, it's cinema, then theater."

Ehsan's support of young musicians and artists reflects his belief that the current generation of Iranian youth is yearning to express itself after decades of being muzzled. "Young people want to go out, they want to see, they want to be seen, they want to talk, they want to be heard," he says. "They're not like my father and his generation, who had a platform in the years leading up to the revolution. These days, young people in Iran are hungry to talk, to share their opinions, to raise their voice. They are waiting to be given a brief moment to just talk—and I'm trying to create that in my small way."

Ehsan also observes that the nature of youth in Iran has changed over the past few decades, especially compared to those who came of age before the revolution. "The young people who grew up mainly in the 1980s and 1990s are no longer confrontational and radical like the youth prior to the revolution," he says. "They are less idealistic and more realistic; they no longer believe in grand, farfetched dreams that they may never achieve. Instead, they are much happier with smaller and more tangible goals that they can actually see happen."

⁘

In 2018, a new hashtag took over Twitter, Instagram, and various other social media platforms in Iran. #ZheneKhoob (#GoodGene) referred to young people in Iran who, by virtue of having influential family members in government, had a substantial step up on the societal ladder to success—both professionally and financially—in comparison with the rest of the population. In Iran, the divide between the "government insiders," the "connected," and "regular" people is large—perhaps even greater than in the United States and Europe. As a result, there is enormous resentment toward the elite and their plugged-in kids. Ordinary Iranians who are struggling to make ends meet believe —rightfully so—that the "insiders" have taken away their opportunities—and that there is no such thing as "fair" play.

As someone who grew up in a financially secure household, and whose father was a high-ranking government official, Ehsan certainly could be accused of being a #ZheneKhoob. Yet, he is quite transparent about his financial security. "I'm aware of the bonus that life has given me. I'm mindful of that every day, and, more so, mindful of how few people have the advantages that I may have in life," he says with humility. "I don't produce music or invest in films to become famous; I produce music and films to share common narratives and conversations with my fellow Iranians—those who're my age and from my generation." Ehsan explains. "That's why I've always wanted to use the gifts that life has given me for the cultural benefit of my society. It's an onus—I have to put it to good use."

Make no mistake, Ehsan's passion for the arts and culture is not the result of a noblesse oblige obligation toward bettering his society, but rather a humble sense of responsibility—and perhaps more so, a nationalistic and patriotic sense of duty. "I was always fascinated with the lonely detective in books or the male movie protagonist who lived in some kind of solitude. Don't get me wrong, I like to be with people and friends, but there is just something so profound about their seclusion." If he could cast himself in any movie, he would surely star in a 1940s film noir—no wonder his favorite movie star has always been Humphrey Bogart. "I would have done anything to meet him, or even wait in line for an autograph. There's just something about his character."

Of all the photographs taken by his deceased brother, the one that Ehsan cherishes the most is a picture of a small village boy wearing traditional Kurdish pants and kneeling against a dirt wall. Behind him on the wall are written the words "Hello Life" (*Salam Zendegi* in Farsi). "Life—that's what I learned from Mohsen," Ehsan says. "To go, to see, and to comprehend the depth of living. Life is so much easier and less serious than we make of it. I learned not to control life, to just let it unfold. I learned to live in the *now* because there is no *then*."

For Ehsan, Mohsen is everywhere—in the gallery, in his office, in his home, but most importantly, in his renewed outlook to life. "Maybe starting the gallery was a healing step for me. Maybe I was meant to learn the real meaning of life."

Zahra Nemati

*M*Y MOM JUST WANTED TO BREATHE for a few hours," she recalls with a giggle. "I was one of those kids who was always a ball of energy; I would literally climb up the wall if I could." If you close your eyes and listen to her voice, you can still hear that rambunctious little girl.

Today, she's an incredibly outgoing person, and her full face, rosy cheeks, and sweet dimples make you feel comfortable around her. "I used to get along with everyone and would make friends very quickly," she says. "When I was a little girl, I would play with everyone and just wanted to be around people. It was funny because when I was not around, my absence was strongly felt—so much so that our family or friends would be like, 'Where is Zahra?!'" She giggles again. "I guess I still want to say that I'm the same."

She was recognized for her unique athletic abilities early on. "I'll never forget the first day of class," she says. "I was running around, sweating like there was no tomorrow, and just trying to absorb everything. At the end of the session, the teacher came to me and said that I had strong legs, and that I was tall." Those words made the teenage girl feel unstoppable.

With three older sisters (and a brother), she is the youngest girl in her family. "Growing up, my oldest sister was my role model," she shares. "She's eight years older than me. She was great at school, always did the right thing, always said the right thing. She was my hero."

Today, it is Zahra Nemati who is a hero for millions of Iranians.

Zahra was born and raised in Kerman, Iran's largest province, located in the center of the country. The state's eponymous capital, which covers the entire northeastern part of the province, has over 500,000 residents. The province is also home to over 400 acres of pistachio farms, making it the main producer of one of Iran's most globally known exports. Commercially, some of the largest automobile, tire, and aluminum factories are based here. The presence of a variety of natural resources including coal and iron, as well as the largest copper mine in the Middle East, make Kerman an attractive mining hub for the region, as well as the whole of Asia.

Kerman's beginnings date back over 4000 years, to the Achaemenid and later Sassanian Empires. The crown jewel of Kerman is Arg-e Bam, or the Bam Citadel, which traces its construction to the sixth century BC, and is the largest adobe structure in the world. Located at the western edge of the Lut Desert, for centuries Bam was the epicenter of trade between East Asia and Europe. Registered as a UNESCO World Heritage site, this historic city is regarded as an ancient architectural and urban planning masterpiece, featuring impeccable underground water irrigation canals known as qanats. For many foreigners, especially

Europeans, the city is associated with the fresh and meaty Mazafati dates.

This once-glorious oasis was also the location of one of the worst tragedies to strike modern Iran. On a cold December morning in 2003, an earthquake measuring 6.6 on the Richter scale literally brought the city of Bam to the ground. It took only twelve seconds to destroy what had stood for nearly 3000 years, including the Bam Citadel (which was later somewhat restored.) According to official reports, out of a population of approximately 140,000, 26,000 were killed, and nearly 30,000 were injured; but unofficial and local accounts estimated the loss of life and injuries to be twice that amount. In less than thirty seconds, more than 5000 children were orphaned. All the hospitals, medical facilities, and pharmacies were reduced to rubble. It took more than twenty-four hours for the rescue workers to get to Bam. As usual, the Iranian government's response was poorly coordinated, and as a result of this mismanagement, many lost any chance they had at survival.

But the scope of the tragedy, like most other natural disasters, was about more than the numbers. Every shattered window, every collapsed building, was a story—a person, a slice of life, as well as a chapter in Iran's ancient history.

⊡

That same year, Zahra experienced an unforeseen tragedy—one that changed her life forever. "I was getting really good at Tae Kwon Do," she remembers. "Throughout high school and the beginning of college, it was my entire life. I was more focused on it than school. My dream was to make it to the Olympics—to make it on the national Tae Kwon Do team and be the flag-bearer for my country." Through her almost seven-year-long Tae Kwon Do run, Zahra won numerous local, state, and country-level championships.

Her biggest cheerleader was her mother. "I could have never done it without her," Zahra says. "She was next to me throughout the years.

She would come and watch me at every single game, cheer me on, and just make me believe that I could do it." Unlike in the United States and some European countries, where sports are a pivotal part of a child's life, playing sports in Iran is often considered a casual, "side" thing—especially for women. Therefore, parental support is critical if children are to have any chance at success. "Dad was also supportive," Zahra adds, "but he couldn't watch my games in the stadium." In Iran, men cannot attend women's games, and unless segregated by gender, women are prohibited from watching male tournaments. In recent years, there has been an uproar concerning women being banned from attending male soccer matches—especially in Tehran's Azadi Stadium. For Iranian women, it's about more than the game; they simply want to be have the right to make their own decisions.

Zahra was only nineteen when her world crumbled. "I was enrolled in university outside of Kerman, and often commuted there on the road." One day, en route from Jiroft to Kerman, Zahra's bus crashed. While she survived the crash, as the result of a spinal injury, her both legs were paralyzed. With that, she lost all her dreams—of Tae Kwon Do, the Olympics, and the gold medal. Initially, she tried to hide how distraught she was. "My tears were all under the blanket, my sobbing was done in quiet," she recalls. "None of it was easy for me. I was constantly acting, pretending that I was okay. I didn't want others to feel sorry for me or get sad. The only thing I wanted was to regain my strength, to show that I was not defeated."

It took a long time for Zahra to be "okay." She was bedridden for several weeks after the accident, and spent years struggling to regain her physical and emotional strength. "I did two years of nonstop physiotherapy, but more than the physical agony, I was emotionally distraught," she shares bravely. "I would see other people's worry, my mother's pain, and hear the whispers of my family. They were all so sad for me, and that sadness was unbearable for me at the time."

According to official reports, there are over 25,000 patients suffering from spinal cord injuries in Iran, with car accidents being the main cause of such injuries. This is one of the highest rates of spinal injuries in the world. Unfortunately, government support for disabled individuals is minimal—so much so that unless a person's family supports them financially, the patient will have a difficult time. In Iran, the number of people living with intellectual, mental and neurological disabilities is much higher than those with physical disabilities. Among them, people with Down syndrome and autism make up a large number of such cases; but sadly, much of the assistance for these people comes from the private sector, which is not enough to build a robust nationwide system.

While Zahra received support from her family, her greatest challenge was finding a new purpose for her still young life. "The idea that 'No, I can't' or 'No, it's hard' was not acceptable to me," she says defiantly. "I just wanted to find a way to move forward. To find a way to restart." That strong zeal helped Zahra slowly come back to life.

Nearly two years after her accident, in collaboration with some new friends who had also suffered spinal injuries, Zahra launched a small non-profit organization called Kerman's Organization for Spinal Injuries. "We all came together to start this group," Zahra says. "The first few months after my accident, I realized how little I knew about the disabled community. We were all people who met as the result of our condition. We wanted to create a safe space that would enable us to learn from each other's experiences, and to also welcome others who faced conditions similar to ours."

At first, the modest group ran art, computer, and English courses, until one day, when they decided to set up sports classes. "Some of us really wanted to do sports, but there were not that many women in the group," Zahra remembers. "Also, quite a few of the women were a bit older, and there were not enough girls around my age. That's why we decided to start with men's sports." The group kickstarted a male basketball team—making Zahra yearn for a time when she could once again play sports or be part of a team.

In Iran, Islamic law prohibits men—unless they are your father, brother, husband, or a doctor—from touching a woman in public. "I would beg the guys to let me play, beg them I say," Zahra recalls with a laugh. "I would watch them play with such a deep sense of remorse—wishing I too could take part in the game." Because of the law, men and women can't even train together. "They'd see me watch them day after day. They were worried that if I fell, they couldn't help me get up, or what would they do if something happened to me during the game?" Zahra explains how those were some of the hardest days of her life: "The idea of not being able to do what I loved for so many years was more painful than you can imagine."

Things changed for Zahra when, one day, the welfare agency in Kerman donated a few sets of bow and arrows to her organization. "It was very random. They sent a few bows and arrows for us to play with. They really didn't intend for them to be used for training or archery, it was really just for recreational use." Zahra remembers the rest of the day vividly. "I got permission for the men and women to train together with the new bows and arrows. I then went to the guys and said, 'Now are you going to let me play?'" she recalls. "All the guys started laughing at me. Even though they were being silly and didn't mean to hurt my feelings, I still didn't like their reaction. They started teasing me and telling me, 'What are you doing with the bow, you should go play with dolls.' I knew they were joking, but I took their jokes seriously and promised myself that I was going to prove them wrong."

It didn't take long for Zahra to prove the men very wrong. She quickly mastered the sport, and within six months, was the third-place finisher at the National Championships in archery (competing against able-bodied athletes.) "There is no one, simply no one, who has made it onto the national Olympic team in Iran in six months," Zahra says with a mixture of confidence and surprise. "I'm not talking about Paralympic;

I'm talking about playing next to able bodies."

As a result of her shocking success, Zahra was asked to join the Iranian National Archery team. In 2011, in her first international appearance in para-archery, in Italy, she broke the world record in four distances, earning a slot at the 2012 Olympic games in London. "You see, the amazing thing about all this was that I was competing with people who could walk and had no disability; I was competing with *able* people, and to me that was the most satisfying thing," she shares proudly about her performance. "I guess this was the initial reason I fell in love with archery—it's a sport that doesn't discriminate. Everyone's equal and I didn't feel I was any less than my counterparts."

Like those in many other countries throughout the world, Iranians revere their athletes. It's not necessarily because of the particular sport the athlete plays, but because sports in general unites the population in a positive and honorable way. In the triumphs of their athletes, people see perseverance, passion, and courage. These are very strong ideals for Iranians, who are hungry to be recognized on the world stage for anything that humanizes, depoliticizes, and demilitarizes them and their country. For Iranians, it's more than a game—it's an opportunity to be part of the international community, at least for a few moments.

Unfortunately, fostering the talents of the country's athletes is not a priority for the regime. The Ministry for Sport and Youth Affairs, the organization in charge of sports programs, is predominantly made up of incompetent managers and policymakers. In Iran, an athlete's growth, salary, and job-security are always at risk. Almost all female athletes are constantly grappling with the constraints posed by the compulsory hijab. In other instances, many athletes have been forced to concede or not to compete against their Israeli counterparts. There are even cases of Iranian champions and medalists ending up homeless, while others are forced to take on side jobs to make ends meet. On numerous occasions such financial and societal restraints have led athletes— both Paralympic and able-bodied professionals—to leave Iran and defect; stars like Olympic medalist Kimia Alizadeh and chess champion Alireza Firouzja are now competing under foreign flags. In addition, many athletes aren't paid on time by international federations, and can't access international sponsors due to the long- standing sanctions against Iran. For example, in 2018, the Iranian national soccer team was unable to get their shoes from Nike due to the latest round of sanctions against the country.

Training for the 2012 games meant that Zahra had to leave her hometown of Kerman for the nation's capital. It was the first time since the accident that she would be living on her own. "It was a very hard moment," she recalls. "At that time, I still didn't have a full sense of independence; I was still relying on my family and my mom. She was next to me every step of the way, and it was the hardest thing to say goodbye." Ultimately, living on her own in Tehran helped Zahra recapture her lost confidence. "It was so hard leaving home, but that experience made me become the independent woman I am today. It helped me regain my self-esteem and learn how to live by myself."

Zahra was looking forward to the upcoming Olympics with great anticipation—until she found herself a victim of discrimination because of her disability. "Even though I qualified for the national team, I was never sent overseas," she shares, the annoyance still clear in her tone of voice. "I felt as if I was being used as a strong opponent for my teammates to compete against—just so they could get stronger." Every time Zahra asked about the Olympics, her Korean coach at the time would ignore her. "I asked him, I asked the federation, I asked everyone: Why am I not being sent? My scores were higher than anyone else on the team, but I was always told that I had to stay back." Eventually, Zahra learned that the other athletes and coaches found it "difficult" to travel with her, and they did not think it was worth the challenge to send a disabled member of team to the games. "I finally said goodbye to the Olympic team and left to join the Paralympics," she says with a hint of fury. "I didn't look back for a while. I was truly hurt. More than feeling celebrated for what I'd achieved in such a short time, I felt disappointed and rejected."

However, ahead of the games, the Iranian Olympic team came back to Zahra, asking her to rejoin the team. "They told me that, 'Oh, we thought you might get tired during the travels and miss the opportunity to perform well.' They were trying to persuade me to get them an Olympic qualifier." But this time, it was Zahra who rejected them. "I was still very heartbroken and felt that I was being used. They had no woman on their team and needed me to perform, but I promised myself that I was going to stay with the Paralympics and fight for the gold."

And so she did; the once Tae Kwon Do champion shone in London, winning an individual gold medal in para-archery, as well as a bronze in the team event, in the process becoming the first Iranian woman to win a gold Olympic or Paralympic medal. "My heartbreak had gradually turned into strength and I knew I wanted to make history," she says with satisfaction. "When I got my first gold, I felt I broke the glass ceiling. I was able to break that barrier that everyone dreams of breaking. It was then that I realized that these are barriers that we create for ourselves—mental barriers that prevent us from reaching our fullest potential. I always loved breaking these walls; and that day, I truly felt that I did."

After her triumph in London, Zahra decided to rejoin the Olympic team. "I wanted to test myself and decided to qualify for both the Olympics and the Paralympics in Rio." It was her performance at the 2016 Olympic games in Rio de Janeiro that forever cemented Zahra as an icon in the eyes of her fellow Iranians. Sitting in her wheelchair, wearing the same beautiful smile she used to share in her youth, Zahra made history as the flag-bearer of her country during the game's opening ceremonies. "At that moment, I was just thinking about my mom," Zahra states with buoyant pride. "All I could think about was how happy she was. There was and is nothing more joyous and beautiful than the ability to make other people happy—and that's what I felt inside. I was truly making my family, the people, and my country proud, and that remains a privilege." It's hard to find an Iranian who did not feel an all-consuming sense of national pride after watching Zahra carry the Iranian flag on the world stage in Rio.

Ironically, one of the men who had initially doubted Zahra's abilities back in Kerman ended up becoming her husband. "We initially met in that group in Kerman," she says. "We all became friends and later got to train together. He was also interested in archery, so we grew closer. It was funny because our friends suggested that we get married; everyone

thought we'd be a good match." Her now ex-husband, also an archer, had lost his legs three years prior to Zahra's accident. He had been a contractor for Kerman's electricity company when he fell off a pole after being electrocuted, damaging his spinal cord and losing the ability to walk. The two got married right after Zahra's 2012 win in London. However, her happiness with her new husband was short-lived, as, because of him, she ended up experiencing the pain of life under a patriarchal society.

In 1962, nearly forty years after their American counterparts, Iranian women were granted the right to vote. Since then, while there have been some reforms to the invidious laws against women in Iran, many archaic legal hurdles still exist that allow men to maintain control. One such discriminatory law is a husband's ability to revoke his wife's travel rights. Even if a couple has been separated for years, unless they are officially divorced, the man still has the right to subjugate his wife to this travel ban.

In Iran, revoking a woman's right to travel is a pressure point that men often use against their wives. This tragic phenomenon was the subject of the 2018 Iranian film, *Cold Sweat*—a powerful drama that focused on the helpless fate of a *futsal* (an indoor version of soccer played on a handball court) player whose husband restricts her ability to travel to a big match. This tactic was used by Zahra's then-husband right before she was to depart for the 2016 Rio Olympic games. "You know, I feel men are intimidated by a woman's independence; somehow they can't see her strength, they can't accept her success," Zahra says. There are hundreds of thousands of women—from housewives to athletes, academics, artists, and students—who are victims of such inequalities. While Zahra successfully fought to regain her travel permit, the emotional and mental harm of that episode traveled with her all the way to the Olympic stage. For the brave athlete, it became another barrier that she had to overcome.

When Zahra looks back at her life-altering accident, she often asks herself if it happened for a reason. "My accident happened while I was working toward my dreams," she says. "Sometimes I wonder if what happened to me was destined to happen so I could actually achieve my dreams. One of those dreams was to enter and win a gold medal in the Olympics; but who would have thought that dream would come true in a wheelchair?"

That same type of dream exists in the hearts and minds of many female Iranian athletes who, due to various societal, family, and financial restraints, will never realize their full potential, as Zahra has. Like her, these pioneering athletes are an inspiration to millions of women inside the country and beyond. In addition to being champions in sports, they are also the embodiment of female resilience in a country where women are still deprived of some of their most fundamental civil rights. "Iranian women are some of the strongest women in the world," Zahra states. "They are women who don't easily lose their hope; women who, despite all existing challenges, aspire to live a happy life. Iranian women try their hardest to have a better life and to create something beautiful for their children. I think every single Iranian woman is a champion—a winner in her own right. They are the champions of their lives."

Zahra has become a champion not only of her own life, but for the lives of countless other women across Iran. In addition to lending her voice to women's civil rights issues, she is a compassionate ambassador for children suffering from autism. Her authentic kindness, humility, and advocacy for women and the disabled won her the 2013 Spirit of Sport Individual Award for "her achievements, her determination, courage, and self-motivation." In 2017, the World Archery Organization nominated Zahra for Athlete of the Year. The following year, she was shortlisted for the International Women's Day Recognition award. In 2014, Zahra spoke at the United Nations on behalf of women and people with disabilities worldwide.[1] Her words won the hearts of the

---

1.. Billie Marshall, "No. 42 Nemati Addresses UN Panel on Sport," International Paralympic Committee, November 20, 2014, https://www.paralympic.org/feature/no-42-nemati-addresses-un-panel-sport.

global community, proving that the dreams, hopes, and wishes of the Iranian people are no different than those of everyone else in the world. "I believe that sport is one of the best ways of empowerment for people with disabilities all over the world," she said at the UN, adding that by 2030, she hoped that all persons with disabilities would have full employment and job security, and that cities around the world would be accessible for disabled individuals. "Never surrender to your disabilities." It was with this powerful statement that the then twenty-nine-year-old closed her remarks—underscoring her belief that sports knows no boundaries or borders.

Today, Zahra is a United Nations Ambassador for women with disabilities, and lives in Kish—an island that, according to her, is the only place in Iran that's truly suitable for people with disabilities. "After Rio, I moved to Kish. It's the one place that I can live independently and go anywhere I want and do whatever I need to do without anyone's assistance," she says. "I just wish more cities were transformed into places that are accessible and safe for the disabled community."

Like so many other athletes in Iran whose salaries from sports are an unreliable source of income and financial security, Zahra has a side business in her hometown of Kerman, a bridal boutique that she owns and runs with her sister. "It's the most beautiful business," she says. "I used to be more involved, but these days I'm a bit busy with my trainings; but whenever I'm in Kerman, I go to the store. I used to do all the shopping myself. We'd go to Turkey, I'd bring inventory from Tehran. It's just so much fun."

When you look at this internationally known female archer, you can't help but to think of another famous Iranian hero, Arash the Archer—the mythical hero whose courage, altruism, and strength helped bring peace to his country and helped determine the borders of Iran. Legend has it that in order to end a war between Persia and Turan, a Persian archer had to come forth to do the impossible. Wherever his arrow fell would mark the border between the two countries. Young Arash volunteered for the task. Atop Mount Damavand, the highest mountain in Iran, he released his arrow with all his might, fell to the ground and died—giving his life for his country. The Turanian king, Afrasiab, believed that the arrow would not reach far, thus presuming a loss for Iran; but to his dismay — Arash's mighty arrow flew over 2200 kilometers, until it finally landed near the Amu Darya river between modern-day Turkmenistan and Uzbekistan. It was a miraculous victory for Iran—one that cost the life of her bravest warrior.

Listening to Zahra, and learning of the many challenges faced by athletes in Iran, especially female athletes, you can't help but wonder what grounds they could conquer, if only given the chance.

Sonia Abdollahi

S HE READS THE SENTENCE OUT LOUD IN perfect English: *"From now on, I'm going to live like tomorrow doesn't exist."* The hairdresser quickly inscribes the words on her body with a tattoo machine. It is an impulsive decision in the aftermath of another impulsive decision that nearly ended her life at the age of twenty-five. "I took around ninety Metoprolol to try and commit suicide," she says. "I felt I had no other choice. I didn't care about my university or my degree, and I thought I had been completely humiliated in front of my friends, family, and anyone who knew me." She continues: "What's funny is that if you would've told me that you were thinking of killing yourself, I would probably have slapped you in the face and said you were an idiot; but somehow, in a split second, I turned into that idiot myself and didn't care about anything else."

It took her three days to recover from her failed suicide attempt; it would take nearly a year to fully recuperate from the pain of the sudden breakup. "He messaged me out of nowhere on Instagram," she says, still incredulous at how it all started. "I took a long time to respond and completely ignored him for almost four months." Out of sheer curiosity, she finally decided to write back to the young medical student from Kerman. "I don't even know why I responded to someone like him. I had no idea who he was, what kind of family he had, or what his deal was. He would just continue to follow up no matter what."

Their first meeting occurred when he surprised her as she was going to the library to study for her exams. "I used to be super active on

Instagram and would constantly post pictures, stories, and add locations, so it wasn't really hard to figure out my routines. One morning, I got a message from him asking why I hadn't looked across the street when I was getting out of the car. I was shocked. He had come to surprise me with a humongous bouquet of flowers. That was the first time I met him in person."

Enthralled by his passionate spontaneity, she began to fall for him. "It was an impulsive reaction," she recalls. "He didn't come from a good family, he had no money, no backing, lived in a small town, and was just not someone I'd normally want to be with. I pretty much took care of him all the time, would pay for things, plan things, and just think about our future. I think I fell in love with the idea of him. I fell in love with the idea of how passionately he came after me for months, and that he was as impulsive a person as I was."

Little did she imagine that the spontaneous love affair would be extinguished just as quickly as it had begun. It was a cold autumn evening, and the two had kissed goodbye after a long day of roaming the streets of old Tehran and visiting the the buzzing Jomeh Bazaar (Friday Bazaar in Farsi)—a staple destination for many residents and tourists near the infamous Cafe Naderi in the nostalgic Lalezar districtof the capital. It's a four-story parking garage that every Friday turns into a marketplace

filled with young artists and old vendors who sell handicraft, artwork, and antiques. "Around 10:00 p.m. I received a text message from him saying that I was 'the angel' of his life," she remembers. "The next morning, I got another text message saying that we needed to talk." Perplexed by the sudden change in tone, she immediately called him— only to learn that he wanted out of the relationship. "He told me he was afraid things might not work out between us and that this might all be a big mistake. I had no idea what he was talking about and was completely taken aback." As soon as he hung up, the once-relentless suitor blocked her from his phone as well as all social media platforms. "I don't know what happened to him; I never found out," she shares, still feeling the deep-seated shame of his sudden and unexplained rejection. "I was shattered. At that moment all I could think about was how humiliated I was in front of everyone. You need to understand that I was so serious about this guy that I even told my mom about him. My family, friends, everyone knew that we were together. I just couldn't understand or accept that someone could so abruptly change face."

Though the torrid and heartbreaking relationship nearly killed the young woman, it would eventually give her the courage to strive for independence and growth. "After the incident, I turned into a completely new person, someone who had regained all her strength and was not going to let anyone stop her from living her life to the fullest." From the despair of trying to take her own life, she came to appreciate the value of living life. "It took me almost a year to get to that point, but somehow I did," she says proudly. "After that experience, I decided that I was only going to live by one motto, which is the sentence I've inscribed on my body. From then on, I decided to live in the moment and enjoy every second. I realized that while life is filled with ups and downs, I was not going to let those turbulent waves disturb my peace. I know deep in my heart that at the end of the day, things will be all right."

Things have certainly turned out all right for Sonia Abdollahi, who today is a doctor with a specialty in emergency medicine.

⊡

Sonia has always been a fragile soul who savored her solitude. Her problems were always her own, as were her dreams. "I had friends, I still do—in fact plenty," she says, "but I was always the listener, not the talker. My world was mine; it still is." To this day, the young ER doctor seldom allows others into her isolation—which for her remains an enticing space filled with untraveled adventures, exciting dreams, and an unbound imagination that helped her survive the confining attitudes of her family; in particular, her mother. "My mother was obsessed with becoming a doctor, but it was during the revolution and she only got accepted to nursing and you couldn't retake the konkoor back then," Sonia explains. "For as long as I remember, she wanted both me and my older sister to become doctors—there was no other option, as far as she was concerned."

Even though she laughs after that last remark, it's not hard to detect an undeniable sense of fear toward the matriarch who, according to Sonia, was the "general" while the rest of their small family were her "little soldiers." "Dad worked for the traffic police in Tehran and was the real general; but it was my mom who acted like one in our house," Sonia chuckles. "Whenever something bad would happen, the first thing I'd think about was how to tell my mom or how to deal with her. Until I was in my early twenties, I thought of her as God. She is the only person I've ever feared in life."

Sonia recalls the time she got into a car accident and all she could think about was how to break the news to her mother. "I never liked the eastern part of Tehran, but that day I had to drop off a friend at her house. I slowly and cautiously entered a narrow one-way street. Suddenly, an idiot motorcyclist came from the opposite side and crashed into my front window. He was thrown down onto the street. I later found that he was fifteen years old and had no driver's license. He ended up being fine except for a few fractures, but at that moment, I only had two thoughts: one, to see if he was dead or alive; and two, how on earth was I going to deal with my mom." She laughs again.

Sonia was born in Tabriz. When she was three, her family moved to Tehran. She grew up in a wage-earning family that, while not religiously conservative, was severely regulated by her mother. "We had satellite TV," Sonia remembers, "but were only allowed to watch it for an hour a day, and only when my mother would permit it; otherwise she'd threaten to uninstall it."

Sonia went to a public elementary school in Fatemi Square, a heavily trafficked and central part of Tehran that's adjacent to the Ministry of Interior and surrounded by many of the capital's oldest hospitals. There, in comparison to the other students, who mainly came from financially vulnerable backgrounds, Sonia was considered a "cool kid." But suddenly, everything changed for her in middle school: "Everything fell apart once my mom sent me to Aboureihan for middle school. (Named after the tenth-century Iranian polymath, Aboureihan is one of the most highly respected and competitive private schools in the country.) Suddenly, I found myself in a classroom where the girl sitting in front of me would travel to Europe or the States every month; the one next to me, her dad owned so-and-so factory; the one behind me was the daughter of such-and-such doctor; and another would tell us about the games she'd play on her computer after school—bear in mind that this was at a time where I'd only seen computers in films. I was no longer relevant. The first two years were very difficult, until finally I settled in." Sonia's experience is a vivid reality of life in Iran—especially in Tehran, where the large gap between the rich and the rest of the society is an indisputable rift that has only widened over time.

Sonia got good grades in high school, but did not enjoy studying, and only did so because of her mother. "I only studied because I was scared of my mom," she says. "I was never the most studious girl in the class, but usually managed to scramble at the last minute, and somehow, I managed to get by with high grades." While Sonia may not have liked to study, there was one activity she did enjoy. "The one thing we all liked was writing in our diaries," she remembers. "We would write little poems and blurbs for one another and just pour our hearts out on the paper."

Sonia remembers her school days as being a carefree time: "Everything we did was so innocent and silly. All we cared about was if a guy talked to us in a restaurant, or gave us his telephone number in the park or at the hookah café," she says. "Of course, you can just imagine how terrible we looked with those ugly school uniforms and awful headscarves. Aaah, who can forget those headscarves," she recalls with a giggle. In mid-2000s Tehran, an era before social media, the most daring thing many teenagers did was skipping after school classes to go to a coffee shop or hookah place—though there were those who pushed farther, ditching school all together to go out and about, maybe planning a half day ski trip, or a date with their boyfriend. Of course, all hell would break loose if the school principal called the house and found out that the student had not only skipped school, but had also lied to their parents.

Sonia believes that much of that innocence has been lost for today's generation. "Over the last couple of years, things have rapidly changed," she explains. "It's only natural. Teenagers now grow up in front of American and European satellite shows and can access whatever content they want with a click. I didn't have a mobile phone until I was eighteen years old, but these days, every twelve-year-old has a cell phone."

Sonia was fourteen when she fell in love for the first time. In one of those classic moments of childlike naiveté, she developed an intense crush on a man who sold compact discs and videotapes at a shopping center near her house. "The guy was probably in his early thirties," she remembers with a smile. "He was tall, super buff, and had dark long hair. Back then, I thought he was the hottest guy ever. I couldn't stop obsessing over him. I literally turned into a movie buff and had seen everything from new releases to old Hollywood classics. You know why?

Simply because I wanted to go see him. I would find any excuse to go to his shop and buy films from him."

Back in the 1980s, 1990s, and early 2000s, people in Iran would call a guy known as a *filmi*—"the guy who brings films"—to get ahold of the latest foreign releases. A few days later, he'd show up at your doorstep with suitcases filled with VHS tapes—and later CDs and DVDs— that you could rent. (This was before the internet made piracy much easier.) Back then, government policing was more invasive, and the *filmi* was always afraid of being caught by the morality police. Eventually, small shops started selling CDs and DVDs containing "government-approved" music and films, though the shopkeepers—often computer geeks and students—would illegally download and sell what was popular and in demand. "I remember watching *American Pie* 1 and 2 and thinking to myself, are you freaking kidding me?" Sonia says. "Is it like this in the US? It was interesting to watch such scenes for the first time at that age. It was quite shocking, but I quickly got used to the cultural and societal differences, and of course, I learned a lot."

⊡

Despite her mother's controlling nature, the heavy load of her schoolwork, and her passive attitude toward her studies, at the age of eighteen, Sonia was accepted into medical school in Tehran. "It was crazy, absolutely crazy," she recalls with a disbelieving laugh. "I had a feeling I was not going to get accepted, and as usual, all I could think about was how to deal with my mom. I did study for the konkoor, but when I heard my classmates talk about how well they did, I was like, 'No way I did as well as those girls.'"

One night her cellphone rang at four in the morning. Sonia picked it up to hear crying on the other end. Her friend—the top student in her class—had just seen the konkoor results online and had not gotten a high enough score for medicine. "I was like, '*Shit! If this girl didn't make it, then there is no way on earth I've passed.*'" Sonia turned on her recently bought PC and tried to connect to the internet. "The crackling noise of the modem was so annoying and woke up my mom," she remembers. "I was super nervous, so I asked her to come and look at the score. I had my eyes shut; I didn't dare look myself." It was then that her mother screamed "133!"—an incredibly high score that would get Sonia admitted into medicine.

Sonia soon found her way to Shahid Beheshti University to embark on her medical training. By then, her sister had finished medical school and was about to get married—something that was not a priority for Sonia. "At that time, I was slowly finding myself," she says. "I was gradually becoming independent, and just learning about life. Honestly, even today, I don't want to get married or even have a relationship anytime soon. I feel relationships confine you, and God knows how much I hate to be confined."

⊡

Medical school graduates in Iran are required to fulfill a two-year service commitment in a vulnerable and distant part of the country, known as a *tarh*. For Sonia, this was a chance to finally travel around the nation. "My mom was always OCD, so we didn't travel much because she was always fussing over hotel cleanliness and so forth," Sonia says. "I always wanted to take advantage of my tarh. You work for a few weeks, then travel in between your shifts."

The medical services in Iran's small towns and villages are generally far below the luxury and modernity of those in larger cities like Tehran. For the longest time, the government has tried to remedy this inequality by establishing a national healthcare system that would cover the entire population. While public employees have always been covered, providing adequate healthcare for more than eighty million people is no simple task. In 2014, then-newly elected President Hassan Rouhani rolled out his version of the US Affordable Care Act, which was nicknamed "Rouhanicare." With the promise of leaving no Iranian without medical care, the Rouhani policy pledged to pay more than 90 percent of a patient's medical bills at public hospitals, and cover any additional fees or charges for special equipment and medication. In addition, the *Tarhe Salamat* (Health Plan) would also cover any extra costs for those already benefitting from standard public health insurance.

Unfortunately, someone had to pay for all these new healthcare commitments. At the outset, a considerable amount was allocated from energy subsidies. Soon after, however, newly imposed foreign sanctions, low oil prices, and regional turbulence led the blanket promise of "free healthcare for all" to fall into a whirlwind of financial shortcomings and uncertainties. As a result of the sanctions, Iran's commercial relations with many of its European and Asian counterparts took a hard hit. Consequently, business transactions with foreign companies that sold medical equipment, medicine, and products used for domestic medicinal production stopped. While Iran has long manufactured much of its medicine domestically, the raw materials needed for production are bought overseas. This crisis has led to the creation of an extensive black market through which expired, fake, and unapproved medicines circulate, which are bought by desperate patients. The most at-risk people are those battling cancer, hemophilia, thalassemia, epilepsy, multiple sclerosis and diabetes, among other diseases. "I saw

it firsthand, especially for cancer patients and those suffering from MS," Sonia shares. "I remember when if someone had to pay 100,000 toman for a session of chemo, after the sanctions, they suddenly had to pay 1 million toman. It was truly horrifying to witness the impact of the sanctions. The hardest part was watching children whose parents couldn't afford their cancer treatment."

The Iranian authorities' mismanagement and the volatility of the medical sector were further exposed when the Covid-19 pandemic swept through the nation in 2020. This occured in conjunction with the United State's continuing sanctions against the Islamic Republic, which are killing untold numbers of ordinary Iranians—children, mothers, fathers, and grandparents who fall victim to Washington's policies toward a regime that has not cracked against such harsh measures.

⊡⋮⊡

While Sonia is passionate about her work, one thing that bothers her is how often she fails to receive equal treatment from her male patients because she is a woman. For example, there are male patients who only respect male doctors and will call female doctors nurse or *khanoum*, which means *Miss* in Farsi. "It's like, are you serious?" Sonia asks with exasperation. "Why can't you accept that a woman can also be a doctor? Some people are just ridiculous." And it's not just the patients who are guilty of these attitudes. "Every now and then, my stupid scarf will fall and cause a problem when I'm in the middle of dealing with an emergency patient. When someone is rushed in and is about to have cardiac arrest or when you're seeing a patient who's literally about to die, the last thing you can—and honestly should—think about is your scarf!" Nothing angers Sonia more than when the hospital *herasat* (the morality officers of the hospital) admonish her. "I mean, are you kidding me? I just think our outfits are not suitable for hospital work—especially in the emergency ward. Similar to men, I think female doctors should also wear scrubs around the hospital, and not just for surgery."

Like with any other job, Sonia has her good days and bad days, but for the most part, she enjoys what she is doing and takes pride in her work. "Every day you're solving a puzzle, and I find this super exciting." This problem-solving attitude has made her a fan of one of America's favorite asocial television doctors: "Imagine if you were Doctor House," she says with delight. "It's incredible to think about having the ability to solve every single problem and puzzle that comes your way. Sure, he's socially weird and an awkward person, but I don't believe there's anything more amazing than being so effective and useful for your patients." It's quite sweet listening to her talk about fictional American characters as if they were real people. "I want to be like Jack Shephard in *Lost*," she says with a smile. "Just picture a plane crash and the following chaos. You should be able to act like Jack Shephard and know how to lead the way. As a doctor, I want to take the lead and guide my team, my group, my people back to safety."

Unlike the television doctor, Sonia doesn't always know how to lead the way—especially in an environment where societal taboos and cultural nuances can often skew one's judgment. "Unlike Iranians, I always thought Americans and Europeans were nonjudgmental people," Sonia says. "I truly admired that quality, and I thought I was like them. But an eye-opening experience with a patient made me realize that I'm far from that." That moment happened when Sonia was working in Tehran's top toxicology hospital. "As soon as he came in, I was like, 'Oh my goodness, what the hell does he think he's doing?' He had perfectly plucked and shaped eyebrows, lovely skin, and was super girly. The first thing that came to my mind was, 'Look at our guys these days.' But I soon discovered that he was transgender, and had tried to commit suicide." This all-too-familiar situation made the young doctor realize how judgmental she had become. "I felt a strong shiver through my entire body. It was as if I had been woken up by a slap in my face." In speaking to the woman, Sonia discovered that her family had been abusive toward her ever since she announced she was a woman and wanted to get a sex change. "Her family was not accepting of him—to the point where she felt that his only option was to take her own life."

Right then and there, Sonia made a promise to herself to never judge another soul. "I swore that I was never going to laugh at anyone, judge anyone, or condemn anyone before hearing the truth."

The long hours spent working with other doctors as well as her patients has opened Sonia's eyes to what she believes to be the biggest problem in Iran today: "Lying, lying, lying—this is the biggest problem in our society." You can hear the disgust in her voice. "It's as if we're interrogators. We ask patients, 'Have you done this, have you done that, have you taken this, have you eaten that?' And all along, they deny the truth." She believes this goes back to the deeply rooted chasms and crippling dualities that permeate contemporary Iranian society. "We're all stuck in this anomalous dualism in Iran," she says. "On one hand, you can be boyfriend-girlfriend, but having sex is forbidden—this is just one example. We're half modern and half conservative, half up-to-date but half traditional, and this has created an abnormal polarization in our society."

Sonia recalls a tragic occasion where simple honesty was the only treatment needed to save a life. A fifteen-year-old girl was brought into the hospital by her parents with severe stomach pain and bleeding. "From what I could tell, they looked like a normal family," Sonia remembers, "but I decided to see the girl alone without her parents. I asked her the basics and whether or not her periods were regular. She said yes, so naturally I asked her if she had had intercourse. She freaked out and said, 'No, what kind of question is that? How could you think of such a thing?'" Three hours later, the teenager died of cardiac arrest—a death that could have easily been averted had she only been honest with her doctor. "We later found out that she had an ectopic pregnancy, but how were we supposed to know? We didn't even think about that. In a short amount of time her bleeding increased, and she was gone."

In Iran, sex is a taboo subject that is not publicly talked about, especially if it happens outside of marriage. Every year, many Iranians die, suffer abuse, and are preyed upon because the greater society doesn't have the cultural capacity to have an open and honest discussion about sex and sexual violence. "I'll never forget the day they brought in a girl and her aunt," Sonia recalls. "They had both committed suicide. I later found out that they were both rape victims. The woman had been raped by her brother, who was the father of the young girl; and the young girl had been raped by her brother—the son of the rapist." She continues, her voice filled with rage: "I don't understand why those two disgusting animals should live while those two innocent victims died for the abuse

they suffered by their own brothers. You know what it was? They just couldn't talk about it; they just couldn't live with it. All I could think about was why? Why can't we talk about these issues out loud? Why can't we be honest and open? Why is it that the victim is always scared? Why?"

Both her personal and professional experiences have taught Sonia some of the most valuable lessons of life—lessons that are absorbed deep in her heart. This has helped her morph into a vibrant girl with an exuberant joie de vivre that she didn't possess when she was twenty-five. She speaks English, a bit of French, and of course Farsi. Her latest obsession is to learn Korean and to travel across Asia. "I'm learning Korean online and also by watching Korean soap operas," Sonia says with a laugh. "I started falling in love with Japanese and Korean animation, and I want to have a Korean boyfriend at some point." Even after all these years, she still chases the dreams and adventures that live inside her head. "I'm still an imaginative person," she shares. "I'm in love with the world of fantasy, magic, and animation. I've always drowned myself in mythology and fiction. From *The Three Musketeers* and Nostradamus to *Lord of The Rings* and *Game Of Thrones*, I live in those magical places with those people; in my mind I've traveled to faraway lands and I plan to do that in real life." The Giza Pyramids, Greece, and China are at the top of her travel agenda. "I want to travel the world. I feel I can use my profession to be of use for others while reaching my own dreams."

While Sonia still lives with her mother, her life is no longer controlled by the older woman's vision of a "perfect future" for her little girl. "These days, I pretty much do whatever I want to do without being afraid of my mom; and truthfully the only reason I don't share things with her is simply because I don't want to see her hurt. It's just that we're two very different people. And besides, what is she going to do to me? Whether I choose to get ten piercings in one ear and six in the other, or get tattoos, or dye my hair cherry red—it's my life. While I still have to respect my mom since I live under her roof, I'm my own person now."

Beyond her vast imagination, Sonia is also quite veracious—a combination that make you feel certain that eventually she will attain all her far-fetched dreams. "I don't want a kid or a husband—maybe down the line a partner who fully gets me—but for now, I just want to go hitchhiking in Asia, clubbing in Europe, excavating with archaeologists in Africa. I don't want to be restrained by anything or anyone. There are plenty of closed doors in the world for me to open, and I have no doubt that I can. I want to make sure that when I'm dying, there is nothing

Nima

*H*OW CAN IT BE POSSIBLE FOR SOMEONE to not fall in love?" He titters, bemused at the impossibility of a life without love. "It's the most beautiful thing, to be in love and to be loved."

His first love was also the first person he ever slept with. He was sixteen, and for him, the boundless romance was an extraordinary *affaire de coeur* that surpassed the physical and rushed straight into the hearts of both men. "He loved me, cared for me, worried about me, and was there for me no matter what," he says with deep emotion. "We spent a lot of time together, just hanging out, talking, and loving one other—we were each other's best friend. He was our neighbor and we knew each other very well. He was someone who loved me way beyond the 'sex.' It was real love—until he was forced to get married."

The groom was twenty years old when his parents made him marry his cousin. "I truly hated her," he says. "But what could I do? I was even invited to the wedding, but of course, I didn't go. I never wanted to see the girl and I never did. I couldn't." Despite the heartbreak he had had to endure, he still helped his lover get ready for the wedding. "I picked out his suit myself and helped him get ready on his wedding night. It was the most bitter and forlorn moment of my life. It was as if I lost a part of myself that evening."

At first, even marriage couldn't prevent the two of them from being together. "After the wedding was over, he dropped off his wife at their house and came straight to me," he remembers. "We went out and talked until dawn." That night, the two men made a promise to never stop loving one another.

They continued their relationship for well over a year. "The girl was always in Dubai," he says. "Her dad had a business there, so she was living there a few weeks out of the month. We saw each other when she wasn't around, but ultimately, our relationship wasn't sustainable." A year and half into the marriage, she got pregnant, and that was when the teenager realized it was time to say goodbye. "It was then that I knew that I had to let go of him. I could no longer go on like that. It wasn't fair to anyone. He was becoming a father. I didn't want the emotional stress. I couldn't handle it. It was time for me to move on and find someone else—someone who could truly be mine and mine alone."

Nearly 800 years ago, the famous Persian poet Rumi found his light in another man—a Sufi and a mystic named Shams. Some of Rumi's most glorious poems were written after his encounter with Shams and his subsequent departure, which nearly turned the poet mad. The result is over 40,000 lyric verses that remain some of the greatest masterpieces of Persian literature—all fueled by the relationship between two men that to this day remains a subject of much speculation among scholars.

Despite there being no conclusive evidence that the two men had any type of physical relationship, the single most important gift that Shams gave to Rumi—and by extension, the world—was the concept of a true selfless and divine love. "Rumi and Shams, I was always fascinated by their story. I respect them so much; their poetry is just magnificent," he says, sitting comfortably on a modern sofa in the cozy apartment where he lives with his boyfriend. "I sometimes think that love is more profound than marriage," he adds. "I just want to love the person I'm with. I want to feel that I miss him when I don't see him and love him more with each day that goes by."

Fast forward from thirteenth century Persia to twenty-first century

Iran, and you'll find ideologies in stark contrast to Rumi's values of love and humanity. In 2007, Iran's then-president, Mahmoud Ahmadinejad, told a crowded room of young students and academics at Columbia University in New York that, "In Iran, we don't have homosexuals like in your country. We don't have that in our country. In Iran, we do not have this phenomenon. I don't know who's told you that we have it."[1] Iranian officials tried to do damage control by alleging that Ahmadinejad was misinterpreted and in reality meant that the homosexual scene in Iran was nothing like what it is in the United States.[2]

Political semantics aside, since 1979, Iran's gay community has been forced to live a largely concealed existence. Before the revolution, gay people were slightly more comfortable and open in public—especially within the upper echelons of the then-Americanized Iranian society—often working as hair stylists, makeup artists, and similar jobs. Nonetheless, they were still not accepted by the conservative and more traditional factions of society, could not legally get married, and were looked down upon by many as "others."

This is of course not exclusively an Iranian phenomenon. In the United States, for example, many evangelical Christians and right-wing politicians oppose gay marriage and equal rights, and have voted for discriminatory policies toward the LGBTQ community. Many right-wing leaders in Europe, Latin America, and Asia have followed suit. In the United Kingdom, up until 1967, gay and bisexual people could get life in prison for engaging in homosexual conduct. The point is that the rights of the LGBTQ community have long been at risk throughout the world, mainly because of religious opposition. "In every part of the world, whether now or historically, the people who hate the gays are the

---

1. "Full Transcript of Ahmadinejad Speech at Columbia University," Global Research, September 25, 2007, https://www.globalresearch.ca/full-transcript-of-ahmadinejad-speech-at-columbia-university/6889.

2. "President Misquoted Over Gays in Iran: Aide," *Reuters*, October 10, 2007, https://www.reuters.com/article/us-iran-gays/president-misquoted-over-gays-in-iran-aide-idUSBLA05294620071010.

religious people," he says. "The problem is that they are everywhere and most of the time they are the most powerful people. The same is true in Iran."

Unlike in many Western nations, gay people in Iran have no legal rights whatsoever. "I feel there are so many similar problems between the LGBTQ community in Iran and in the United States and other parts of the world," he states. "Of course, the legal system in the US and Europe is not even comparable to Iran. Here, it's pretty much nonexistent and we have no legal rights." Still, that doesn't mean progress cannot be made. "You have to look at how change came about in those countries," he explains. "Progress was made over time; nothing happened overnight." However, he doesn't believe that it is the law alone that is restricting the rights of the gay community in Iran. "Our biggest problem is not the government or the laws; we have in ways accepted that that's how they are. Our main problem is our culture, people's behavior, their attitudes, and their way of thinking. These are the root causes of all the bigotry and hate in our society, which of course is amplified by the government." He goes on to opine that a public fight for gay rights in Iran would be unsuccessful. "You need to understand that if at this very moment, we, as the LGBTQ community, end up going loud and big, we're not going to succeed. We'd be heavily scrutinized once again and be placed under a meticulous magnifying glass. Things were not like this thirty years ago, and we can't risk losing what we have right now. Why should we jeopardize everything we have for something that we know cannot come in the short-term?"

This cautious outlook toward the possibility of "change" is a common attitude among Iranians—especially the youth. "In Iran, people have so many problems in their lives that LGBTQ rights are the least of their worries," he says. "They have more important issues to be concerned about than whether or not gay people have full civil or employment rights. People are occupied with their own day-to-day challenges."

He's handsome, well-groomed, and charismatic, with a witty sense of humor that mixes well with his stern charm. He instantly strikes you as someone who has seen a lot—both inside his home country and abroad.

Nima is one of the hundreds of thousands of gay people currently living in the Islamic Republic of Iran.* While he's open about his sexuality around his friends and family, in public he downplays his identity. When you speak with him, it's hard to imagine that this charming man was born into a family where both his parents were revolutionary insiders who fought on the frontlines of the Iran-Iraq War and then worked in Ayatollah Khomeini's regime, climbing the ranks of the Islamic Revolutionary Guard Corps (IRGC), or Sepah. "My mom was a high-ranking female commander, and my dad held many high-level posts within the Sepah and the military," Nima says. "My dad was on a terrorist watch list a few times." Based on their high-level positions within the regime, it is not surprising to learn that Nima's parents were ultra-religious. "My dad was super strict. You can't imagine how tough he was.

---

*In order to protect him from potential harassment, I used a pseudonym for "Nima."

Both my parents were very conservative, to a point that we were not even allowed to play music—any kind of music—in the house."

Nima was born in 1983, during the height of the Iran-Iraq War. He was the only boy out of six children, and for the most part, was raised by his two older sisters. "My parents were always away," he remembers. "They were never around, especially when I was young. Up until the end of the war, my mom was constantly in war zones—same with my dad." Eventually, his two older sisters got married, and Nima was left to care for his younger siblings.

By the time he reached his thirteenth birthday, Nima knew "something was different" about him. Once he turned fourteen, he began to understand that he was gay. "I guess I didn't know the classic definition of gay or homosexual," he recalls, "but I knew I was not interested in girls and that I wanted to be with boys."

In Iran, the mid-1990s was a difficult time for a boy to discover his sexuality. There was no internet, no cellphones, and more importantly, no one to trust. Unlike today, where a click of a button in the West can trigger a soft revolution in the East, and an Instagram post in one continent can cause an uproar in another, young people were nowhere near as connected, and daily communication was generally limited to close friends and family members. "Middle school was the hardest time of my life," Nima recalls. "I had no one to talk to and nowhere to find information. Can you imagine the level of confusion I and many others like me had growing up?" His classmates would tease him and call him *evakhahar*, a derogatory slur in Farsi that refers to an effeminate man. "They used to tease me all the time and tell me, 'Oh, you are like a girl, you sound like them.' They used to call me evakahar and I hated it. My only defense was to yell at them and say that I was not evakhahar."

In an effort to prove his masculinity and keep his secret from being discovered, Nima would frequently get into fistfights. "I was feisty and would always get into fights. I just thought it would help me look more like a boy. There were a few cases were some boys were exposed and in order to protect themselves were bullied into forced sex with the boys who had found out about their secret. I wanted to protect myself. I didn't want to chance anything."

But then came along his neighbor—another homosexual boy who would play a pivotal role in Nima's life. "Our passion and sexual energy conquered all my fears," he shares with longing in his voice. "Our love prevailed, and I was no longer scared of anything. I just wanted to immerse myself into that experience. It was amazing." While the euphoria of that first love consumed the then-high schooler, at the same time, he was having a hard time understanding his relationship with God. "During high school, religion classes (known as *dini* class in Farsi) were the most difficult classes for me," Nima remembers. "The teachers would tell us how masturbation was a sin or having sex outside of marriage was sinful and how men were only allowed to marry women, and only after that could they experience sex. In the dini classes, we were constantly told that God didn't love those who didn't follow his rules."

For a time, Nima was consumed by his fear of God. "Whenever I would have sex or engage in any sexual activity, I would end up feeling terribly guilty and ashamed afterward," he admits. "I was terrified of God, of how he no longer loved me, and that I had committed an unforgivable sin." Eventually, Nima learned how to cope with his fear by understanding that he was created in God's image. "The more time passed, the more I was able to learn about gay life and the truth about my nature," he shares. "I came to grips with the fact that my homosexuality was part of who I was as a human being. Then I thought, 'How can a God who says we as people are part of him be upset at me for being true to the way I came to life?' God created me this way, so how could he get mad at me for being the way I had been created?"

▪▫

As the new millennium dawned in 2000, the Iranian people were beginning to access a whole new world through the internet. Even though some of

Iran's universities had been connected in the early 1990s, most ordinary citizens did not get online until the late 1990s and early 2000s. Suddenly, the youth of Iran were connected to a world beyond their schools, teachers, and family. "You need to understand how little information we had growing up," Nima explains. "Back then, who could we talk to about sex? Our parents? We couldn't. So, when the internet came and things opened up, we were suddenly introduced to a whole new world." Online chatrooms immediately turned into a major communication network for youth in Iran. This exciting environment was a major platform for young boys and girls who would spend hours in virtual flirtations with the opposite—or same—sex. "It was the internet. That's where we got all of our information from," Nima recalls. "Every single thing I learned was from the internet; it was my single source of information. And that was the case for pretty much everyone."

However, this new freedom to communicate came with concerns about government monitoring. "Back then, things were done in secrecy; you never knew who was watching," Nima says. "In the beginning, we were so afraid of the virtual space. Some people would say that the Basij would log in to the chatrooms to monitor conversations. Setting up a date was not easy; we were all scared and intimidated. It would take a while for people to trust each other and be willing to reveal their true identity and show up for a date." To this day, the government's "morality apparatus" blocks websites it deems "un-Islamic" and often roams the virtual space in a largely failed effort to regulate the ever-vibrant Iranian youth.

In those early days of the internet, Nima and a few of his friends— many of whom he had met in chatrooms—started an online newsletter in an effort to provide some basic information for the LGBTQ community. "There was no information about this, so we figured we had to do something," Nima says. "It was a monthly publication that we created as a PDF file and would share with people online. We would circulate it in the chatrooms and by email." They called their small magazine *Cheragh* (lamp in Farsi), writing its enlightening content against a backdrop of angst and fear. "When I was doing the magazine, I heard about this guy in northern Iran whose family had set him on fire when they found out that he was gay, and other stories like that," Nima remembers. "Even if the stories like that were never proven, you were still stuck in this fearful state. You were constantly thinking that what you were doing was wrong and that at any moment you could be caught."

Even though it was a terrifying time in many ways, Nima and his gay friends had some wonderful experiences. "We managed to set up dates, go out, and see other people like us," he recalls fondly. "Despite all the angst and anxiety of those early years, we still managed to find moments of happiness."

After the establishment of the Islamic legal and judiciary system in post-revolution Iran, homosexuality began to be tried under "sodomy laws" and could be punished by the death penalty. Despite this, the laws around homosexuality are quite complicated. In essence, the death penalty can only be carried out if there are four male witnesses at the time of "intercourse," among other meticulous measures that make it quite challenging to prove that "sodomy" has in fact taken place.

According to Nima, the reality on the ground is far different than what the law says. "These are exaggerated versions of the reality," he says. "Some of my LGBTQ friends may be like, 'Why are you saying this' and 'This is not going to help us gain more freedom,' but the reality is that no one is being dragged out of their house and hung just because someone heard that they were gay. There are a lot of steps that need to be taken in order to execute someone on homosexuality charges." The complex nature of the law does not negate the inhumane, discriminatory, and often violent treatment of the gay community in Iran by the government, and to an even greater extent, by people's families. "It's the families that destroy their children's lives," Nima states. "Shame, embarrassment, society's ignorance and bigotry, these are the core elements of why we live in a backward society."

On the other hand, in Iran, transsexuality is regarded as a mental illness and it is not as frowned upon. In the early days of the revolution, Ayatollah Khomeini signed a religious amendment (fatwa) stating that transgender people had the right to seek treatment and that their condition was not because of an "immoral nature," but instead was considered a "medical condition." Unfortunately, there are many gay people in Iran who undergo the surgery. Some are not aware that they are gay, while others feel that they will be less ostracized if they receive a sex change.

In addition to Iran, Saudi Arabia, the United Arab Emirates, Afghanistan, Pakistan, Brunei, Qatar, Sudan, and Somalia are among the Muslim countries where homosexuality is illegal and can be punishable by death. This illiberality has led to a massive influx of asylum seekers from these countries into Turkey, who use the country as a stopping point on their eventual way to Europe or North America. This lack of tolerance toward the gay and trans community has also led to an uptick in human trafficking in many Gulf countries, where gay men are being prostituted and abused.

Nima was eighteen years old when he decided to reveal his true identity to his family. It was not an easy decision, but the idea of living a double life was an unbearable burden that he could no longer endure. "I was always very close to my two younger sisters; they were my best friends, so naturally I told them first," Nima recalls. "I'll never forget the face of my youngest sister; she was fourteen at the time. She looked at me with excitement and said, 'Oh, so you're like me?' and I said, 'No, I'm not a girl, I'm still a boy, but I like boys.'" Nima still laughs when he remembers her reaction. "After I told them everything, both were like, 'Okay, whatever.' It was as if I told them I was going to order lunch. They were so nonchalant, as if nothing had changed."

But then he had to tell his parents. "I told my mom first," he says. "We sat down, and I asked her, 'Mom, would you love me no matter what?' I remember her placid face when she looked me in the eye and said, 'You're my child; one always loves their children.' I then told her, 'Well, what if I killed someone or was thrown in prison?' She said, 'Listen, no matter what, you're still my child; you are part of me, and you always will be.'" It was at that moment that Nima felt he could tell his mother the truth. "I told her, 'Mom, in my heart, I don't like girls, I feel different and my feelings are strong for boys.' I remember telling her how that I didn't want to marry a girl and that I couldn't change my feelings." To his surprise, the conservative woman looked at her only son and said, "I know." "I was shocked when my mom told me that she had known for many years and had always feared this moment. The look in her eyes was as if she felt sorry for me—a piteous gaze that left me feeling sad and lonely."

While he was straightforward with his mother, Nima hesitated on coming out to his strict father. "I didn't really see eye to eye with my dad. Between my mom and myself, we managed to break the news to him step by step. There was no way I could have had a heart-to-heart with him. It was best to tell him slowly; and when he finally knew, he thought I was transsexual. In fact, for a very long time, both my parents thought or at least wanted to think that I was transgender. Maybe that was easier for them."

Unlike many other gay people, Nima wasn't abandoned by his family—or worse. For a while, his parents kept things within the family, but they eventually decided to send their son for "treatment" in Europe. "The way they dealt with me and coped with the whole thing was to treat me as if I was sick, and that I'd get better," Nima says. "I guess this was the only way they could handle the situation in their heads."

Guided by the belief that Nima's condition could be treated by mental health professionals, his parents sent him to Prague, where his oldest sister and her husband were living at the time. "My parents had zero information about gay people and thought that transsexuals could be treated," Nima shares. "The only reason they thought I was transsexual is because in Iran, people know more about transsexuals, given its legality."

It was the first time that Nima had ever stepped foot in Europe. Once in Prague, he was taken to several doctors who all confirmed his mental and physical health and told him that there was nothing wrong with him—he was just gay. "The doctors would all say the same thing," he recalls with a smirk. "I remember that my dad would call from Iran every day and ask me, 'Are you feeling better son?' In order not to hurt his feelings, I'd respond, 'Yes Dad, yes, I'm much better.' He'd then say, 'Oh well, great. Thank God.'"

The person who most helped Nima's parents come to grips with the reality of their son's homosexuality was his brother-in-law. "I'll never forget the first time I told him my story," Nima remembers. "We were in the car together and he was driving. He suddenly went through a dark tunnel and when he came out, he pulled over and got out of the car. He screamed for a few seconds and started talking to himself, saying, 'Why God? Why?' He didn't get mad at me, but was just complaining to God and asking him, 'Why?'"

After the car ride, Nima's brother-in-law began to research homosexuality—believing that the more he learned about it, the better equipped he would be to help. "He researched so much and educated himself," Nima says with a smile. "He is an open-minded man and is not afraid to learn. That's what led him to understand and accept my homosexuality. From that point on, he became my biggest ally—my friend—and the main reason why my parents began to comprehend the reality of my situation."

While in Prague, Nima continued to help with the online publication back home, and became more deeply engaged with the gay community in Iran. "All we were doing was giving information to people; we weren't doing anything political," he says. "All we wanted was for people to know about our community. We also wanted the LGBTQ community to have access to information about HIV, safe sex, and how to cope with their family's intolerance and a host of other issues that my other friends and I had faced."

⬚⬚

In 2005, the fiercely conservative Mahmoud Ahmadinejad took office as President of Iran. By then, Nima had returned to his homeland, and along with a few members of the LGBTQ community, decided to cooperate with a documentary filmmaker who wanted to produce the first ever foreign film on gays and transsexuals in the Islamic Republic. "I was quite outspoken, so much of the film was about me," Nima says. His main reason for participating in the documentary was to raise awareness about the LGBTQ community in Iran. "I wanted to open up and provide information about gay life, my situation, and how there were homosexuals in each and every corner of the country who were struggling to get in touch with who they really were. There were people who had gotten married and divorced but still didn't have the courage to come out. There were men in their forties and fifties who had never had the pleasure of sex—even once. They all needed to know that it was okay to be gay. I wanted them to know that they were not alone."

While the documentary opened a rare window into the LGBTQ world in Iran—especially the asylum seekers who leave their families and home country—it had negative repercussions for Nima, particularly from his father. "The documentary got really bold," Nima recalls. "People were talking about it in Iran, and my parents, especially my dad, was livid. There were many reasons for his anger. One, because of my parents' jobs and their position in the society and government, and second, because now everyone knew. It was no longer a family secret."

Paranoid about his son's safety and concerned about the public embarrassment and his job and social status, Nima's father sent him away to Holland. "I didn't want to go, but I had to," Nima says sadly. "The film had become too public, and in those days, it could have gotten my family and I into a lot of trouble." In spite of the problems the film caused him and his family, Nima has no regrets about doing it, or any of the other activism he has engaged in. "I'm proud of everything I did," he shares confidently. "I'm proud of every article we wrote, every online publication we produced, and I'm especially proud of coming out in front of the camera. It was a shake-up that helped others learn about the reality of gay life in Iran. Sure, my dad was furious, but after so many years, I'm seeing the results of our work. Had we been quiet and stayed in our little mousetrap back then, we wouldn't have this tiny bit of openness that we have today. I'm proud of everything I stood for."

Leaving Iran was one of the most painful experiences of Nima's life. "I didn't want to leave," he says bluntly. "Not because I was so in love with the country, but because I was being forced to leave. Because some people thought that me being myself and speaking out was not okay. I never experienced anything worse than those days." Nima was studying pharmacy at the time, but was forced to quit school. In Holland, he continued to write about his gay experiences in Europe and share his insights with the LGBTQ community back home. "I didn't stop campaigning. I was experiencing so much and wanted to pass all that information on to others in Iran."

Living in one of the most liberal countries in the world taught Nima the most precious lessons of his young life. "I learned that just being human is valued. That's incredible—it's something I first saw in Holland." When he was in Iran, Nima had always been doubtful of his future, but living in a free society enabled him to push aside those doubts and embrace a newfound acceptance and optimism. "I was afraid of my future, but in Holland, I realized that everywhere in the world there are those who don't like gays and that's not going to change. But I also learned that despite the haters, there are others who support us, who accept us, and love us for who we are. From that moment on, I realized that the way I lived was fully up to me. I stopped being scared, stopped being afraid of being myself and being gay. All my fears, anxiety and worries gave way to a new perspective toward life."

When he returned to Iran a few years later, Nima was a new person.

He had partied in the hottest gay clubs in Europe, met some of the most vulnerable Iranian asylum seekers on the streets of Istanbul, and had encountered European, Turkish, and other Middle East LGBTQ people whose struggles, worries, and fears were the same as his.

⌗

Today, Nima is a confident man who is proud to be making a life in his home country, despite the many challenges gay people face in Iran. "I don't get involved so much in public," he says calmly. "All I want is to live a quiet and peaceful life in the calmness of my home." He has built that peace and quiet with his boyfriend, who is nine years his junior. The two live together in an apartment owned by Nima's boyfriend. "I still have my stuff at my parents' house, but I'm here most of the time." While from the outside the couple appear to live a pleasant life, there are still invisible wounds that hurt both men. "Obviously, my parents know that I'm gay," Nima says. "But they're now too old to cause drama and be mad at me. But my boyfriend's parents don't know he's gay. They are too old to be bothered, and he's too afraid to break their hearts. I don't blame him; it's not worth the pain they would endure."

Nima's parents are now retired, and he spends a lot of his time caring

for them. "They're sick," he shares. "Dad has had a few surgeries and has a heart condition, and Mom has issues with her back. I try to be there for them as much as I can." The former government insiders now spend most of their days at their country house, gardening, and living a quiet life. "Oh gosh, they have changed a lot," Nima exclaims. "We never talk about politics and never really engage in any discussion, but I see how different they are today—especially Dad. Sometimes when I'm watching satellite TV or a foreign film, he'll sit next to me and watch with me. Remember, this was a man who didn't even let us listen to music."

Both Nima and his boyfriend work in the gaming and app industry; he is in sales and his partner works in marketing. They're both well dressed and fashion conscious. "I'm obsessed with cleanliness," Nima laughs. "My boyfriend and I are also fanatically crazy about perfumes and colognes. If you come to our bedroom and look at the vanity, you'll see a million bottles of perfume. It's just this magical idea of leaving a scent behind when we pass by and seeing people wonder who we are or take note of what are we wearing."

While Nima believes things have changed for the better in many ways since he first came out, he states that there is still a lot of work to be done, particularly with regard to intergenerational communication about sex. "Things have changed so much compared to twenty years ago," he says. "Things are much more open and easy to navigate, but we still have a long way to go. Why can't parents talk about sex with their kids? Why can't a mom talk to her daughter about condoms? If we don't talk about these things with our kids, the taboos will only continue."

Unlike many members of the LGBTQ community in Iran, Nima has no interest in leaving his country to live outside—especially in the United States. "Life in the US is different and hard," he says decisively. "I feel the liberties and social values that you have in Europe you don't have in the US. People are not valued the same way they are in Europe. I have never wanted to live in the US."

The love he once had and lost as a teenage boy he has now found with someone else. This time it's a mature commitment—something that no one can take away from him. "You know, life has taught me to live now, to live and breathe in the moment," he says. "The past is gone, and I can't do anything about it; the future is out of my control. The best I can do is to live now, to be happy now, to love now. I've been lucky in life and I know that; all I can do is appreciate the now."

Though Nima may have settled down into a stable life with his partner, the old activist still lives inside him. He's a huge admirer of Hillary Clinton, who has always fascinated the Iranian man for her "resilience, strength, and conviction." "We just need to continue fighting the fight and not being scared," he says defiantly. "That is the only way we can keep hope alive. Hey, maybe one day we'll have an open society where gorgeous American guys can also come to Iran." He laughs. "But honestly, it's all about creating change one family at a time."

Taraneh Aram

With her bold and colorful makeup, bright shawls, and perfectly manicured nails, no one would mistake her for being religious; however, this full-figured woman once dreamt of becoming a cleric. In her youthful mind, a cleric had the "the power to gather a crowd," as well as the ability to bring about "change"—something that she desperately needed growing up.

There's a dejected yearn for belonging in her voice, accompanied by an inhibited effort to prove that she does. Those teenage thoughts of becoming a cleric later blurred into a new dream of becoming an actor—like being a cleric, acting promised relevance, reverence, and the "power to gather a crowd." While this dream went unfulfilled, she has become a public performer in another, more important way: as an activist for transgender rights in Iran. "If I had one dream," she shares, "I would want to become someone like Miss Oprah or a famous actress. Then I could spend all my money on transgender kids in Iran—opening a center, giving something back . . . and then go (by which she means death)."

Today, she is a vivacious figure who through her brittle confidence, sees herself as a leading voice for the transgender community in Iran."I always knew I was different. I played with dolls, I loved girly things," she says, reminiscing about her childhood. "I was lucky that God loved me so much because I was born with a size thirty-seven shoe (women's size seven in the United States) and my height is 160 cm (five foot two), so I was meant to be a girl. And, compared to other transgendered people, I am much prettier."

Beneath her confident talk is a meek sense of sincerity that attests to the pain she endured growing up. "It was like being the ugly duckling," she says of her formative years struggling to come to terms with who she really was. "No one talked to me, not even my own family. They all blamed me for undergoing the surgery and coming out as a woman. My aunts would say, 'You're neither a man nor a woman. Who's ever going to marry you? No one can ever understand want I went through—what all transgender people go through."

For most people, that kind of treatment would make them bitter. But instead, she is full of love and a sense of obligation toward others in the LGBTQ community. "Anyone who went through what I did—having no family, no father, no mother, being lonely, being a man and woman in one life, being isolated, hated—would kill herself, or at the very least, lose their ability to love," she says. "The only reason I'm not like that is the work of God."

⊡

Taraneh was born into an upper middle-class family in Tehran. Her birth name was Amir—a common name for boys in Iran that means *prince*. Amir's father was a teacher who left his homeland for the United States when his son was very young. His mother—a nurse—carried on with her life, giving birth to a daughter from another man. She offered her son financial support, and little else. Today, Taraneh has no recollection of her father, and no emotional ties to her mother. "I only speak to my mom three or four times a year." The indifference in her voice is obvious. "I could care less. I think now that she sees that I'm happy, pretty, and actually have suitors, she wants to get close to me, but I don't believe her," she adds with a daunting smirk. "I told her, Mother, taking me to this restaurant or that coffee shop once every few weeks won't change anything between us. If you really want to be useful, give me money—otherwise, seeing you, connecting with you, doesn't make a difference anymore."

Amir decided to undergo sex-change surgery when he was twenty-two years old. He got the money from an inheritance he received after his father's death—a father who never knew his son's real identity. "When I decided to get my surgery, my mom was the head nurse at this super fancy private hospital in Tehran," she shares. "You know what she said? 'Don't get near my hospital for this or I'll kill you.'"

Iran is the only Muslim country in the region that grants legal rights to transgender people, providing them with financial subsidies toward gender reassignment surgery, as well as giving them new identities. It is believed that after Thailand, Iran ranks second in the world in the number of sex-change operations, with flocks of people coming to the Islamic Republic from Europe and other parts of the Middle East to undergo the surgery.[1] The reason for the regime's "openness" toward the surgery is the belief that transgender people are "ill" and that the operation will "fix" them by turning them into either a man or a woman. This view dates back to 1982, when a transgender woman named Maryam Khatoon Molkara sought out Ayatollah Khomeini in search of an answer to her pain. Sneaking past his guards while dressed as a man, Molkara told the country's supreme leader that her gender and her physical sex where two different things. After consultations with doctors, Khomeini did the inevitable—issuing a fatwa legalizing sex-change surgery in the Republic of Iran.

⊡

After undergoing the surgery, Amir took the name Taraneh Aram; in Farsi, *Taraneh* means *melody*, and *Aram* means *calm*. In reality, she is far from a calm melody, but a vivacious volcano who is a passionate advocate for the transgender community in Iran. "Growing up, I was

---

1. Vanessa Barford, "Iran's 'Diagnosed Transsexuals,'" BBC News, February 25, 2008, http://news.bbc.co.uk/2/hi/7259057.stm.

confused—to this day many LGBTQ kids are," Taraneh says. "People don't talk about these issues openly. It wasn't until a few years ago when social media apps like Telegram and WhatsApp came out that we were allowed to speak freely to one another. It wasn't like this when I

was growing up. Everything was in the dark; everything was hush-hush. I didn't even know that people had surgeries."

Amir grew up without ever having sex with a female. She detested the thought of sleeping with a woman—even though women were attracted to "Amir." "I was so cute when I was Amir," she snickers. "Women were attracted to me left and right." The first time Amir had sex was with a straight teenage classmate during his freshman year in high school (they are still friends.) Unlike in the United States, Canada, Latin America or Europe, most Iranian parents did not—and still don't—talk to their children about sex. There is no sex ed in school, and there's certainly no one to educate you about STDs, safe sex, or anything else that has to do with sex. This "hush hush" attitude toward sex has led many teenagers to start having intercourse at an incredibly young age in Iran—as early as thirteen. The more the government and society has tried to prevent the youth from having anopen dialogue about sex, the more they have rebelled in their sexual escapades.

On what turned into a life-changing stroll in the park, Amir ran into a woman—a prostitute—who was fishing for clients. "She came up to me and asked if I wanted to have sex with her—I was a very attractive boy, you know," Taraneh recalls with a small grin. "But as soon as she saw me, she said, 'Oh my goodness! You're not a boy, you're like me, a transgender. You need to become a woman, honey.'" Unfortunately, in Iran, many transsexuals are involved in the sex industry and work as prostitutes. While some people, including Taraneh, believe the number to be as high as 60 to 70 percent, it is impossible to get accurate statistics from the government.

There are multiple factors that blur the reality of one of the country's most common practices—prostitution and sex work. First, it's illegal; however, by ignoring it, the government leverages its denial into a strong PR campaign to portray a chaste society free of what they label "immoral" behavior. There are also no public agencies that properly handle issues as such, and the majority of aid and rehabilitation are done by private organization and nonprofits, which really don't publicize their work. To make matters worse, you have the private vs. public phenomena that exists in Iran—a centuries old, equivocal, and at points sickening nuance that's embedded in Persian culture. Much of it has nothing to do with the government, and is rooted in the duality that an Iranian person, family, or even the society, does one thing behind closed doors, but something different in public.

"After the prostitute told me I needed to have a sex change, my life changed in the blink of an eye." It took two years to get all the legal paperwork done, go through the proper medical process, and save enough money for the operation, which was helped by the inheritance from her father. "You don't understand the pain," Taraneh says plaintively. "I had nothing, no one, nothing but a flat that I rented. After the surgery, my friends came and took me to my home. I didn't even have a bed and had to lie on the floor. Can you imagine that? Can you imagine trying to get up from the floor after that intense of a surgery?" The feeling in her voice is harsh—offering a glimpse into the nightmare that was her transformation.

Despite the pain, Taraneh recalls several beautiful moments from right after her surgery, such as the first time she opened her eyes to view life as a woman, or when she felt milk coming out of her breasts. "It was a dream. I couldn't believe it," she says through tears.

⁛

During her transition, Taraneh was studying law, beginning her studies as a man, but finishing her law degree as a woman. Today, she dates, throws parties, and celebrates her life a woman. "It's so fabulous to see how many men want to be with me," she laughs. "You know those aunts who said I'd never find a husband, now I have more suitors than my cousins." But deep beneath her volcanic spirit is a quiet person who reads poetry, lights candles, and spends time alone in her apartment listening to Celine Dion—particularly her French songs.

Without any close familial relations, the transgender community has become her family. "We were all a colony," Taraneh says. "All the transgenders know each other—it's like a family in a society that doesn't know what to do with us." Her support for the transgender

community deeply influences her politics, causing her alliances to shift to whom she feels has the best interests of the community at heart. Back in 2009, for example, she was detained for supporting the "green movement"; yet in 2017, she was supportive of the ultra-conservative cleric Ibrahim Raisi—whose anti-reformist position is resented by more progressive Iranians. Taraneh says she is not political, but rather determined to get things done for the transgender community. "I don't care about politics, what I care about is who supports the transgender community," she says bluntly. "Back then, the reformist candidates were vocal, and this time Raisi was vocal."

She tears up as she recalls an event where she was the guest of honor at one of Tehran's universities. An ayatollah was speaking to the students, and during his speech, he mentioned her name and congratulated her for her advocacy and bravery. "I never thought the day would come that an ayatollah would say my name in public," Taraneh says emotionally.

These days, she keeps up her social media presence on her Telegram channel, which serves as an advocacy tool for the transgender community; and of course her aspirations to act are still ongoing. It seems that she has accepted society's prejudice, despite the legality of her sex-change. She acts like a butterfly who is now living a free life—in fact she tells me that the butterfly is a strong symbol for many transgenders in Iran. However, there are still moments that weaken her wings. "It hurts when a man sits in front of you and tells you that you're half a woman because you can't bear children. You know how that feels? It kills." But, in the next breath she laughs, and says that the most powerful men in history were enslaved by women. "The power of the woman is that she is always desired, and the weakness of the man is that he is beneath her because of his desire."

I asked if she could meet one person in history, who would it be. She said the Prophet Mohammad: "I would express all my pain and grievances to him."

Acknowledgments

Cover Photographer: Sabrina Rynas
Couture Designer: Ali Karoui
Location: Persian Gulf, Kuwait

A Very Special Thanks To Amir Sadeghi, who tirelessly journeyed through Iran to capture the photographs of its people. Without his passion, commitment and genuine support, these stories would have not come to life.

My sincerest gratitude to each and every person who trusted me with their life story and gave me the opportunity to share their voice with the rest of the world. I am forever humbled by your trust, sincerity, and generosity to invite me and millions of others into your life, your home. I hope that your stories will inspire, empower, and shed light on a society that's often seen through a dark narrow window.

May this book serve as a small reminder that beyond our skin color, religion, and passport, we all share similar dreams, fears, and aspirations—and are all bound to one another through our joint humanity.

Tara Kangarlou is an award-winning American journalist who has previously worked with news outlets such as NBC-LA, CNN, and Al Jazeera America. Her writing and reporting has also appeared in Al Monitor, *TIME*, *Vanity Fair*, and The Huffington Post. While at CNN, Tara was involved in covering major domestic and international news stories. In 2015, she led Al Jazeera America's team from inside Iran during the historic nuclear negotiations. She is a frequent on-air contributor for various international news outlets covering the MENA region, foreign affairs, and humanitarian issues. As a journalist, she has interviewed many high ranking government officials, heads of state, and newsmakers in the US and around the world. In recent years, she has spent much time in the Syrian border regions of Lebanon, Turkey and Jordan reporting on issues that impact Syrian refugees, host countries and the Middle East at large. Born out of her extensive reporting and firsthand knowledge of the global refugee crisis, in 2016, she founded Art Of Hope, the first American nonprofit that solely focuses on supporting the psycho-social and mental health needs of war-torn refugees in vulnerable communities. In 2018, she was the recipient of the Ted Sorensen Award from Network 20/20 for her impact journalism and humanitarian work. Tara was born and raised in Tehran, and currently splits her time between London and New York. She has a Bachelor's Degree in English from UCLA, and a Master's Degree in Journalism from USC.